Mortal Adhesions

Mortal Adhesions

A Surgeon Battles the Seven Deadly Sins
to Find Faith, Happiness, and Inner Peace

John Sottosanti

RESOURCE *Publications* · Eugene, Oregon

MORTAL ADHESIONS
A Surgeon Battles the Seven Deadly Sins to Find Faith, Happiness,
and Inner Peace

Resource Publications
An Imprint of Wipf and Stock Publishers
199 W. 8th Ave., Suite 3
Eugene, OR 97401

www.wipfandstock.com

PAPERBACK ISBN: 978-1-6667-7446-7
HARDCOVER ISBN: 978-1-6667-7447-4
EBOOK ISBN: 978-1-6667-7448-1

05/17/23

Margaret and John, circa 1988

To Margaret, who endured my transgressions with prayer
and patience. May God reward her.

The true object of all human life is play. Earth is a task garden. Heaven is a playground.

—G. K. CHESTERTON

Contents

Introduction

THESE ARE DIFFICULT TIMES, compelling millions around the world to pursue happiness however they can.

In January of 2022, almost two years into the COVID pandemic, more than three and a half million people had enrolled in Yale's "happiness" course, which had to move online to meet the overwhelming demand. It all began early in 2018, when Laurie Santos, a Yale psychology professor—concerned about the depression, anxiety, and stress she witnessed in the student population—offered *Psyc 157: Psychology and the Good Life*. What happened next surprised her.

According to *The New York Times*, soon after registration opened on January 12, several hundred students signed up for the course. Within days the number doubled, then doubled again, until twelve hundred students—nearly a fourth of Yale undergraduates—had enrolled. The student body realized it needed help. A 2013 study from the Yale College Council agreed, finding that almost 50 percent of recent undergraduates had received mental health therapy during their time on campus.

Santos emphasizes that neither money, beauty, nor even true love can guarantee long-term happiness. Students learn a variety of techniques to foster happiness—savoring the moment, expressing gratitude for the good things, and practicing meditation. While this is certainly helpful, no one knows how effective these approaches will be later in life when the inevitable stressors become more powerful and excessive.

I used many of Santos' recommended techniques in my own search for happiness, and they worked for a while. But when financial insolvency, marriage issues, and a serious medical diagnosis loomed large, I was submerged by a tidal wave of doubt, anxiety, and despair. Frustrated and despondent, I felt happiness flee my psyche. The result was a series of emotional crises during which my intelligence, cunning, fortitude, and perseverance, which I'd relied on for years, failed to extricate me from the dark abyss into which I'd fallen.

I had it all—money, prestige, a beautiful wife, three smart kids, a home overlooking the Pacific Ocean, titles, awards, travel to exotic places, and encounters with movie stars and Nobel Prize winners. Shouldn't these have protected me from psychological trauma? They didn't. It took me a quarter of a century to learn that I needed stronger armor to blunt the adversity that has plagued modern man for centuries. My goal in writing this book is to enable you, the reader, to profit from my experiences and strive for a more loving, happy, and peaceful life.

Why would I—a successful, scientifically-trained surgeon, without need of further remuneration, prestige, or acclaim—write a book detailing my embarrassments and failures? I wish to help others avoid what Viktor Frankl, in *Man's Search for Meaning*, calls the "existential vacuum," which is what remains when individual experience becomes meaningless. As the saying goes, nature abhors a vacuum, so depression, anxiety, and addictions flood the soul.

Seven years ago, as president of the San Diego chapter of Legatus, a religious organization comprised of CEOs of major businesses, I welcomed our speaker, Robert J. Spitzer, to the podium. He is the author of *Finding True Happiness: Satisfying Our Restless Hearts*. In the following half an hour, I learned that the principles of happiness can be divided into four levels, and as I listened, I placed the critical events of my life into each of the levels Spitzer delineated. It's essential for readers of this book to understand these levels and do likewise.

We achieve Level One Happiness—pleasure and material-based— when our desires or senses are satisfied. I'm happy for a moment when I eat a scoop of chocolate chip cookie dough ice cream on a sugar cone. Extended periods of this Level One "bliss" may be achieved by nice cars, beautiful homes, stylish clothes, and sufficient money, yet the excitement wanes. My life was filled with Level One Happiness for many years.

Level Two Happiness involves our ego in comparison to others. I found myself thinking: my house is bigger, surgical practice more lucrative, and foreign travel more extensive than yours. If I received an award at a professional meeting, most in the room did not. If I won the tennis match, you lost. By its very nature, Level Two Happiness is competitive and can result in excessive pride, power conflicts, and control issues. It lasts longer than Level One because it often involves higher levels of education, status, credibility, and self-esteem. It may be uplifting for a while but can give way to fear and jealousy.

In Level Three Happiness, one chooses to have concern for others, to desire to make a difference in the world, and to do good beyond oneself. Here we are contributive and empathetic, with concern for others and society at large. Living at this level, we go beyond our own pleasure. We donate to the poor, visit the sick and elderly, or volunteer for unpaid leadership positions in benevolent organizations. We want to make a positive difference. Many consider this the highest level of happiness.

But there is one more level, attainable only by those who admit that they are not entirely in control of their own lives—that their existence is more than a random product of nature. Level Four happiness is transcendent happiness. We look for perfect truth, goodness, justice, and beauty, while at peace with ourselves and those around us. We look for evidence that a spiritual world exists. We believe in the existence of God, eternal souls, and the presence of the sacred in all of nature and humanity. We understand that happiness can be found in the first three levels, but in Level Four, we experience something more profound and longer lasting, worth enormous sacrifices. This level of happiness is enduring and eternal.

Throughout my life, I have searched for peace and happiness, conditions that are inextricably and intimately related. *Inner peace* refers to the state of psychological calmness in the presence of stress, and it is doubtful it can always be achieved. But as a goal, it is definitely worthwhile.

My story begins with my parents, who planted and nurtured the seeds of my existence, and whose beliefs, habits, and quirks—for better or worse—for a time became my own. My father, mother, and then my wife were the dominating influences in my life, and I have attempted to portray them candidly.

Finally, against all that my extensive education has taught me about logic, the scientific method, and rational thinking, I believe that the universe is ultimately concerned with our existence. Once I rejected the belief that I am in command of my own life, the universe responded with events that can only be called miraculous, the source of which is a loving God. As you become aware of the ascending happiness levels in your life, I believe you will also experience them. Look for the mysteries—where the Divine becomes visible.

Chapter 1   A Kid from Italy

HE WAS A SEVEN-YEAR-OLD boy, arrived from Italy less than a year ago, walking along the railroad tracks, pulling a child's wagon. He tripped, maintained his balance, walked a few feet, and then tripped again. The right sole of his Buster Browns had detached, folding beneath his foot with every step. It snapped as he flicked his foot, returning to where it belonged. At home, he would have cut it off at the base were it not for the stones along the tracks that curved through the weeds of Greenwich. The rocks were hard, sharp, and always a hazard, like the ends of the railway ties that extended into them. The boy liked the shoes and passed the time by repeating the popular Buster Brown jingle: "I'm Buster Brown! I live in a shoe! That's my dog, Tige! He lives in there, too!"

The wagon, originally red, was now rusted. The cold, wet Connecticut winters took their toll on anything left outside. It was empty now, easier to pull, but if their home in the Chickahominy section of Greenwich—the Italian neighborhood—was to be warm this evening, he had work to do before dark.

The boy stopped at a faint sound, like rain hitting a metal roof in the distance. Except this sound was rhythmic, almost to the beat of a metronome, with a slight pause between every fourth and fifth beat. The sound grew louder every second. Knowing a train was coming, the boy stopped and pulled his wagon aside, away from the stones and ties, then turned his head to the approaching black monster. Its face was a circle, a plume of smoke spewing above its forehead, unfurling into a massive cloud like those from the factory smokestacks of neighboring industrial towns.

The shrill whistle screamed intermittently, the sight and sound enough to send the young boy running home to mama had he not witnessed it many times before. As the train sped by, the boy saw the engineer on one side of the cab, pulling on a rope connected to the whistle.

On the other side, the stoker shoveled coal into the firebox, heating the water to create the steam that moved the train. The stoker worked feverishly, thrusting his shovel into the coal in the tinderbox, then rotating his body to propel the black chunks into the open firebox. Some flew from his shovel to the ground, and some disappeared into the weeds. To the boy, those chunks were black gold, a fish on the end of a taut line, an ice cream cone in the dog days of a hot New England summer.

It took him nearly an hour to fill the bottom of the wagon. The chunks of coal would go into the brazier around which he, his brother, and their parents would gather, before sleeping under thick covers in the same room, their body heat adding warmth, an arrangement better than the privacy of the frigid living room couch.

The winter sun was setting, and the boy hastened towards home. First, he crossed the muddy path to Bruce Park Avenue, then headed north on Davis Avenue to the tiny brick duplex his parents rented. Bursting through the front door, he hugged his mama, Vincenza Sottosanti, and then his pop, Biagio. "Mangia, Giuon!" his mother exclaimed, removing his threadbare jacket and muddy shoes, and leading him to the dinner table. Mama only spoke Italian, with such a distinct Sicilian dialect that the Milanese in the north of Italy would have difficulty comprehending her.

In 1920, the pregnant Vincenza, her husband Biagio, and their son Giovanni had made the long trip by ferry and bus from Mistretta, near the north coast of Sicily, to Naples, where they boarded the steamship Pesaro. Directed to the steerage section, they crossed the Atlantic in eleven days, landing at the Port of New York. From there, they were ferried to Ellis Island for medical examinations and processing.

Like millions of Italians of their generation, they were fleeing poverty, the destruction wrought by the great 1908 earthquake, and organized crime. America welcomed them because they represented cheap labor. But the friendly reception depended on living in the Little Italy sections of American towns and cities. Chickahominy in the southern end of exclusive Greenwich, near the railroad tracks, was such an area.

Giovanni's classmates at the nearby Mason Street Elementary School called him "Johnny." His intelligence made up for what he lacked in physical stature and attractiveness. Within a year, he spoke conversational English without an "old country" accent. Though initially placed with classmates a year younger, he skipped a grade at Mason Street Elementary School and another at Greenwich High.

Meanwhile, his father, Biagio, worked in the construction industry as a common laborer with no extraordinary skills. Giovanni saw him return from work each day in filthy, sometimes torn clothing and blistered hands. He worked mostly outside, in freezing temperatures and snowstorms in winter. Temporary layoffs were common, putting the cost of heating fuel beyond their means. Biagio would tell Johnny to study hard, so he wouldn't have to work so hard for such little money when he finished school. Collecting coal by the tracks convinced "Johnny" that there had to be a better way.

Vincenza was a survivor. She had several more children as Johnny grew up. She watched newspaper ads for items on sale, and some suspected her of occasionally shoplifting to feed her family if the need was great. Though she was never formally accused, her forceful personality and frequent lying betrayed her.

Johnny was a fast learner. He understood that sometimes you needed to push boundaries to succeed, especially since life was stacked against the Italian immigrant. At the onset of his senior year, his teachers told him that he should attend college and that there were scholarships available for bright young students. His father said that engineers in the construction industry wore white shirts and ties, even on the job site, since they didn't have to dirty their hands. There were so many laborers available.

The Sottosanti family in Greenwich frequently visited their close relatives in Brooklyn. Biagio's brother, Louie, and his wife, Liboria, had a son also named Giovanni, called "Cousin John from Brooklyn." He told Johnny that he should apply for a full tuition scholarship from Cooper Union, a private college in New York City founded by Peter Cooper, a prominent inventor, entrepreneur, and one of the wealthiest men in the United States in the 19th century. Its engineering program ranked among the top ten in the country.

"Now ya gotta be livin' in New York State to get da scholarship," Cousin Johnny said. "If ya worried, fuggedaboutit. See da couch ova dare? Dat's your bed when you wannit. Whose agonna count da nights you sleep in it? You now canna say you live in Brooklyn." Living in Aunt Liboria's home was impractical for Johnny—it was not very close to Cooper Union—but its address met the scholarship requirements.

Johnny applied and was accepted. All correspondence from the college was addressed to Aunt Liboria's house in Brooklyn, which she forwarded to Davis Avenue in Greenwich. The cost of room and board at Cooper Union was prohibitive, so Johnny decided to commute from Greenwich to Manhattan on the New Haven Railroad. He was pleased to be in the train rather than alongside the tracks looking for coal. In his mind, this was real progress, not much, because there was still a problem. How to pay for the daily train tickets?

Johnny's first trips to and from college allowed time for reading chapters in his textbooks and listening to the clackety-clack of the train and its shrill whistle. Another sound came from the conductor in the rail-car up ahead. "Tickets . . . tickets . . . have your tickets ready!" When the conductor reached his seat, Johnny handed him his ticket. Before long, he realized that once he heard the conductor in the forward car, it took five minutes before he entered the next. The following day, when he heard the conductor's voice, he went to the toilet at the front end of the car, sitting with his physics book on his lap, until the conductor walked by, calling, "Tickets . . . tickets . . . have your tickets ready!" When the sound disappeared, Johnny returned to his seat.

It didn't take long for him to determine how much money he could save by timing his trips to the toilet. When stressing the enormity of his poverty and how it could be avoided through a college education, Johnny later would tell his own family, "I think that conductor knew I was in there but felt sorry for me."

Members of the Sottosanti family from Brooklyn and Greenwich attended Johnny's graduation from Cooper Union. It was 1934, in the middle of the Great Depression. Now called simply "John" by family and friends, Giovanni found a job in the engineering department of the Sontag Company, a small contractor in the Connecticut arms manufacturing industry. He met his future wife, Frances, a beautiful though somewhat prudish brunette, at the annual August Feast of Saint Roch, in the church of the same name in Chickahominy. The event featured delicacies such as pizza fritta, cannolis, and lasagna—eaten with white plastic forks, sold on paper plates, and covered with aluminum foil to keep in the heat. There were games of chance, carnival rides, and an opportunity to see not only Italians from Chicka-hominy but some who came on the train from Little Italy in Manhattan. Those Italians, more gentrified, purchased their tickets with "city money," forgoing the toilet unless they actually needed it.

Born in Greenwich, Frances was the oldest child of Charley and Min-nie Russo, from Reggio, Calabria, near the tip of the boot of Italy. It's well known that opposites attract, which must have been the case with John and Frances. Many said the Sicilians and Calabrese were "cutthroats" who hated each other due to historical warfare before the 1861 unification of Italy. Italians do not easily forget their grievances. Charley, a gardener on wealthy estates in north Greenwich, was an honorable man. His mantras, which he adhered to, were simple: "Always tell the truth, do not dishonor your family, obey the laws, be kind to people, respect your elders, be a good Catholic, confess your sins, and invite your parish priest over for dinner once a year." Frances adored Charley, and anyone who disparaged her father received a scolding.

John and Frances were married on the 4th of July 1936 in St. Roch's Church. They were an impassioned couple, both stubborn and with strong personalities. A passerby could hear their arguments when they disagreed, even in winter with closed windows. John believed that the stresses of the day needed to be offset by two beers after work. One bottle brought a smile to his face, and the second often provoked off-color jokes such as: "What's the difference between snowmen and snowwomen?" Then, after a pause, he would laugh and answer, "Snowballs!" Then Frances would scream, saying he'd embarrass her if he ever did that in front of others. But this would only spur him to do it even more—unless Charley was within earshot.

An unusual event occurred at their wedding reception, with the custom of the groom kissing the bride whenever attendees clinked their spoons against their wine glasses. Frances, according to John, certainly was a good kisser in the "Tunnel of Love" at Coney Island, but she didn't like being kissed in public, especially not in the presence of Charley and Minnie. John's buddies started clinking their glasses, and even their wives and girlfriends participated. Now the pride, virility, and self-esteem of Sicilian men depend on being the dominant partner in a public display of their relationship with their spouse. So with the tumultuous clinking and a beer or two as motivation, John grabbed Frances by the shoulders and planted a prolonged kiss dead center on her lips. Unable to pull away, Frances used her right arm to smack John's left cheek as hard as she could with the flat of her hand. Stunned, John released her, and Frances fled to the ladies' room. John then stood, cussed softly in Sicilian, paced the floor, and finally sat down.

The raucous room was now silent. Frances returned a few minutes later, the noise level gradually increased, and for the remainder of the reception, it appeared that nothing had happened. The wedding guests did not know "The John and Frances 4th of July Fireworks Show" would become an annual event.

Chapter 2   In the Shadows

JOHN AND FRANCES WERE my parents.

I must have been conceived in a moment of passion, a burst of heat in an often wintry relationship, though it was not an indifferent one. They loved each other. Romantic reconciliations followed angry arguments, evidence of an alternating current, electricity that lasted fifty-two years before the unusual occurred. But more on that later.

As I recall my earliest memories, a fog envelops me, with occasional moments providing clarity.

According to Mom, when I was six months old, my pediatrician stood on his toes, stretched, and, using his long arms and a pencil, circled a spot of urine on the ceiling, recording: *Sottosanti 9/3/42*. "Frances," he exclaimed, "in my forty-plus years of practice, I've never had a baby do that! It deserves recognition!"

I presume the table was tall and the ceiling low. This event was my only claim to fame for many years, as I lived in the shadow of a talented older sister, Janet, the favorite of all her teachers.

Dad doted on Janet, a cute, blue-eyed blonde born three years before me, but since Mom lavished attention on me, neither of us was deprived of affection. He was offered a job teaching mathematics and architectural drawing at Greenwich High. He was a natural, and during his first year, his students won awards at several state contests. Intelligent and artistic, Dad earned the admiration of his students and faculty. Two years later, his fame among educators reached the town of Stratford, thirty miles to the east, and he accepted a job at Stratford High.

A salary increase made the move worthwhile, allowing Dad to qualify for a loan to purchase a small two-story Cape Cod. He supplemented his teaching job by drawing house plans at night and on weekends, which minimized our playtime with him. Owning property was a milestone for an Italian immigrant, and he took the responsibility seriously.

Dad had never played football or baseball but was an expert at bocce. He could toss the heavy ball thirty feet in the air and land it on a dime. He did teach me bocce, but it was a game the neighborhood kids didn't play. I'd listen to the New York Yankees on the radio at night while Mom and Janet did the dishes.

Concerned with money and status, Dad frequently asked Janet and me, "What are the three secrets of success in America?" And without missing a beat, he'd answer the question himself: "Education, education, and more education!" Italian fathers wanted their children to achieve beyond what they had. Having Janet and me addressed as "Dr. Sottosanti" one day would be the fulfillment of his dream.

Founded in 1639 by Puritans from England, Stratford was a town of thirty thousand residents, a mixture of blue- and white-collar workers, along the southern coast of Connecticut on Long Island Sound. Its residents were mostly European Caucasians, with a smattering of Puerto Ricans and Black Americans. The wealthy lived in stately homes near the beach or in the northern communities of Oronoque and Putney, where large lots and houses were typical. The remainder of us lived in small homes huddled in the middle of town, bounded on the north by Paradise Green—several acres of trees and grass where the Continental Army had marched to the fife and drum two centuries earlier. Farther south, just beyond the same railroad tracks that ran through Greenwich, Stratford Town Center bisected similar neighborhoods, with its white-steepled Congregational Church, movie theater, bar, and essential stores.

The names in my neighborhood were short—Smith, Stinson, May, Twist, and Leddy, many of them "WASPish"—White Anglo-Saxon Protestants, the founders of New England. Besides Sottosanti, the one long name in the neighborhood was Rackiewicz, a Polish name. "Jay-Jay" Rackiewicz, a slender boy with a big smile that exposed the wide gap between his two front teeth, lived nearby with his mother, Sophie, a woman divorced from her alcoholic husband, and his sister, Mandy, a tomboy our age, endowed with a square jaw, pale skin, and short curly strawberry blonde hair.

The neighborhood kids told Italian or Polish jokes. "Hey, Jay-Jay. How many Poles does it take to change a light bulb?" "Dunno," he responded. "Three! One to hold the bulb, and two to turn the chair!" Jay-Jay grinned in self-defense. Ralphie Stinson, who'd been stricken with polio at an early age, shouted at me from his wheelchair, "Hey, Johnny-Boy, what sound does a Sikorsky helicopter make before it takes off?" The Sikorsky plant, in Stratford since 1929, was the largest in town, its choppers world-renowned. Ralphie screamed, fast and rhythmically, "Guinea, Wop Wop! Guinea, Wop Wop!" I thought his polio should have made him more compassionate.

Guinea was an Italian slur, likening darker-skinned Italians to Blacks from the Guinea region of the West African coast. *Wop* was short for "without papers," based on accusations that some Italians were illegal immigrants. It may seem that the neighborhood boys were cruel, but they were just spouting words they'd heard from their parents. Brian and Buddy Smith, my best friends, never used those words. I was fully accepted by them, as was Jay-Jay. We were the Four Amigos. The Smith boys lived several blocks away, but Granny Smith lived just across the street. She was a short, fragile lady with hair like Little Orphan Annie. And she was sweet, with a sweet tooth, making us Kool-Aid from pouches of colored powder, two gallons of water, and several cups of sugar, all mixed in the largest pitcher I'd ever seen. Granny's Smith's regular supply of Kool-Aid—and Milky Ways as well—resulted in serious tooth decay for all of us.

Twice a year, I had to visit "Dr. Two Cavities," a name we'd given Dr. Paul Fisher, a dentist located down the hill in Paradise Green. He'd discover two cavities at every appointment, which he promptly filled. I never met anyone who went to Dr. Fisher and didn't have two cavities. We all drank Kool-Aid and ate candy bars, and the forty-five-minute time slot allowed for filling just the two worst teeth. Each time I left, Dr. Fisher would grin and say, "See you in six months!" Our teeth needed to be fixed, and Dr. Fisher needed to pay his mortgage.

My mother was overbearing in her protection of me. At the first drop of rain, she'd drive her Chrysler sedan—a sign of upward mobility—to Garden School to pick me up, while the others walked home. I soon learned to peer out the school window, and if I spied her car, I'd exit from a side door and take the back streets home. I needed to fit in with the other kids, and I would do whatever it took to achieve that goal.

Mom was a religious fanatic. She never missed Sunday Mass, and as soon as I entered the second grade, she sent me off on Tuesday afternoons to Baltimore Catechism classes at St. James Church, where we memorized answers to standard religious questions. "Who made us?" "*God made us!*" "Why did God make us?" "*To show His goodness and to share with us His everlasting happiness in heaven.*" None of this rote memorization, taught by nuns robed in black, with rounded white bibs on their chests, was meaningful to me. Their mumbo jumbo made me late for dinner, and my knees hurt from the hard wooden kneelers.

I joined the Cub Scouts at a time when I felt like a foreigner. When short, heavyset Grandma Sottosanti, with her nylon stockings rolled to her ankles, said to me, "Johnutz, why you no wanna speak Italiano?" I said,

"Grandma, I only want to speak English." Sad and frustrated, she said, "Some-a-day, you be sorry."

But my Cub Scout uniform gave me a sense of belonging. It was like being in the American military. I wore a blue shirt with a gold neckerchief and an oval slide that tightened it to four inches below the neck. Gold letters above the right pocket said CUB SCOUTS USA. The left pocket bore merit badge patches my mom had sewn on. These were earned for completing different activities. I wore long blue pants and a blue cap with the Cub Scouts emblem showing my rank—Wolf, Bear, then Webelos. Still, my most vivid memory was one of humiliation. It happened during the Cub Scout Jamboree at Stratford's Raybestos Field.

Raybestos made brake linings and was the second largest plant in town, home to the Raybestos Brakettes, a world champion women's softball team. They played at a celebrated facility with light towers and bleachers holding thousands. In several games I attended with Brian and Buddy, Joanie Joyce faced twenty-one batters and struck out each one. Like Sikorsky, the name Raybestos was synonymous with worldwide success. Raybestos sponsored Saturday morning baseball games for the kids in town on the very field where Joanie Joyce played. And Raybestos hosted the Cub Scout Jamboree.

At one pack meeting, our scoutmaster announced, "Next month, we're going to attend the Fairfield County Jamboree, right here in Stratford. It's an honor for our town to be selected. You can compete against other scouts at Raybestos Field in various events. Winners will be awarded special badges."

I was so excited that I tossed and turned the night before, waking early to shower, comb my hair, and make sure my uniform looked good. But a feeling of awe overtook me as I stepped onto Raybestos Field, where we were asked to pick a competition. I selected "Pounding A Nail." Since my father's hobby was carpentry, I thought I might be good with a hammer, although I rarely worked with my dad. Dad did his carpentry on a table saw in the basement late at night, accompanied by several beers and a radio playing Italian operas. Twice I remember him yelling, "Frances, get me a towel! Quick!" After which, Mom ran down with a towel that he wrapped around his hand. Dad had several short fingers, and Mom didn't want me to lose mine. She'd decided I'd become an accordion player instead of an athlete.

For the "Pounding A Nail" contest, we gathered around home plate, which added to the excitement. Six boys were competing, each given a hammer, nail, and piece of wood. When the scout leader shouted, "Go!" I took one big swing, striking the head of the nail with a glancing blow. I can still see that nail in slow motion, spinning upward, end over end, into the blue sky and white clouds. It came down just as slowly, landing behind the backstop. Contest over. Everyone laughed, and my self-esteem suffered.

"'The Sotes' launched a rocket at the Jamboree," Jay-Jay later told Ralphie Stinson. "I thought it was going to the moon!"

When not playing ball, we amused ourselves playing "cowboys and Indians." The shallow woods behind our houses were ideal for hiding and then jumping out, six-shooter in hand, to shout, "Bang! Bang! You're dead!" I was tall for my age, chubby and baby-faced, with short curly blond hair and a demeanor that wouldn't scare a crow. For my tenth birthday, my mother's sister, my Aunt Josephine, had bought me a Hopalong Cassidy cowboy outfit. Aunt Jo had saved for months to purchase it because it was expensive, and identical to the one Hoppy wore on TV. Jay-Jay, Brian, and Buddy simply wore jeans, a plaid shirt, and a cowboy hat and carried but a single-holstered gun. Of all the famous cowboys, only Hopalong Cassidy wore distinctive clothing—a wide-brimmed black hat with an extra-tall crown and deep crease, a black shirt with a speckled black-and-gray bandana, black pants, and a belt with a silver buckle. His double holsters sported silver studs, and his twin six-shooters had pearl handles. I had it all— except for the boots. With their slightly elevated heels and silver spurs, they were too expensive. So, instead, I wore my brown-and-white saddle shoes, the only shoes I owned besides my sneakers.

Dressed like Hoppy, I sauntered down the block, spying Jay-Jay, Brian, and Buddy in the backyard of Granny Smith's house. So I threw back my shoulders, straightened my spine, and burst through the bushes with both guns drawn. Glaring at each of them in turn, I shouted, "Don't move! Got ya covered!" But they just grinned at me and burst out laughing. Probably everything would have been fine if I'd simply said, "Hey, I got a new Hopalong Cassidy outfit for my birthday." But I felt helpless in the face of their laughter. There was nothing to do but run home. I never wore that outfit again.

* * *

About the time I turned twelve, I began noticing the changing shape of the girls at school. They began filling out their sweaters, some more than others, and it was exciting to look at them without getting caught. Dad had some photography books in the basement—mostly scenery and portrait shots— but interspersed among them were a few glamour photos of topless women. I now knew what was filling out those sweaters.

Sophie Rackiewicz, mother of Jay-Jay and Mandy, was always throwing birthday parties for her two kids. When we were younger, the best game was "Pin the Tail on the Donkey." But when we were twelve, someone suggested that we play "Spin the Bottle," Within minutes, Sophie was there with an empty Coke bottle, hoping her daughter Mandy would show an interest in boys. One of the players was a prematurely developed girl who resembled a teenage Elizabeth Taylor, with full sexy lips like Marilyn Monroe. Her name was Evelyn Scalia, and she was the object of the Amigos' attention. Thanks to my dad, we knew what pinups were. That birthday party was my first experience of a kiss on the lips.

I noticed that if the bottle pointed at Mandy or one of her friends, the kiss was a quick peck on the cheek. But Evelyn knew how to smooch. We adjusted the spin to point the bottle her way, and when we were successful, she gave us the full treatment. It was a first for all of us, but obviously not for her. I enjoyed my kiss in turn, and that did it for the Cub Scouts and six-shooters.

Mom had told me that God created mankind. He was an artist of the highest order when he made Evelyn Scalia.

Chapter 3   Music Lessons

AT THE CRACK OF the bat, I ran back to the wall and made a two-handed grab. Three outs—we're up—one run down, bottom of the ninth. Gary Vinci, a slightly-built boy with a mop of dark brown hair, swung hard and sent a dribbler down the first base line. Safe! Up next, laying off the first two pitches, I took a full swing. The ball shot off, missed the chandelier, struck the far wall, and bounced away from the lone outfielder, who retrieved it in the corner as I circled the bases. Game over! Gary hugged me. He was excited because the losers had to treat the winners to a soda at the corner pharmacy later in the day.

This was our version of stickball, a popular game we borrowed from the streets of New York. We used a Wiffle Ball—invented in 1953 in nearby Fairfield—with a broomstick handle for a bat. The "park" was a deserted second-floor ballroom with a sixteen-foot ceiling and ornate chandeliers on two-foot chains draped with cobwebs from a bygone era. Burnt-out bulbs added to the feeling of a twilight contest, although the arched windows fronting the building behind home plate gave sufficient light for our secret game.

We were young teenagers, students at the Rudy Molinaro Accordion School in Bridgeport, ten miles from home. It was June 1956, and we were preparing for a national competition on July 22 in New York City—at the Annual Meeting of the American Accordionists' Association. Nineteen of us, ages fourteen to eighteen, were members of an all-accordion symphonic orchestra, ten boys and nine girls. But Rudy didn't trust six of the youngest boys—me among them—to practice four hours daily in summertime. So he told our parents we needed to be at his studio at 7:45 a.m., Monday through Friday, to work under his supervision.

His studio was on the first floor of a defunct hotel on busy Fairfield Avenue, just north of the railroad tracks. These tracks of the New Haven Railroad were a prominent image in my early life, perhaps planting in me a latent desire to someday cross, from one side to the other, those long rails that separated impoverished neighborhoods from the more affluent ones in Connecticut towns of the twentieth century.

The hotel's ground floor had been converted into storefronts, and the Rudy Molinaro Accordion School occupied one of them. It consisted of a reception area, a long hallway, and a series of eight-by-twelve rooms for music lessons. The second floor contained the ballroom, unused since the hotel's demise. The rooms adjacent to the ballroom—former guestrooms with solid doors and walls—were perfect for individual practice rooms.

Rudy taught one-hour lessons beginning at 8 a.m. At 7:50 every morning, he would escort us to our assigned rooms to practice independently. The six of us had agreed upon two time slots for our stickball games—9:15 to 9:45 and 10:15 to 10:45—when we knew Mr. Molinaro would be occupied. Ending at 10:45 assured us that our sweat would be dry when he checked on us at noon. Because the ballroom was situated over two vacant storefronts, our footsteps, as we ran the bases, went undetected. Such deceit was not difficult for me. I felt my father would understand.

Immediately after our victory, Gary asked if he could join me in my room for a joint practice session. We played similar parts in the "brass" section of the orchestra, since our accordions, by the flick of a switch, could be made to mimic the sounds of different instruments.

At age fourteen, the last two years for me had been a period of growth and maturation. I was no longer the chubby pushover kid of the Paradise Green neighborhood. Slightly over six feet tall, slender, and with a deeper voice, some called me "Big John."

Gary and I sat adjacent, playing in unison before the sheet music on the stand. At the end of the first page, I reached to flip it. A full-size accordion is a heavy, bulky instrument, which I supported on my separated thighs, and I was shocked as Gary deftly reached between them. I grabbed his hand, jerked it away, and glared at him, saying in a deep, strong voice, "Don't you ever do that again!"

This act of attempted molestation is fixed in my memory, undistorted by the clouds of aging. Gary's grinning baby face turned to one of intense fear, and I was proud of my forceful refutation. Subsequently, I wondered what had prompted his behavior. Was I projecting an effeminate image? At a precipitous moment between childhood and manhood, someone was invading my space. Remaining silent about the incident, we kept our distance. But who *was* I? I was about to find out.

Early in the morning on July 22, Rudy Molinaro met us on the sidewalk outside his studio for the trip to the contest in New York City—nineteen teenagers and one adult on a bus that seated 40. We arrived on time at the

Stuyvesant High School auditorium on the south end of Manhattan, ready to demonstrate to the judges that we were one of the best accordion orchestras in the country. In the previous year, two of our members had won first place in individual performances, giving us a sense of confidence.

I was awestruck by the skyscrapers and the energy of the city. The school was a five-story stone building, and the sculpted face of a Greek god, with wreath-like strands extending right and left, rose above the main entrance. Like the school's impressive entrance, the Stuyvesant auditorium was huge—twenty-five rows deep and forty seats wide, with an expansive balcony and a capacity of sixteen hundred. The first-class acoustics would enhance our performance.

One by one, the accordion orchestras took the stage for a fifteen-minute warm-up and tuning session. We were the last group to perform. After a thirty-minute break, Charles Magnante, the president of the American Accordionists' Association, announced the winners. "Our winning national champion senior accordion orchestra award goes to the Rudy Molinaro Symphonic Accordion Orchestra." We thrust our hands in the air and exchanged congratulatory handshakes and pats on the back. Beaming, Rudy greeted Magnante in the middle of the stage to receive the Senior Band Winner—First Place Certificate award.

After dinner at a nearby restaurant, our bus arrived at the curb at a designated time. After a long day and a full stomach, I planned to stretch out in a double seat and sleep all the way home. Climbing aboard, I rushed past Gary Vinci, who had taken the seat behind the driver, and found one halfway down on the right. But for the first half hour, sleep was impossible. Horns honked, and the bus made quick stops. Once we entered the first of a series of nonstop parkways, it would be a smooth ride for an hour and a half to Bridgeport, the victors returning home. Satisfaction filled me—body and soul—and I closed my eyes.

Minutes later, I felt a tap on my shoulder. It was fourteen-year-old Joan Lisi. She was slender, with the most striking dark eyes I'd ever seen. I had noticed her in our practice sessions, dressed casually, her face devoid of makeup. But tonight, her eyebrows, wide and arching, were as dark as her eyes, her brown pupils offset by eye shadow. She wore a clinging blue evening dress, revealing a developing figure. Her dark brown hair, cut in a medium bob, had just enough curl to make it alluring. She wore rose-colored lipstick, and her small slim nose was more like that of an Irish lassie than what you'd expect of an Italian accordion player. Perfectly symmetrical and shaped like a narrow heart, her face had a smooth, tapered jawline. Had I died and gone to Heaven?

"Wake up, John," she whispered. "The back seat's empty. Join me and be comfortable?" Following her silently, we sat down, our shoulders touching, and she planted an Evelyn Scalia-quality kiss on my lips. The remaining trip seemed short. As we left the Merritt Parkway on the Route 25 exit to Bridgeport, the bus took an abrupt right turn at the foot of the ramp, throwing me momentarily on top of Joan. She sat up, removed a tissue and small mirror from her purse, scrubbed her lips and lower face, and reapplied her lipstick in the dim light of the fleeting streetlamps. Then, with a quick hand-check of her hair, she disappeared down the aisle to her original seat. I beamed with pride—like Rudy accepting our award—as I now knew who I was.

I never saw Joan Lisi again; we'd be attending different schools, and I had relinquished the accordion for a saxophone and the Molinaro orchestra for the Stratford High band. The incident would be revealed to my mom the next day. After church, I called my friend Brian Smith, asking if he'd come over to walk to Hamilton's Drugstore at Paradise Green for cherry Cokes. Then I whispered, "You'll never believe what happened last night." Forgetting the part about winning the contest, I told him every detail about Joan, believing I was disclosing this in confidence.

When he arrived, I was late getting ready, a characteristic of my ritual laziness, but Brian was happy to talk to my mom, who must have been trained by the FBI. I could hear her asking, ". . . and then what happened?" Brian's voice droned on, prompting me to pick up my pace to minimize the damage.

Late that afternoon, Mom came into my room and told me I must go to confession, even though it was not time for my annual Easter duty, which required a Saturday afternoon trip to Saint James. I couldn't imagine myself saying—in a creepy wooden box with hard kneelers—"Bless me, Father, for I have sinned. It has been three months since my last confession, and these are my sins: I swore three times, disobeyed my father twice, and then there was this thing with Joan Lisi." *If my real father could fool a conductor on the New Haven Railroad for four years, I could fool a priest by leaving Joan out of it.* All a good Catholic boy had to do was memorize the Our Father, Hail Mary, and Act of Contrition, and once a year, make a pilgrimage to the confessional, and he could survive nicely.

On Sunday mornings, Mom held her rosary beads in church, and Dad scrutinized the walls, ceilings, and beams with an engineer's eye. She recited prayers while he calculated the pounds per square foot each beam had to support. Dad always dressed in his finest suit and crisp white shirt, with a matching tie and pocket handkerchief, his hair slicked down and shiny. Smelling of strong aftershave, he'd parked the Chrysler, washed earlier that morning, right in front of the church whenever a space was available. It was the perfect time for an Italian immigrant to strut his stuff. For me, Communion was a chance to get out of my hard seat. Fortunately, kneeling at the railing in front of the altar wasn't uncomfortable, as the step had a thick cushion. The most difficult part was sticking out my tongue far enough for the placement of the wafer, knowing that if it fell to the floor, I'd still have to eat it as Mom had told me it was "holy" and could not be thrown away.

I soon became a pawn in a chess game between Calabrese and Sicilian parents. Mom supported my laziness, allowing me to sleep till noon on Saturdays while she and Janet cleaned the house, avoiding vacuuming until 11:30. I could hear her arguing with Dad about me. He'd yell, "You get that lazy *scoubine*"—street cleaner, in English—"up and have him come out to the garden to help me!" And she'd retort, "He needs his sleep. You planted the tomatoes. Pull the weeds yourself!" I was content with pulling the covers—not the weeds—over my head and returning to sleep. Dad thought I went to sleep at 11 on Friday night, but hiding my new transistor radio under my pillow, I'd listened to the midnight Long John Nebel show out of New York. Nebel interviewed oddballs who talked about UFOs and other paranormal phenomena. If the show was interesting, I could be awake half the night.

Janet graduated from Stratford High as the salutatorian in a class of five hundred, and my prospects brightened when she fell in love her freshman year and left college to marry and raise a family. There was now money for my education. Janet was bright and a hard worker, and I believed I'd inherited Dad's intelligence, just as she had. But I was pure laziness, and Mom did nothing to alter it.

Senior year, through our school's aptitude test, I qualified for honors math. Because of my high SAT scores, I was accepted into the University of Pennsylvania—an Ivy League college—in early April. In the middle of the month, my math teacher scheduled a midterm calculus exam, but I hadn't studied the material. Realizing that failure would be inevitable, I woke up that morning and told my mother I had a sore throat. Without further questioning, she said, "I'll call the school and let them know."

Mr. Hathaway, a very tall, slender man with a prominent Adam's apple, was enraged that I'd missed the first semester's midterm for a similar "illness"—and now, once again, requiring him to create a make-up exam. He queried the class, "Does anyone know where Sottosanti's going to college?" "I do," said Brian Smith, who was always ready to speak. "He's going to the University of Pennsylvania." Founded by Benjamin Franklin in 1740, Penn didn't have the status of Harvard or Yale but was still ranked as one of the top ten universities in the nation. It was unusual for a student at Stratford High to go to an Ivy League college.

Mr. Hathaway became visibly angry, his Adam's apple bobbing: "I'll give him one semester before he flunks out of Penn!" As Brian reported to me, the usually reserved teacher had made an uncharacteristically dire prediction. It may have been one of the most important statements in my entire life because it became a necessity for me to prove Mr. Hathaway wrong. Not just at Penn but in any subsequent endeavor.

In five months, Penn would be my home, devoid of the protection of my mother. Would I be ready?

Chapter 4   Shipwrecked

DESCENDING THE STAIRCASE WITH my date, I saw, on the bottom step, Andy "Bones" Camara, the lanky social director of the Alpha Tau Omega fraternity, holding a spear. Naked except for a loincloth over a skimpy bathing suit, he was skinny—the obvious source of his nickname—with ATΩ inked on both biceps beneath crudely drawn skulls. "Welcome to the Shipwreck, mates! The bar's in the far corner!" A slight smile belied his fierceness.

My date for Homecoming Weekend that early November was Maryann O'Brien, an Irish girl I'd met in Stratford the previous summer. She was pretty, with long straight brown hair, a delicate nose, enchanting eyes, and a winning smile. Her mom, a widow raising three attractive daughters, was religious and protective, hoping her girls would all marry nice Catholic boys. Maryann was only seventeen, a senior at Notre Dame Catholic High School in Fairfield, and several weeks into our relationship, she'd told me of her mother's concern. "He's *Italian*," Mrs. O'Brien had said. "Aren't there any Irish boys you can date?" Here was another person whose attitude I was determined to overcome, just like Mr. Hathaway's. So I behaved well whenever in her presence, and before long, Maryann reported, "Mom really likes you now."

Late for the Shipwreck party, we approached the three-story brick mansion at 3914 Walnut Street in West Philadelphia, the former home of the president of the Pennsylvania Railroad. ATΩ was emblazoned in large white letters on the facade, centered above the second-floor windows. Ascending three steps onto a large side porch, we entered via the unlocked door and headed directly to the basement.

Warm air engulfed us as we squeezed by Bones, who was yelling to each new arrival over the blaring music—*The Twist*, by Chubby Checker. In 1959 this dance craze swept the world, reaching Philly a year later. Couples faced off, feet shoulder-width apart, arms extended, hips, torso, and legs madly rotating. Tossing our coats into a corner pile, we dodged flying elbows as I led Maryann to the bar adjacent to a palm branch hut with a thatched roof.

The pungent smell of beer filled our nostrils while the low ceiling retained the heat from packed bodies in Bermuda shorts, tee shirts and halters, pirate hats, captain hats, and baseball caps. Considering the temperature, Maryann and I were overdressed—she wore a long sleeve white blouse and gray wool skirt; I was in khakis and a button-down shirt with a narrow tie.

Cold beer was on tap, accessible from two kegs packed in ice-filled metal tubs. I handed Maryann a large paper cup filled with amber liquid and foam. "No thanks," she said. "I'll have the ginger ale." Thirsty, I chugged the beer myself, then drank the other while Maryann looked on. Spilling beer was not a problem—some of the brothers had spread the floor with a four-inch layer of sawdust, the "sand" for our Shipwreck party.

Mrs. O'Brien would never have allowed her oldest daughter to take the train to Philadelphia had it not been for a Penn brochure touting the measures the University had instituted for protecting the young women who visited on weekends. The school provided overnight housing at Hill House, the freshman women's dorm—a new structure designed by the acclaimed Finnish-American architect Eero Saarinen. Made of prison-like red brick, it featured sleek lines, a surrounding moat, an immovable drawbridge, and—for dramatic effect—a black, wrought iron fence topped by vertical steel spikes. The curfew was midnight.

Transitioning from blue-collar Stratford to the massive City of Brotherly Love would have been difficult for me except for the welcome extended by Gary Jacopian, a friendly fellow who'd graduated from Stratford High two years earlier. He was a devotee of fraternity life, and the day we met on campus, he said, "I'll introduce you to Alpha Tau Omega—in my opinion, the best fraternity at Penn. We've got most of the jocks, and our president is captain of the football team." Of course, I didn't tell him I'd been a star on the Rudy Molinaro Wiffle Ball Team.

Attending several rush parties, I'd felt comfortable with the ATO brothers. Many of them had been to elite college-prep schools like Philips Exeter and Choate, where the tuition and room and board were similar to Penn's. I'd overheard one of the guys asking, "Where do you get your clothes?" The answer was "Brooks Brothers in Manhattan," the oldest haberdashery in the nation, dating back to 1818. "They've got great jackets, ties, and the best underwear." (My underwear was from Sears Roebuck.) A prep school diploma, classy boxer shorts, and a Jaguar XKE were what the prettiest coeds in Philly hoped to find in a guy at Penn. And in late October, despite my inadequate self-esteem, I was offered a bid to pledge the fraternity, thanks to the endorsement of Gary Jacopian.

I took Maryann to the Homecoming football game against Columbia on Saturday afternoon. We sat high in the stands at Franklin Field, cozily wrapped in Penn's colors—a red-and-blue-striped wool blanket. Built in 1922, Franklin Field was the oldest college stadium in the country, erected when Harvard, Yale, and Penn—three of the oldest educational institutions—were dominating collegiate football, vying for national titles each season. The Ivy League had been formed in the late fifties, composed of eight schools known for academic excellence, exclusivity, and selective admissions. Soon after, the League decided to deemphasize football, banning athletic scholarships to stress academics. Home of the Philadelphia Eagles from 1958 to 1970, Franklin Field was a two-tiered stadium holding fifty-five thousand fans who had cheered for Penn before the Ivy League even existed. Only fifteen thousand attended the day I took Maryann.

Walking into the stadium, I had a flashback to the "Pound the Nail" contest at Raybestos Field, increasing the awe I was experiencing in attending an Ivy League university with a world-class football stadium. Although Penn lost to Columbia that day, I enjoyed cheering for our team as I taught Maryann the Penn Quaker songs. According to tradition, between the third and fourth quarter, everyone stood and sang "Drink a Highball," written in 1906. At that moment, many students pulled out a hip flask and took a swig of alcohol, their idea of the Penn highball. Maryann was pleased I didn't join in—she seemed to be making mental notes of the rowdy drunks in the stands—but it didn't matter. I believed I was in love. I wanted to marry Maryann O'Brien and raise six kids in Stratford.

* * *

I was amazed at the décor of the Shipwreck party. Fishnets and sea urchin shells hung low from the ceiling. Occasionally, couples disappeared into the thatched hut, not at all embarrassed when they emerged and adjusted their clothing. Avoiding the hut, Maryann and I "twisted" the night away. Although under the drinking age in Pennsylvania, I drank my fill of beer—the kegs had been purchased by the brothers who were twenty-one. But I could tell that the heat, noise, smoke, and stench were becoming unpleasant for Maryann, so we left early to get her back to Hill House before the curfew.

Maryann wanted to attend Mass on Sunday. Looking up local churches in the phonebook, I discovered that St. James, at nearby 38th and Chestnut Streets, had services at 9:00 and 11:30 a.m. We chose the earlier one, arriving in time to look around. In the Gothic style of Penn's campus buildings, St. James was a mini "Notre Dame of Paris," absent the flying buttresses and gargoyles. I'd been mailed a brochure from St. James early in the semester and—at the urging of my mother—attended a welcome reception at the adjacent Newman Center. But I hadn't gone back. Nor had I been attending church on Sunday.

After Mass, I would have taken Maryann on the trolley from Penn to the classic 30th Street Station to catch her train home, but the tracks had recently been torn up and replaced with a bus line. So we walked, enjoying the fresh autumn chill and the colorful leaves blowing in the wind, arriving a few minutes before departure with just enough time for one short kiss. "Write soon," I called as Maryann boarded.

Engulfed in sadness, I remained on the platform long enough to see her wave from the window. Then the train pulled away, leaving me thinking of how far behind I was in my courses. I'd brought my laziness from Stratford to Philadelphia, and suddenly the image of Mr. Hathaway flashed through my mind. I left the station resolved to study hard since I wouldn't be seeing Maryann until Christmas break.

* * *

I'd chosen Penn over the University of Connecticut because of the academics, but fraternity life and the associated alcohol threatened my ability to remain there. The first semester I'd registered for a pre-med/pre-dental curriculum that included advanced calculus, chemistry, physics, sociology, and Russian history courses. I quickly fell behind in the math and science courses but not in sociology and history because I liked the classes and the professors.

Dr. Digby Baltzell, my sociology professor—an intellectual dapper man who wore Harris Tweed jackets, bow ties, and pocket squares—was fascinating. Descended from an upper-class Episcopalian family, he had distinguished himself in many ways, one of which was coining the word *WASP* as the designation for White Anglo-Saxon Protestants. During my time in his class, he was writing *The Protestant Establishment*, published in 1964, expressing his belief in a classless society. But as he told the *New York Times*, aristocracy is necessary for democracy. What he doesn't like is *caste*. He believed equality of opportunity, based on merit, is better supported by a fluid and open class system. This made sense to me—my Italian immigrant father had risen from the lowest class and ascended in the social system while pushing his son beyond the level he'd achieved. A sense of guilt overwhelmed me as Dr. Baltzell's course forced me to entertain ideas I'd never considered before. It got me wondering if Dad would consider drinking highballs at nightfall a good use of his hard-earned resources. He'd certainly earned his two evening beers. But had I?

Russian history was of no interest to me until I took the class of Dr. Alexander Riasanovsky, who'd been born in Manchuria to Russian parents, studied at Oxford, and earned a Ph.D. at Stanford. He made the subject come alive through his entertaining dramatizations of the men and women who'd made Russia the country it is today—Peter the Great, Catherine the Great, Lenin, Trotsky, and Stalin. In one class, he treated us to a theatrical rendition of the lengthy murder of Rasputin, who, on his final day, survived multiple attempts of poisoning and point-blank shootings before his murderers tossed him into the Neva River, where he eventually drowned.

I was proud of my main achievements—being admitted to Penn, pledging Alpha Tau Omega, and becoming a successful and avid student of Professors Baltzell and Riasanovsky. But I'd neglected to fully realize that I was falling further behind in science and math. I hadn't heard from Maryann in weeks, and final exams were approaching, scheduled for the last week of the semester before Christmas break. The university reserved one week without classes for study, during which I needed to read half of the calculus book and much of the chemistry and physics texts. But I was confident. I felt I'd been gifted with a brain that allowed me to do in days what it took others to do in weeks. It had always worked in the past, extricating me from many difficult situations. I felt in control of my life. So why not, I figured, have fun along the way? In one semester, I'd become addicted to parties, alcohol, and procrastination. This attachment to pleasure was deep-seated, and it was threatening my future.

The day before the beginning of "study week," I excitedly tore open an envelope I received at my dorm, addressed to me in Maryann's handwriting. After an initial greeting, the letter stated: *After my weekend at Penn, I realized that our lives are taking different directions. I have begun dating someone else. I wish you the best in the future. Maryann.*

I was devastated! Depression and anxiety overwhelmed me. I couldn't concentrate on anything except my loss of Maryann— the future mother of my children, the girl I felt had been made for me.

Dejected, I walked to the McClelland Study Hall in the Big Quad. Given its private desks and cubicles, it had always been an ideal environment for studying. I'd managed to map out a schedule—eighty hours of study during the week before finals. But sitting at one of the desks, I was overwhelmed by my rejection, the first one in my life that really mattered. *What could I have done differently? Would Maryann consent to see me? Would she let me explain? Is she kissing someone else as she had kissed me? How could she?* These thoughts would not cease punishing me. I'd convinced myself that I had complete control over my mind. And now it was clear that I didn't.

A full day passed, and I lost many hours of study time. I was unable to overcome the melancholy and anxiety that held me prisoner. Besides those of Maryann, only one thought could push its way to the forefront of my brain—I couldn't let Mr. Hathaway's prediction come true. It would be the ultimate failure.

But where could I turn for help? Before I left for Penn, my mother said, "Johnny, when you go to college, I will pray to Saint Jude every day for you. He is the saint of hopeless cases." No doubt she had a predilection for what the future would hold for me at Penn, an eerie echo to Mr. Hathaway's.

For me, prayer seemed irrational and unscientific, but I figured it might be my only hope, so I walked to St. James. Though the church was locked, a small chapel was open in the adjacent Catholic Newman Center.

I'd been at Penn for over three months and never felt the need to enter a house of worship—except to please Maryann. For me, such places were built on superstition and myth. *Who needs God when you control your own destiny? God is but the fabrication of a needy humanity and, according to Karl Marx, the opiate of the masses.*

I entered the empty chapel and sat in the front pew. Two square wooden columns supported the simple altar. On the left one was the alpha symbol, "A." The right held the omega symbol, "Ω." According to my Baltimore Catechism class, these symbols in Christianity meant "the beginning" and "the end," the symbol for Christ. A white cloth covered the middle of the altar, hanging down in front. In the center, it was embossed with a gold twelve-inch cross. Right before my eyes, the three symbols spelled "AΤΩ"—a stunning coincidence, and they looked just like the large letters on the outside of the fraternity house. The altar held a gold tabernacle and an adjacent red candle—eight inches tall and three inches in diameter—set into a beautiful gold base. Its flickering flame had a mesmerizing effect on me.

I was vaguely aware that flames are very much a part of the Judeo-Christian experience, the most famous of which is Moses and the burning bush. In many instances, fire represents the presence of God. As I would later learn, fire occurs in hundreds of Bible verses, including the descent of the Holy Spirit, as tongues of flame, upon the Apostles after the Ascension. But for the moment, there was simply the flickering flame of a large red candle.

I began to think that the party at the ATO house was responsible for Maryann deciding I wasn't the man for her. An intense melancholy returned, the same I'd experienced at the McClelland Study Hall. I'd come to the chapel to pray, not knowing how to proceed. I decided I should kneel on the uncomfortable wooden kneelers and repeated the only prayers I knew—the *Our Father*, the *Hail Mary*, and the *Act of Contrition*.

An hour passed, the anxiety persisted, my knees ached, and my back hurt, but I knew of no other hope. Then something happened around the two-hour mark: while I was totally engaged in the repetitive prayers, a warm feeling invaded my body, a sense of peace and calm. A sense of wisdom, fortitude, and certainty. It didn't happen slowly—it seemed to occur within seconds, like the warmth that had engulfed Maryann and me as we descended to the Shipwreck party. But those sources of warmth couldn't have been more different.

Don't get me wrong—I didn't believe the heavens had opened to shower me with light. I'd read somewhere that the effects of a meditative approach to stress were transient. With that in mind, I immediately left for McClelland Study Hall to take advantage of whatever time might remain of this tranquility. *When would the effects decline? Would I be able to study? Was flunking out now avoidable?* These questions ran through my mind, momentarily troubling me. Yet the buoyancy and confidence I was experiencing kept them at bay.

Arriving at McClelland Hall, I sat at a desk and began to study.

Chapter 5   Penn in Hand

THE FIRST AMERICANS TO die from enemy fire in the Vietnam War were Major Dale R. Ruis and Master Sergeant Chester M. Ovnand on July 8, 1959. They had been military advisors helping the South Vietnamese in their conflict with the North. In 1960, President John Kennedy began a program of increasing U.S. involvement in the conflict—expanding the number of advisors and, eventually, the number of combat troops.

Just after midnight on a Sunday morning in early December 1961, a projectile whizzed by my ear, striking the wall behind me. Crouching behind an overturned table, I peered above it, spied an enemy target, and returned fire. Our adversaries countered, five in number, less than thirty feet away, well protected by their defenses. As seconds passed, my four fellow combatants and I stood as one, letting loose a ferocious volley that would have subdued any ordinary enemy. But this was not the case.

All ten fighters engaged in the battle were fraternity brothers—bonded not by blood but by a secret handshake, clandestine rituals, a secret password, and a black-and-gold pin in the shape of a Maltese cross bearing a crescent moon, three stars, and two hands clasped in that handshake. We were survivors of paddling and hazing, lovers of drink and women, and residents of a three-story mansion in west Philadelphia. The battle raged in the early morning in an oversized dining room designed not for war but to serve dinner to forty people.

Reaching down for more ammo—ice cubes at the start, at first easy to find, now melting and rare—I looked up and spied something tumbling toward my head, many times the size of an ice cube. I ducked before it shattered on the wall behind me. It was a cocktail glass. This battle wasn't fueled by hatred of an enemy or support of a cause but by alcohol, dulling our senses and decimating our rationality.

The battle followed the last fraternity party of the first semester of my sophomore year. Held annually, the "Make the Rounds Party" was the most notorious event at the ATO house, second in popularity to the annual Homecoming Shipwreck Party. The residents of the house, in their respective bedrooms, filled large punch bowls with various concoctions of fruit juice, alcohol, and ice, gave their drink a name, then painted that name on a sign hung outside the door to entice other brothers and their dates to enter and drink. Typical names were "Jungle Juice," "Jingle Juice" (popular in December), and, most notorious of all, "Let's Skip and Go Naked"—which nobody did—but it was the most intriguing drink of the party.

After the glass hit the wall behind my head, I searched the floor for more ice cubes. Finding none, I gathered large shards of the shattered glass and hurled them against the far wall, well above the heads of the enemy, to scare them to their senses in order to end the ridiculous battle. Voices came from both sides—"Truce! Stop! This is crazy!" Simultaneously we dropped our ammo, got up, and met in the middle to shake hands, like soldiers in the famous World War I Christmas truce in "No Man's Land."

I was the last to rise. My shirt was stained red. Eager to shake hands, I ignored my shirt, but I was bleeding profusely from a gaping wound across my palm. James McDougal, our chapter's "Worthy Chaplain" and, fortunately, the son of a nurse, ran with me to the kitchen, held the palm of my hand under cold tap water, and grabbed the first aid kit from the cupboard. He tightly wrapped the wound with gauze and adhesive tape, making multiple passes around my hand's thumb, forefinger, and heel.

When Frank Godfrey, our "Worthy Master"—or "President," that is, in any organization besides a Greek fraternity—entered, having just returned from driving his date back to Bryn Mawr, he screamed, "Take John to the hospital and get that hand stitched!" But I resisted. "No way! I'm not going!"

I'd hated hospitals since I was seven, when I spent the night at Bridgeport Hospital following a tonsillectomy. At bedtime, the nurse, who I'd one day liken to Nurse Ratched in *One Flew Over the Cuckoo's Nest*, had handed me a bedpan and said, "Pee in this before you go to sleep. I'll be back in a few minutes." I'd finished by the time she returned, but as I tried to remove the bedpan from under the covers, it snagged, spilling urine all over the sheets. Nurse Ratched yelled, "You wet the bed! Shame on you! For your punishment, you'll have to sleep in it all night long!" Turning off the light, she slammed the door on her way out.

James had stopped the bleeding from the gash in my palm. Such was my introduction to human anatomy. I briefly glanced at the wound and saw tendons under the separated skin. It took months for the wound to heal, but I was pleased to avoid the hospital.

As I lay in bed that night, suffering from a terrible headache and sharp pain in my hand, I began to reflect on the events of the past year. The calmness that had engulfed me in the Newman Center chapel remained with me for two weeks, sufficient time to study for my final exams. But my consternation had gradually returned, albeit at a reduced level, increasing when I drove by Maryann's house during that Christmas break. Returning to Penn in mid-January, I was mildly anxious and depressed. I'd escaped academic probation by the thinnest of margins, but as I began a new semester of science and liberal arts courses, I continued to attend alcohol-fueled fraternity parties—at once the salve for my despondence and the source of my chagrin because alcohol, or any drug for that matter, cannot root out the cause of disquiet.

In the spring of freshman year, I met Patty Dalman, a student at the Jefferson College of Nursing, located at 901 Walnut Street, thirty blocks from the ATO house and on the same street, a transfer-free bus ride away. Patty helped fill, but not eliminate, the void created by Maryann. She was from Lancaster, Pennsylvania, eighty miles west of the University of Pennsylvania.

Lancaster County is the site of America's oldest and largest Amish settlement. Many thousands, engaged in farming and small-business ownership, resided there in the 1960s. Known for simple living and avoiding modern technology, they traveled by horse and buggy. Members of the Amish church required their baptized members between the ages of sixteen and twenty-three to marry another member. Surprisingly, for a conservative society, many of the Amish towns of Lancaster County had risqué names. A popular saying among Penn guys, although not geographically correct, was that "The town of 'Blue Ball' leads to 'Bareville,' which leads to 'Mount Joy,' which leads to 'Intercourse,' which leads to 'Paradise,' which leads to 'Fertility,' which leads to 'Fatigue,' which is not a town." The actual distance from Mount Joy to Intercourse was twenty-two miles, but some liked to describe it in terms of minutes. Generations of Amish would make that journey, and the Amish sect would continue to thrive—as well as survive the common fraternity hazing assignment that ordered pledges to steal the town sign of Intercourse, costing the community money every time it went missing. Patty and I never mentioned these town names. It was beneath her dignity, and I respected her.

Was Patty Dalman Amish? I doubt it—we never discussed it. She was pretty, had a lovely figure, dark hair, high cheekbones, and full red lips—just the type of date to generate the admiration of my fraternity brothers. Patty and I never mentioned religion, and in some ways, although she became a steady date, we knew very little about each other. I was still mired in memories of

Maryann, and although I enjoyed Patty's company, I created a wall around my intimate thoughts that she was unable to penetrate.

Although I remained conscious of the role the Newman Center chapel had played in my ability to study, pass exams, and remain at Penn, its significance in my mind wasn't sufficient to make me a churchgoer. Three years passed, and I never entered another church in Philadelphia. I simply calculated the amount of academic effort needed to avoid Mr. Hathaway's prophecy. When it came time to select a major during sophomore year, I decided on history. My grades were too poor for the sciences, and I'm sure my parents—especially my dad—were disappointed. There was no way I was going to be a doctor.

Each summer during my years at Penn, I returned home to Connecticut to work and spend time with family and friends. Dad had left the teaching profession—the salary was inadequate to cover my Ivy League tuition and fraternity bills—becoming an engineer at a large Italian-owned construction company, a key player in the building of modern high schools in local communities. My first summer, he secured me a job as a common laborer in his company, E & F Construction, co-owned by Messrs. Epifano and Frasinelli. Dad believed he needed to teach me, still under the strong protective arm of my mom, that the jobs of an unskilled laborer, as performed by my grandfather and uncles, were something to avoid.

So he gave the site superintendent, Tony Mancini, specific instructions to saddle me with the dirtiest and most demanding tasks to convince me to stay in college. My job was to pour concrete from a cement truck into wooden forms. On my first day, before the truck's arrival, Tony gave me a pail, mop, liquid soap, toilet brush, and rags and told me to clean the nearby latrines used by the workers. When the truck arrived, I could hear the sound of its huge rotating cylindrical drum mixing cement, gravel, sand, and water into a homogenous concoction. Tony guided the truck as it backed in. Then a chute, extending from the rear of the truck, unfolded and rotated, its end placed above a heavy-duty wheelbarrow.

"John, watch Joey," Tony said. "And do what he does." Joey Lipari was a young man in his mid-twenties, not tall, but with massive shoulders and upper arms. The truck driver flipped a switch, and concrete entered the chute while Joey used a rounded hoe to guide it into the wheelbarrow. When it was almost full, the driver hit the switch again, and the flow stopped. Then Joey rotated the wheelbarrow one hundred eighty degrees and pushed it toward the wooden forms, quickening his pace to get it up a wooden ramp before dumping it. "The key," he said, "is when you get to the top of the ramp, keep your knuckles down. Then pull up as hard as you can, push forward with your palms, and dump the load. Don't lose your balance."

It seemed easy enough—until I reached the top of the ramp, where it took every ounce of my strength to complete the task. I couldn't imagine doing this for the rest of the day, but it's exactly what I did—for that day and every day for the next three months.

* * *

Early senior year, the conversations among my fraternity brothers at Penn included work, graduate school, and the War. President Kennedy was assassinated in Dallas on Friday, November 22, 1963, at 1:30 p.m. EST. I'd been sitting on a bench in the locker room after a workout in the Hutchinson Gymnasium when someone entered and broke the news. Everyone was devastated. I'd lost beloved grandparents and aunts and uncles while at Penn, but my mother, ever protective, had always urged me to remain in Philadelphia, avoid the funerals, and continue my studies. The souls of these relatives, she said, were "happy in heaven"—as if they'd floated away like helium-filled balloons in a gentle wind, growing smaller and smaller until they disappeared into a place my mom referred to as "eternity." These relatives were old and expected to die. But Kennedy had been young and dynamic. He'd stared down Nikita Khrushchev, the Russian bear, in the Cuban Missile Crisis of October 1962 and had won. How could an American hero, responsible for the lives of so many, be taken so quickly, with three bullets inflicting mortal wounds to the head and neck? I watched television for the remainder of the day, switching channels between CBS, NBC, and ABC, pondering the question of mortality for the first time in my life. Although subdued, our weekly fraternity party that Friday night temporarily suspended my thoughts about the meaning of life. And how quickly life could end.

In early December, responding to solicitations from prospective employers, I'd accepted interviews for the holiday break at corporate offices of two of the nation's largest insurers, both based in Hartford—The Hartford Group and Connecticut General. In February, three months before graduation, I accepted an offer to be in charge of a Connecticut General regional office in Stamford, twenty-five miles west of Stratford. I would have twelve salesmen to supervise, my own company car, and an office in a new building just south of the High Ridge Road exit on the Merritt Parkway.

At the ATO house that March, as our cook James Sproles, a gentle Black man, cleared the dinner plates from the table and brought out coffee and cake, Bill Bagnato, sitting across from me, asked what I was doing after graduation. Bill was a pragmatic guy, a senior at Penn's Wharton School of

Business, and he'd planned his future well in advance. He was headed to law school at the University of Buffalo.

"I'll be an insurance executive with Connecticut General," I said.

"There's a rumor," Bill said, "that Johnson's gonna increase our involvement in Vietnam. I'll give you three months before you're drafted. Law school gives me three more years of academic deferment."

This guy, I remember thinking, has his act together.

The following day, I picked up *The Philadelphia Inquirer*. The large headline in bold print said: 8 Americans Killed, 62 Hurt in Vietnam. The Viet Cong had launched coordinated attacks on several U.S. compounds, destroying airplanes on the ground and killing and maiming many Americans. The following day, the front page declared: Landmines Deadly in Vietnam Jungles.

That night I pictured a helmeted infantryman—Private John Sottosanti, Jr.—carrying an automatic weapon, a bandolier of bullets draped across his chest, traipsing through water up to his knees, one man in front, one in back, the humid air threatening to turn torrential at any moment. The shores of the riverbed were lined with palm trees, their branches intertwined with vines, moss, and ferns. The leaves of a banana plant concealed an eight-inch Vietnamese Jungle Centipede, which—as described in a recent newspaper article—was ready to spring onto the neck of the next American passing by. This was an awake, eyes-wide-open nightmare.

I jumped out of bed at 8:00 a.m.—my first class wasn't until eleven—and rifled through a pile of unopened mail on my desk. A check from my parents, and March birthday cards, had been the only envelopes worth opening ever since my letters from Maryann had stopped coming freshman year. And there it was! *"Discover the Navy! Start Your Journey! Apply to Officer's Candidate School!"* The fine print detailed sixteen weeks of training with pay—grade E-2 (whatever that was)—in Newport, Rhode Island, only hours from Stratford, with commissioning as a Lieutenant Junior Grade at the completion of the program. Requirements included a college degree (obtainable unless Mr. Hathaway planned to exercise powers of which I was unaware), an application, a comprehensive physical examination, and a signed agreement to serve six years of active duty. I immediately sent for an application.

In early May, a government letter arrived. I opened it immediately, rejoicing to read: "Congratulations, you have been accepted into the August 1964 class of the Naval Officer's Candidate School in Newport, Rhode Island. You will be inducted into the U.S. Navy at a brief ceremony in Philadelphia on Tuesday, June 2, 1964." Thoughts flooded my mind: *This is great! . . . no Vietnam jungles . . . you'll be on a ship . . . the food will be good . . . no landmines or centipedes . . . a respected officer . . . enlisted personnel will salute you, call you "sir" . . . the pay is good . . . Mom and Dad will be proud . . .*

Then the flood reversed course: *You'll be twenty-eight when you get out . . . most guys will already have tied the knot . . . all the pretty girls will be married . . . when Dad took you fishing on Long Island Sound, you got seasick . . . and that wasn't even the ocean . . . you barfed . . . no fun . . . six years is a long time . . . you should have stayed in pre-med . . . but you don't like dealing with death . . . dentistry isn't a bad career . . . there's respect . . . good money . . . remember Dr. Two Cavities? . . . maybe you could get into dental school and keep your deferment . . . no chance . . . why not try anyway? . . . Penn's a cohesive school . . . all graduates bond in camaraderie, pride, loyalty . . . and love of the red and the blue.*

That day, a week before graduation, I composed a letter to Dr. Lester Burkett, Dean of the University of Pennsylvania School of Dental Medicine, telling him my grades were poor my first years at Penn because I had no academic goals, but things were different now as I had decided upon a career in dentistry. "Would you be so kind as to grant me an interview on Monday, June 1st?" I asked.

I wasn't exactly lying about having an interest in dental school. I'd initially registered for the pre-med/pre-dental curriculum, wherein the early course requirements were identical. Either was fine with dad since they were both respected careers—each having the title "Doctor."

That afternoon I watched the news about the war on television, switching channels between CBS, NBC, and ABC, pondering the question of my own mortality for the first time in my life. How quickly and unexpectedly life can end.

Chapter 6   Interlude

I'D BEEN DRIVING FOR hours when a splotch of white goo hit the windshield, then another, and another—about ten spots in as many seconds. They were elongated vertical smears, broad at the base, thin, and waving above. More appeared, like a giant army of semen-covered spermatozoa, completely coating the windshield. Then I made a mistake—I squirted wiper fluid, but the sweeping blades only smeared the glass, further blocking my visibility. I was doing fifty on a two-lane highway separated by a broken yellow line, heading west on Highway 90 from New Orleans to Lafayette. Trees on the right narrowed the width of the shoulder. "Hold on!" I shouted suddenly, startling Richard, who was asleep in the back, awaiting his turn at the wheel to take us to Laredo near the Mexican border. Signaling a right turn, I pumped the brakes and edged onto the shoulder. The car whipped against tree branches before skidding to a stop.

* * *

I'd met with Dean Burkett on June 1st. After reviewing my transcript, he told me I needed three advanced lab science courses, plus one in statistics, to be admitted to dental school. I asked if I could attend the University of Bridgeport and live at home in Stratford since Penn was so expensive. He agreed but added, "You'll need good grades. Straight A's would help." Because of his positive attitude, I'd called the naval office the next day—June 2nd—to notify them that I'd changed my mind.

Despite the heavy course load, I would manage the requirements simultaneously that fall. It was time to prove to my parents, professors, and most of all, myself—that I was a capable individual, born not just for amusement but for achievement. It was time to emerge from the shadows, assert myself, and realize I had a choice. Time to get pummeled by the wind or become the wind, blowing obstacles from my path.

Earlier, Richard Lipman, an adventurous friend and fellow history major at Penn, had called me in Connecticut. He had two weeks before starting a new job and was looking for someone to share expenses on a two-week trip south. We agreed to meet at the ATO house on June 3rd, where I stood out front when a shiny white Buick pulled up to the curb.

Richard smiled. "My dad's new Riviera. He was afraid we'd never make it in my Ford."

I tossed my suitcase in the trunk and hopped into the leather bucket seat.

To me, "Riviera" meant vacations, luxury, and palm trees. I'd heard of the French Riviera, Italian Riviera, and Spanish Riviera, imagining beaches separated from the roadway by rows of towering palms. I was excited—I'd never been south of Philly. I'd been born on the wrong side of the tracks, the son of an Italian immigrant, a father who spent his money on his family's basic needs, except for two beers a day. Palm trees invoked the lives of the privileged and famous, who flew south with their kids over the winter holidays, sparking my jealousy.

"Where we going?" I asked.

"Not Florida. I've been there before. What about New Orleans? I got some TripTiks from Triple-A. The first one's on the dash. They'll show us the route."

"Where will we be tomorrow? I told my mother I'd call her."

"*N'awlins*. Get used to the lingo. We'll have Cajun food at Antoine's on Bourbon Street!"

Had I gone to UConn instead of Penn, I wouldn't be on my way to the land of Louis Armstrong, Pete Fountain, and Al Hirt. If only those Smith brothers and the Rackiewicz kid could see me now. They'd laughed at Hopalong Cassidy, but they'd never been out of Stratford, except for an occasional ballgame at Yankee Stadium. Tomorrow I'd be in "The Big Easy."

"Here's the plan," Richard said. "When I get tired, you drive, and I'll sleep. There's a pillow and blanket in the back."

* * *

Richard woke at the sound of my voice and skidding tires. We inspected the car. It was free of scratches, but those little black bugs, united in pairs, had painted the windshield and entire front end, an insect graveyard turning the Riviera a spotty black and white. The bugs must have been mating. In some cases, one was smashed while the other was still alive and wiggling. A thousand or more were stuck to the hood, headlights, and windshield. I took a bottle of water and a paper towel and cleaned enough of the windshield to get us to the next service station. The attendant—in khakis, bowtie, and short-sleeve shirt with a yellow clamshell above the pocket—took one look at the car and pointed to a spigot and hose. "Pahk ova dere by da wadder," he said. Then he went to work on the windshield. Looking up, he said, "Yah hit wonna da worstest luvbug storms I eva seen. Da men bugs grab da women bugs and hold on fur days."

As I would learn that fall, looking them up in my biology class, lovebugs are flies—order *Diptera*, Latin name *Plecia nearctica*. But a scientific moniker doesn't make them any less of a nuisance. They mate in May and December, and we'd plowed through them at the end of their season. But the attendant's colorful description got me thinking: *Lovebug sex must be something special to make them cling to one another at length so adamantly. Someone should figure out how to extract and bottle those sticky juices.*

Fanciful as it may seem, my whimsical ideas would one day result in several innovative companies I would form. But that was far down the road. As Richard had revealed at Antoine's, the immediate road ahead would lead to Acapulco, the world-famous beach and playground for the stars. "It's more than two thousand miles from Philly," he said, "but it's where celebrities go to escape. It's exotic, sexy, warm, and architecturally stunning. Elizabeth Taylor and Mike Todd honeymooned there. John Kennedy and Jackie, too—in '53—at the famous Las Brisas Hotel. You've gotta see that place. It's got two hundred and fifty private swimming pools. Everything's pink and white. You get your own pink-and-white jeep!"

On the road again with the Riviera cleansed of the lovebugs, I studied the AAA TripTiks for New Orleans to Laredo and Laredo to Acapulco. We'd driven almost thirty hours and hadn't been to bed, so a cheap Laredo motel, just five dollars a night, seemed like a bargain.

"Well," I told Mom when I called, "I'm in Texas. We'll be in Mexico in the morning on our way to Acapulco. It's an international call, so I'll only telephone if it's important."

Mom knew that Mexico was far away but had no idea that Acapulco was on the Pacific coast, which was just as well. "I'll pray to Saint Jude for your safety," she said, leaving me thinking, *I hope Saint Jude won't spoil our fun.*

* * *

Passing through Juarez, I was astonished by the hillside shacks, nothing but odd-sized sections of plywood boards and plastic bags spread out on the roofs.

"We'll go through Mexico City," Richard said, "and won't stop except to pee and grab a sandwich."

Unfortunately, the brand-new Riviera was low to the ground, and every ten miles or so, we descended into an arroyo—a dry riverbed. In a particularly deep one, we scraped the muffler, puncturing a hole in it, which caused a loud throaty rumbling beneath us. After limping into Mexico City, we had to abandon the Riviera for three days to get the muffler replaced and the cooling system overhauled. The lovebugs had coated the radiator with black gunk, inside and out. There was nothing to do but catch a bus to Acapulco.

Avoiding the expensive accommodations, we took a room for three nights in the multi-storied, new-but-cheap *El Presidente*, where our eighth-floor balcony offered a panoramic view of Acapulco Bay, all for nine dollars a night.

After a day on the beach and a seafood meal, I told Richard, "The way you described that Las Brisas place on our way here—I want to see it."

"We'll take a cab first thing tomorrow. It's just five miles up the hill."

Looking around with fresh eyes in the morning light, I saw a worn carpet, torn wallpaper, and thin towels. One was white and another pink. Twisting them into a spiral, I said to Richard, "Pink and white are the colors of Las Brisas, isn't that what you said? Let's go!"

The cab dropped us at the entrance. The hillside *casitas*, with their private pools, were on the upper side of the road, the La Concha Beach Club on the lower. A uniformed guard stood out front under a sizeable pink-and-white umbrella. "Follow me," I said to Richard. Then, thrusting my shoulders back, raising my chin, and avoiding eye contact with the guard, I stepped briskly down the winding road to the beach, thinking of something my father often said. *Sometimes life isn't fair, but you do what you must to get by.*

Below lay a veritable Garden of Eden—palm trees and banana trees lined the street, with bougainvillea and marigolds in between. We approached the shore through dense and humid tropical air. My only goal was to swim in the cool waters at Las Brisas. But the road ended at a large sign—La Concha Beach Club—*Privado.*

We only want to swim, I told myself. *No crime in that. It's so hot. Can't turn back now. It took time and money to get here. Twenty-five hundred miles! What are you willing to risk? Just don't wind up in jail.*

A thin man with dark hair and mustache addressed me without an accent. "Señor, please sign our guestbook." He stood by a table with a large guest register, four columns on each page.

The headings were in English: Room Number. Time-in. Time-out. Signature. Toward the top of the page, I noticed Robert Johnson of Casita 337 had signed in at 8:15 and left at 10:30, so I picked up the pen, and on the first open line, scribbled *casita 337, 11:45*, and forged Mr. Johnson's signature. I had no idea what the penalty might be, but I knew that Mexican judges don't like *gringos*. Dad would be furious if he had to post bail. But I felt I was too smart to get caught. I thought, *Let's do our thing and* get *out of here!*

"Avoid room charges," I told Rich on the narrow path through the bougainvillea to the La Concha Beach Club. At the saltwater pool, beautiful women sunned themselves in skimpy two-piece bathing suits unlike any I'd ever seen at Short Beach in Stratford. "This is heaven!" I whispered. "That bus ride was worth it!"

With sapphire blue water, the pool was round and lined by rock walls, with a twelve-foot channel for the seawater. Around the circumference, pink-and-white umbrellas shaded the chaise lounges and small cocktail tables. A pink bridge over the inlet allowed a beverage cart to slowly circle the deck. Guests signed for their drinks, but Richard and I declined each visit from the charming hostess.

Unwilling to press our luck, we spent the next two days on the public beach adjacent to the *El Presidente*. Then we flew to Mexico City to fetch the Buick. It was my first plane ride—as exciting as my first palm tree. We flew over the stunning pointed peaks of the Sierra Madre, picked up the repaired car, and then we drove back to Philadelphia, nonstop except for food and restrooms, and our sleep-and-drive rotation worked to perfection.

* * *

That fall, the University of Bridgeport was no challenge compared to the academic rigor of the University of Pennsylvania. I earned straight A's in all of my classes, as Dean Burkett had suggested was necessary, and applied to two dental schools—Penn and Georgetown. Then I began looking for full-time employment to save money for grad school. An ad for "a college graduate interested in metallurgy" sent me to the dictionary. *Metallurgy*: "the branch of science and technology concerned with the properties of metals and their production and purification." I applied, and the Huyck Corporation in nearby Milford hired me in early January for eight months, knowing that

I'd be attending dental school. The income allowed me to purchase my first car—a cute little sports car—a red Austin Healey Sprite.

Huyck made fiber metal in its Milford factory. To start the process, rough sandpaper ground the surfaces of various metals to form fibers. These strands were then placed in a rectangular and ¼ inch thick form and *sintered*—made into a porous slab—at high temperatures, which caused them to fuse. Manufacturers used the product in various ways, such as lining jet engines for cooling purposes. The company called its material "Feltmetal."

Huyck employees had to separate the sand from the fibers, a costly part of the fabrication process, for which the engineers had designed an elaborate flotation system. In the slow periods between projects, I became bored on the job and would spend time doing what I characterized as "play." During one such time, I reached into a container of uncleansed fibers, took a handful, and tossed them onto a porous sheet of Feltmetal supported by wooden blocks at the corners. I was curious to discover if air, held above and emitted from a high-pressure hose, would force the fibers flat against the sheet. It did more than that. The sand trickled through the pores, and we had clean metal fibers in seconds.

My "play" resulted in considerable cost savings for the company. They heaped accolades upon me and offered me a permanent, full-time job as a "junior engineer"—with a good salary and benefits—to dissuade me from dental school. I declined, knowing it would disappoint my father and limit my uncertain future.

But once again, with a fanciful idea, I'd demonstrated a creative instinct, a talent not necessarily linked to success in graduate school, creating in me a sense of trepidation for my future.

Chapter 7 Fire and Ice

GRAY SMOKE BILLOWED FROM the fireplace above intense yellow flames, spiraling through the rec room of the new home my father had built. Intent upon conversation, food, and drink, the partygoers I'd invited were oblivious to the impending disaster. The burgeoning fire threatened to engulf me. I'd just lit a match to crumpled balls of newspaper that I'd stuffed between twigs and small logs, but I'd forgotten to open the damper. How could I be so dumb? Clouds of smoke replaced the warm rec room air, creating a haze like a shower in a bathroom, except this fog was scorching and oppressive, causing my eyes to tear.

"Everybody upstairs and out of the house!" I screamed, my voice scratchy from the smoke, as I ran to Dad's workshop for the fire extinguisher, returning in time to see the last legs of my party guests disappear through the murkiness in the stairwell.

The instructions said: *Pull the pin. Point the hose. Squeeze the handle.* I did that, directing a long stream of retardant onto the flames, and the fire went out. But then, a dark ball of smoke surrounded me, making me dizzy. My lungs burned. There was no oxygen in the expanding black cloud. I had to get out of there before I collapsed.

Unable to see the stairs, I stumbled to the rear basement door, opened it, and placed my palms flat against the stainless steel hatchway overhead. I pushed hard, but there was no give. Nothing—no movement, no sound— yet I'd opened those double doors from below many times. I then realized that a winter storm had covered the hatchway the night before with five inches of snow and ice.

Two more attempts left me unable to breathe. On the verge of passing out, I pushed with everything I had left. This produced a cracking sound, and I felt a slight upward movement. One more push left me gazing at the stars.

I paused, then struggled up the three concrete steps and sank to my knees in the snow for the most wondrous breath I'd ever taken. When my head cleared, I trudged around to the front yard into the arms of my friends. They were relieved to see me but soon departed, one by one, the party over. I was lucky to be alive and pleased my parents weren't home.

On that cold March night in 1966, with my parents out for the evening, without telling them, I'd invited friends from the University of Bridgeport and Huyck Manufacturing to party in the basement rec room of our new ranch house. Dad had purchased a double lot near our small home on Park Street, and then, working every weekend for more than a year, with limited help from a few subcontractors, he'd built the largest home on the block. His favorite section was his workshop, behind the rear wall of the rec room, where he'd mounted his skill saw—the cause of his two shortened fingers—on a sturdy workbench. He was proud of the rec room, which featured a fireplace with limestone from an Ontario quarry, a wet sink, and a small refrigerator behind the wooden bar. Knotty pine paneling covered the lower half of the surrounding walls. The red wallpaper above it was stenciled with white outlines of cocktail glasses, shakers, corkscrews, and whiskey bottles. I'd thrown the first party in that lovely room and nearly destroyed it.

When they returned, I told my parents about the fire—as if they couldn't smell it—but omitted my near-death experience. I expected them to be angry, but they were relieved that no one had been injured. The rec room needed extensive cleaning, but insurance would cover the cost. Doing some research, Dad discovered that the fire extinguisher he'd bought, a product of the late '50s, contained carbon tetrachloride, which can become a poisonous gas under certain conditions. In 1960, the government had banned that very type for home use. Unaware of the measure, Dad had mounted it within easy reach on his workshop wall.

Doing some research in our *Encyclopedia Britannica*, I learned that one square foot of snow weighs 1.66 pounds per inch of depth. Then I measured the double doors in the basement hatchway. The area of each side was 13.5 square feet—22 pounds for each inch of snow. A layer five inches thick, accounting for limited melting, would put 110 pounds of weight on each door, not counting the door itself. (Mr. Hathaway would have been pleased with my math.) I'd lifted over 220 pounds of snow and ice, with limited oxygen in my lungs, and I hadn't worked construction or been to the gym in more than a year.

In a biology class, I'd learned of an oddity in which an "adrenaline rush" allows individuals to lift huge weights. One woman, for example, had lifted a car off her father's body, the victim of a failed jack. My mother would have attributed my experience to the intervention of St. Jude, and my father would've told her she was *pazzo*—crazy to believe such a thing. This would have resulted in another of their vicious quarrels, with dad spouting words like *afanabola*, Italian for *Go to Napoli*. Or go to hell. Which he would say but never mean.

Coincidentally, that week I'd read in the paper about a new research hospital that had just opened in Memphis, Tennessee. Named for St. Jude and founded by the entertainer Danny Thomas, it was for young children with catastrophic illnesses, often thought to be hopeless cases. When Thomas was a struggling entertainer with a baby on the way, he'd visited a Detroit church, where he was so moved by the Mass that he'd put his last dollar in the collection box. Realizing what he'd done, he prayed to St. Jude for a way to pay the bills his baby would bring. The next day he was offered a small part—for ten times what he'd given to the church. A few years later, now a believer, as he struggled to move his career to the next level, he prayed to St. Jude once again, asking for help on his path in life, promising to "build you a shrine" in return. And he did.

* * *

I chose the dental school at Georgetown rather than Penn because it was farther south than Philadelphia in an exciting city known for its abundance of beautiful women, many of whom worked in the politically powerful offices of Washington, D.C. The Georgetown campus was also attractive, with gothic spires that overlooked the Potomac River.

As I soon learned, during their first two years, dental students at Georgetown attended classes with the medical students. My initial classes included human gross anatomy, pathology, pharmacology, and biochemistry. Newly arrived in the area, I shared an apartment with three first-year students across the Potomac in Arlington. I realized on the day before my first anatomy class that I'd never seen a single dead body in the 23 years of my life. That was my mother's doing, her way of protecting me from deaths in the family, believing that it was in my best interest. Like it or not, it was time to see one.

At 5:00 p.m., the day before my first dissection class in gross anatomy, I wandered down the hallway stopping at the lab entrance. I'd been assigned to table #87. Then I pushed through those metal doors into a surreal world. More than a hundred rectangular tables, waist high, filled the room, with a zippered body bag on each. The noxious odor of formaldehyde—injected into the cadavers to slow human tissue deterioration—stung my nostrils, and my eyes burned.

The temperature was necessarily chilly—in the fifties, I guessed—as I stood by table #87, wondering if my cadaver was male or female, white or black, killed by a bullet, or ravaged by pathology. I remembered a line from Shakespeare's *Julius Caesar:* "*Death, a necessary end, will come when it will come.*" Now I was confronting death in a new way, far beyond an abstract statement in iambic pentameter. I was no longer "Johnny Boy," the son of an Italian immigrant, the kid who'd sent a nail sailing over the backstop at Raybestos Field, not far from the theater grounds. Instead, I was an adult, acknowledging life as revealed by scientific evidence, shutting out the idea of my own death as some might cover their ears from an obscenity, which is, in a way, what death is.

I realized that we sublimate the contemplation of death, trivializing it on Halloween with visions of skeletons, skulls, and headstones. In Mexico—it seemed like forever since I'd been to Mexico—*Dia de los Muertos* commemorates the departed, an annual October 31st to November 2nd holiday that coincides with the Christian observance of All Souls Day. Many celebrate the day with cemetery visits, shared meals at gravesites, and family remembrances. For others, the Day of the Dead has become so popularized that creepy skulls—or enormous sugar skulls—appear everywhere, and people paint their faces in macabre designs. But what is all this except the Mexican version of sublimation?

Opening the zipper a few inches, I glimpsed a black forehead and coarse black hair. Then I closed the bag and slipped away. I'd get to know that corpse in detail during my first two semesters.

* * *

Memorizing the names, locations, and distributions of nerves and blood vessels was the most demanding aspect of my first year in dental school. One evening, soon after classes began, I'd gone to my desk in our Arlington apartment to focus on the axillary artery branches, starting from the subclavian and ending with the brachial. And as I looked at the diagram in *Gray's Anatomy*, an idea came to mind. The names of nerves, blood vessels, or muscles had to be remembered in their proper sequence. By noting the first letter of each word of an anatomical structure and using that letter to begin a word in a sentence, I could remember them in the proper order.

Superior thoracic, Thoracoacromial, Lateral thoracic, Subscapular, Anterior circumflex humeral, and Posterior circumflex humeral—STLSAP. What would be a good mnemonic device? I thought for a moment, then came up with *Saint Teresa liked some apples and pears.* It would do. Moreover, it was one I could tell my mother—not the ones I soon began forming with four-letter words. I soon realized the more indecent the words in the sentence, the better I'd remember them—a kind of shock factor. My reputation for this approach spread quickly among my fellow students, and many began calling the apartment before exams for my sentences.

Early in that first semester, despite the tremendous academic pressures, I never considered praying or attending church services. Yet occasionally, as I passed the medical school bookstore, I paused to notice a sign. To this day, I remember its size and the exact place in the window, eighteen by three inches, in the lower right corner: "*Smile—God Loves You.*" Georgetown University is a Catholic institution, so it was logical for such a sign to be in the bookstore. But that's not why I'd gone to Georgetown. Still, I began to notice, especially around exam times, myself paying attention to that sign and gaining a small but significant sense of peace in reading it.

But I wasn't sure why.

* * *

An incident during my second year illustrated for me the difficulty of overcoming harmful addictions. An addiction clings like adhesive tape to a hairy arm, knowing it needs to be removed, but the anticipation of the pain in doing so delays the execution. In a pathology class on adenocarcinoma of the lung, Dr. John Henry had lectured passionately as a Kodak Carousel projector, its bright light streaming through colored transparent films, delivered vivid graphics to a large screen suspended from the ceiling. The photographs were from an autopsy—a healthy pink lung adjacent to a black cancer-ridden lung—of a fifty-year-old, two-pack-a-day smoker. For an hour, he'd gone on and on about the significance of motivating patients to cease smoking. Then, when he finished, he added, "If anyone has questions, come up, and I'll do my best to answer them."

Was there a minimal number of daily cigarettes that would do no harm? I didn't smoke; I was just curious. Overcoming my reticence, I walked to the front of the room, where Dr. Henry, lingering in a corner, his back to me, heard my steps. Then he turned to greet me with a cigarette dangling from the corner of his mouth. Given that day's lecture topic, a wave of empathy washed over me. Dr. Henry was a victim of the same addiction he sought to prevent in his patients. His class that day left me thinking about what sort of addictions I might have or come to acquire, aside from my penchant for laziness and how difficult it would be for me to become free of them.

Chapter 8   Debridement

MANY YOUNG WOMEN THOUGHT that my red convertible 1960 Austin Healey Sprite—small, low to the ground, bug-eyed, and with a tooth-like grill—was the cutest car they'd ever seen, as adorable as a King Charles Spaniel. But a Chevy Impala would be more dependable and hold more people. My ad for the Sprite in the *Bridgeport Post* brought only one response. A man and his son would come over that afternoon. Having the title ready, I took one last drive around Stratford, but the muffler suddenly fell off several miles from home. I'd known the moment it happened—the car sounded like the Lipman Riviera emerging from that deep arroyo in Mexico. The noise fluctuated, increasing when I stepped on the gas, and the tires squealed as I made an abrupt U-turn to retrieve the lost part.

Under the car in our driveway, I found a rusted exhaust pipe resulting from road salt meant for winter ice. What to do? My buyers were coming in an hour. Rummaging through my dad's workshop, I settled on pliers and a length of wire and did a quick repair job.

Tom Pritchard and his teenage son, Mike, arrived shortly. "What a beauty!" Tom said, studying the Sprite. Mike looked like the cliché kid in a candy shop. But as he returned from a short test drive, the jerry-rigged muffler fell off when he pulled into the driveway.

"I'm so sorry," I lied. "I had no idea." I'd be leaving for Georgetown in a few days and needed to find a new car. Time was short. I had to sell the Sprite to these people. *Now.*

"Oh, these things happen," Tom said, smiling. "My son loves the car. We'll take it." Then he handed me a check for the full amount, and they backed out of the driveway without the muffler, the grumbling roar resounding through the neighborhood.

As they drove away, I felt ashamed of myself. I had lied, and now I was standing there holding a check for the new car I felt I needed. I would never forget the warmth and understanding of Tom Pritchard, who exuded genuine affection for everyone. It was something I simply couldn't imagine or understand.

How to become that kind of person?

* * *

I explained to Margaret Keil that we were going to the Shoreham. "It's an amazing hotel," I said, "built in 1930. The Roosevelt inaugural ball was held there. All subsequent balls as well." The Beatles had stayed at the Shoreham in 1964, after their famous appearance on the *Ed Sullivan Show.* Liza Minnelli was currently performing in the Blue Room. But she was too expensive for my dental school budget.

"We're seeing Mark Russell," I told Margaret as I followed her into the Marquee Lounge, the place to see and be seen in the '60s in D.C. "He's a fabulous comedian."

Margaret was tall and slender in a fitted black dress cut several inches above the knee. It was not quite a mini-skirt. Mini-skirts were in fashion, appealing to the youth rebelling against the Vietnam War and the older generation responsible for it. Her black high-heeled pumps accentuated her height, and her long legs, sheathed in nylon, had a sensuality all their own. She was turning heads, validating my opinion of her and making me proud, as we made our way through the dark lounge to a table against the far wall.

I loved her smile. It was faultless, except for the imperceptible overlap of a front tooth, something only a student of aesthetic dentistry would notice. For me, it added an authentic touch to her charm. Her blond hair was styled in a modified bob, two parentheses framing her face and pointing to her full lips, which a touch of gloss had turned deep pink, complementing their naturalness. Margaret Keil was a classic beauty—elegant, warm, and confident. Her sparkling blue eyes ignited a fire in my heart. She was a nurse, a kind-hearted and sensitive woman. I could imagine her on the cover of *Vogue.*

"We can see the show for the price of a drink," I said. I needed Margaret to know about my budget.

"That's fine," she said. "One's all I can handle."

Mark Russell came to the raised platform wearing a blue blazer, white pocket square, grey slacks, and pinstriped button-down shirt. His polka dot bowtie and geeky dark glasses were his trademark. Smiling, he stood at the piano, played some unobtrusive background music, and finally acknowledged the crowd.

"Lyndon Johnson was here last week," he said. "Fell asleep right down in front! So I said, very quietly, 'All you men who wanna go to heaven, stand up!' And they all stood, except LBJ. Then I yelled, 'All you men who wanna go to hell, STAND UP!' Johnson stood and said, 'Mark, I don't know what we're voting on, but you and I seem to be the only ones for it!'"

The lounge erupted in laughter. Johnson's unpopularity had risen with each new soldier he sent to Vietnam. Indeed, many young men wanted him to go to hell. And Mark Russell had just voted him in.

I'd met Margaret three months earlier at Whiskey Beach in Rehoboth, Delaware, a popular spot with the D.C. crowd. Contrary to rumor, it wasn't named for the booze imbibed on the sand—it had been the drop-off point for liquor during Prohibition. It was the last Sunday in June when I'd swung by Whiskey Beach en route to Connecticut for summer break. President Johnson's daughter, Lynda Bird, was playing bridge on a blanket with her fiancé, Chuck Robb, and two secret service agents. On a blanket nearby, my friend, Jeff Larson, and I were playing Scrabble with Margaret and her friend, Kathy Murphy—we'd encountered them bodysurfing earlier that afternoon, unaware that the four of us were from Georgetown. Margaret and Kathy worked at the university hospital.

Then, in early October, I'd called Margaret to make a date for the Shoreham, fully expecting her to decline. How could such a beautiful woman go out with a third-year dental student? She undoubtedly had her pick of interns, residents, and staff physicians. But her good friend, Jan Sarmiere, another Georgetown nurse and the wife of Larry Sarmiere, a dental school colleague, had acted as matchmakers, touting our qualities and minimizing our faults.

During our ensuing dates, I learned more about Margaret, all of which I liked. One of six children, she was the daughter of a military physician. She'd been born in Iowa, but the family had moved many times. And she was Catholic. I wasn't consciously looking for Catholic women, although I understood what Freud believed, that men seek their mothers' traits in the women they choose. Margaret was one-quarter Irish, and one-quarter Scottish. The remaining half, German, accounted for her efficiency, diligence, organization, punctuality, and love of routine, traits so different from those of my Sicilian heritage.

Opposites do attract, and as our relationship blossomed, it was obvious that attending Sunday Mass together would be a requirement. Margaret chose the Basilica of the National Shrine of the Immaculate Conception, the largest Catholic facility in the United States. Having no idea what "immaculate conception" even meant, Margaret explained it meant that Mary was conceived without the stain of original sin. I wasn't convinced of the merits of a thirty-minute drive to attend this church. Fortunately, a fellow student had informed me of an abbreviated Mass offered at the nearby George-town Hospital chapel—celebrated without a sermon and all the attendant rubrics—which could be reached in half the driving time, and Mass lasted only twenty minutes. Margaret was considerate and deferred to my wishes—something she would do time and again in our future life together—so we attended service at the chapel, and our relationship continued to flourish. By Thanksgiving, we were phoning daily and dating weekly.

Since September, I'd been sharing an apartment in Arlington across the Potomac River from Georgetown with Bud Smith, my childhood friend from Stratford. Bud now taught high school English and coached basketball in nearby Maryland. On a cold January night in 1968, with Bud out for the evening, Margaret and I were kissing and cooing on a low-slung couch, listening to Johnny Mathis. But soon, I'd had enough of Johnny Mathis and *Chances Are*, so I got up and put on *Sergeant Pepper*. And before long, a question hung in the air: *Would you believe in a love at first sight?* Which Ringo Starr answered in his throaty voice: *Yes. I'm certain that it happens all the time.*

"Margaret," I said suddenly, "what would you say if I asked you to mar-ry me?" Marriage was on my mind, but the question I'd asked Margaret was vague and tentative. It was, as D.C. politicians would say, a trial balloon. My fragile ego simply couldn't tolerate a rejection. But I needn't have worried.

"Ohhhhh, yes!" Margaret screamed, squeezing me tight and planting a lengthy kiss on my lips.

* * *

Within weeks of that night, I rotated into oral surgery, a student of the great Dr. Gustav Krueger, chairman of the department. Editor of the *Textbook of Oral and Maxillofacial Surgery*, the most widely disseminated oral surgery textbook in the world, he stood over my shoulder as I examined a patient with a golf ball-sized swelling in his right cheek, just above the jawline.

"Give him a local," he said, "then make an incision and drain it."

Months earlier, I'd given a local anesthetic to a live patient for the first time—not to the oranges we used for practice. It had been embarrass-ing, and I now recalled every detail. I'd grasped the syringe in my right hand, as my notes from the previous day's lecture raced through my mind. *Injection into a blood vessel can cause angina, precipitating severe chest pain, rapid heart rate, seizures, shortness of breath, and increased blood pressure. Hit the mandibular nerve, and the patient experiences a lightning bolt in the jaw. Damage the nerve, and you cause a lifelong numbness to the tongue and lower lip. Anaphylaxis, with ensuing death, occurs in one of ten thousand oral injections.*

I'm not capable of this, I'd thought. I lack manual dexterity. I remembered hammering the nail at the Cub Scout Jamboree. I'll make a fool of myself. *What am I doing here?*

I'd held the syringe aloft for that first injection, ready to plunge the long needle into the intraoral soft tissues. But my hand was trembling, the needle moving like a windshield wiper on steroids. All I could do was take my left hand away from retracting the patient's cheek and grab my right wrist to steady it. But then, with both hands guiding the syringe, I couldn't see the target. I had to ask the patient to retract his own cheek with his fingers, and he did. I could only imagine what he was thinking. Before injecting the solution, my thumb, through the ring, pulled back the plunger to see if blood from any vessel would be aspirated into the anesthetic carpule. Seeing none, I blindly released 1.8 milliliters of lidocaine and epinephrine. The patient survived, and I did too. I had given my first local anesthetic, a rite of passage recorded forever in the memories of all dental students.

But that was months ago. Now, while Dr. Kruger read the chart, I confidently delivered the anesthetic. Then, using a mirror to move the cheek away, I saw the bulge from the abscess in the valley below the lower right molars. "Take the Bard-Parker 15," Dr. Krueger said, "and make a decisive incision to bone at the superior margin of the swelling."

His instructions swirled in my head. I'd never seen another person's blood other than that of a pinprick—I'd been sent to my room when my father sawed off his fingertips. *Would I pass out?* As I wielded the scalpel and made the incision, a thick mixture of yellow pus and blood burst forth, immediately suctioned away by the surgical assistant. "Press into the tissues with your moving mirror," Dr. Krueger continued, "until all the suppuration is gone."

Once the pus disappeared, bright red blood pulsed from the wound in rhythm to the patient's heartbeat before subsiding. For the remainder of my rotation, patients would come to the clinic with infections—my fingers were continually coated with blood—but I forced myself to concentrate on the help I rendered.

Slowly growing in confidence, I believed I could now tolerate anything. I'd gained experience in my field and the love of a marvelous woman. Our wedding was planned for next summer. But two questions lingered. *Was I ready for marriage? What about active duty in the Vietnam War when my academic deferment ended?*

Chapter 9   The Honeymooners

WE'D FALLEN IN LOVE during turbulent times, including unrest from race riots and anti-war demonstrations. Two weeks after our first date in October 1967, one hundred thousand protestors had camped at the Lincoln Memorial. Later that night, thirty thousand marched on the Pentagon. Assassinated the previous spring, Martin Luther King, Jr. had condemned the war on moral grounds, lamenting the decreased funding for domestic welfare and the disproportionate number of Blacks being killed in Vietnam. Immediately following his death, race riots gripped the District of Columbia. During four days, twelve hundred buildings were burned, and it took over thirteen thousand Federal troops and National Guardsmen to quell the chaos.

We married on August 10, 1968, during the summer break before my final year at Georgetown. Since Margaret was from a military family and accustomed to moving every few years, she'd agreed to a wedding in Stratford so my relatives could attend. Our marriage was to take place at St. James Roman Catholic Church on Main Street, the site of the after-school Catechism studies for my First Holy Communion. Built in the early twentieth-century Gothic revival style, it was an imposing structure of brown bricks with white and gray accents. Concrete arches framed its wooden front doors. Above the twin doors stood a six-foot statue of St. James with a walking stick, an image that would hold no meaning for me until thirty-three years later.

Two hours before the wedding, I experienced a loss of confidence and overwhelming fear. Could I handle being the center of attention of more than a hundred relatives and friends? Was I up to the enormity of my decision—to spend the rest of my life with one person as wonderful as I believed Margaret Keil to be? No Dr. Krueger was standing over me to tell me what to do, so I called Bill Hickman, a high school friend in the wedding party, who met me at O'Reilly's Irish Bar on the corner of East Broadway and Main, half a mile from St. James. O'Reilly's was across the street from the First

Congregational Church, the place of worship for Stratford's many WASPs, with parish records dating to 1682.

Sitting on the bar stool over my third scotch-on-the-rocks, I gazed at the white edifice of the First Congregational Church. The clear windows of this elegant structure were such a contrast to the stained windows of St. James. Yet both churches honored the same Christian God. I imagined that the cross on its two-tiered steeple, which rose sixty feet in the air, was a source of spiritual consolation for many, but—as with the solemn majesty of Saint James—it meant nothing to me.

When we arrived at the church, I learned that Monsignor Anderson, an Irish priest with a delightful brogue, was ill and that the associate pastor, Fr. Marino, a short and portly Italian, would officiate. Perspiring profusely in the heat and humidity of that August day, Fr. Marino briskly spoke the words of the ritual Latin Mass and led us in our vows, the entire event taking just thirty-five minutes. I would later discover, quite by accident, that Fr. Marino had rushed the Mass to be able to place a bet on the daily double before the 1:30 p.m. post time at Aqueduct Raceway in New York, an hour and a half drive from Stratford. I wasn't pleased.

We honeymooned in Bermuda, shunning the glamorous Elbow Beach Hotel—the most popular place for the educated and affluent—for a pink "honeymoon" cottage on the cliffs above a semi-private beach. During the week, we rode mopeds for sightseeing, listened to steel bands, and grilled red snappers—freshly caught from a party boat—while turquoise waves crashed on the pink sand below. It was a romantic, fun-filled time. Then I returned to dental school and Margaret to her nursing, settling into a one-bedroom rental in the Cherry Hill Apartments in Arlington, Virginia, near the Key Bridge on the Potomac.

As a senior dental student, confident of the diagnostic and clinical skills I'd acquired from a dedicated staff of teaching professionals, I applied for one of fifty spots in an Air Force rotating dental internship program. If accepted, I would serve as a Captain in the Air Force Medical Service, with an extra year of education paid for by the government, before two years of active duty at another base.

In March, a thick envelope arrived. *"Congratulations! You have been accepted into a one-year program of dental and medical training. You will report to Keesler Air Force Base Medical Center in Biloxi, Mississippi, on June 2, 1969, at 8 a.m. for orientation, during which you will receive a uniform and instructions on military courtesy. The internship program will provide a foundation in your profession that may lead to a career as a dental officer in the United States Air Force Medical Service. You will rotate through the following areas: plastic surgery, anesthesiology, internal medicine, dermatology, and all the specialty departments of dentistry. This will ensure that upon completing the program, you will be competent to transfer to a clinic lacking a dental specialist in one or more disciplines. Your training will allow you to fill this role."*

* * *

Keesler Air Force Base, home to twenty thousand active-duty personnel, is in Biloxi, Mississippi, a coastal city founded by the French in 1720. Its beachfront motels, tall palms, and swim-up bars attract visitors from all over. Assigned to officer base housing, upon arrival, we moved into a modest, single-story, two-bedroom home, identical to the other adjacent brick houses, in a thinned-out forest of tall pines.

When he welcomed me in his office early Monday morning, June 9, 1969, Major Hank Davies, Chief of Plastic Surgery, was wearing his informal khaki uniform, with gold oak leaves on the collar and US AIR FORCE above the left pocket. He was prematurely bald for someone in his forties. A hint of a beard extended from both ears, surrounding his broad smile right down to his chin. His eyes were serious, but his mouth revealed his warmth, allowing me to relax from the tension I felt as I began my active duty—a fear of the unknown. My mind whispered: *Don't make a fool of yourself.*

"Do you like surgery?" Major Davies asked. I nodded, and he said, "Well, you're in luck. June is a transition month in the service. All department physicians except me have moved to their next base, and you're the only new person that's arrived. When I do surgery, I usually have the medical resident beside me and the medical intern beside him. the dental intern is near the foot of the table. This week it's just you and me. It should be interesting! You up for it?"

I wavered a second. "I think so."

"You'll be my assistant surgeon, and if you show some skill, you'll do some cutting and maybe some sewing. Today we'll do scar revisions and other minor procedures, but the next two days will be more challenging— we'll treat the wives of two officers. One's an older woman having a facelift. The other, much younger, is coming in for a breast augmentation."

I smiled at the thought of the second procedure before concern about my ability to measure up crept in.

"Normally, the Air Force doesn't do elective surgery," Major Davies continued, "but the only way we can keep plastic surgeons for more than their two years is to let 'em hone their skills on procedures they'll do in private practice."

That night in bed, I thought about both procedures, which were elective and not related to any disease. So why would anyone want to submit to invasive cosmetic surgery? The only reason I could think of was vanity.

In dental school, I'd learned about operative morbidity, an unexpected complication during or after surgery. There is a remote chance—one in ten thousand—of a patient dying from general anesthesia. And I understood surgical accidents do occur. For example, severing a nerve can cause permanent numbness. You don't graduate from medical or dental school without learning about such complications. Further, post-surgical adhesions may bind adjacent structures meant to move independently but can create considerable pain when attached.

At breakfast, I asked Margaret what she thought of cosmetic surgery. "I'd never have it," she said. "God made me just the way he wants me. So why would I want to change?"

Her remark got me thinking. *Is self-esteem related to faith?* If so, I could use a good dose of each. A plaque in the Georgetown Medical School bookstore bore a quote from Ecclesiastes: "*Vanity of vanities, all is vanity.*" Of all the things we do, own, or achieve in life, it seems to mean, nothing is permanent. We will live, die, and then are forgotten. Since God exists, we should show our love by following His commandments in hopes of spending eternity with Him. Margaret believed this—but I was too caught up in the moment to do more than notice that sign in the bookstore.

Margaret had gained remarkable faith through her Catholic education, knowledge of Scripture, and Sunday sermons. She went to confession regularly and missed Mass only if she was sick. She had to switch schools often, along with her five siblings, since her father, Colonel Philip Keil, a physician in the Air Force, had served at many bases. Margaret preferred Catholic schools whenever a choice was possible—her faith provided familiarity in the face of change. After attending four high schools, two public and two Catholic, she graduated from St. Cecilia's Academy in D.C. Then she spent four years at St. Joseph College in Emmitsburg, Maryland, earning a B.S. degree in nursing. She became a registered nurse at the Georgetown University Medical Center after graduation.

I had difficulty understanding Margaret's religious faith because it was something I lacked. I'd made fun of the nuns in my Baltimore Catechism class, daydreamed during Mass, never went to Confession, and attended church only to please Margaret. I felt that life was hard. You had to get ahead of the pack by whatever means possible. Make money, accumulate honors, prestige, a lovely house, fancy car, and enjoy yourself. Then, at the end of your life, you could be proud of what you've accomplished.

I thought I'd figured it out. Wasn't this what Dad had taught me? If so, I'd been a good son and student. Although I loved Margaret deeply, I regarded her as an idealist. But I'd always seen myself as a realist.

* * *

When Major Hank Davies and I entered the operating room—scrubbed, gowned, and gloved—the patient was draped, asleep, and attended by an anesthesiologist and surgical assistant.

"This is a fifty-two-year-old colonel's wife," Hank said. "She's here for her first facelift. It'll be easier than some because she's a non-smoker. There won't be any adhesions to worry about from previous surgery. Nothing is worse than scar tissue when trying to separate layers."

With two years of oral surgery at Georgetown behind me, I had improved confidence in my manual dexterity skills. And yet, though I'd successfully relinquished the youthful feelings of inadequacy, self-doubt continued to plague me.

Hank injected the right half of the patient's face with lidocaine and epinephrine and then held up his opened right hand. The assistant promptly slapped a surgical marking pen into his palm. A crisp transfer of surgical instruments lessened the chance of dropping them. Hank then outlined the incision—a critical step—making a thin purple mark along the hairline just above the ear. Then he drew this line downward into the crease in front of the top of the ear and behind the tragus, continuing it under the lobe and ending in the hairline behind the ear. Then he made this first cut with a Bard-Parker handle with a #15 blade.

"The incision is the signature of the plastic surgeon," he said, speaking as he worked. "It can make or break a case. You may get rid of wrinkles, but you'll have an unhappy camper if the scar shows." I was amazed at the length of the incision but soon learned the reason.

"To do a good job," Hank continued, "you need access, plus the ability to retract the skin. It's like pulling a bedspread taut to remove the wrinkles and tucking the ends under the mattress. But we don't tuck. We cut off the excess."

Hank and his highly trained assistant worked harmoniously for the next hour. The latter stretched the tissue upward with forceps. Underneath the flap, Hank used the scalpel to free the skin, then electro-cautery to stop the bleeders. It was a surgical symphony. The surgeon, as the maestro, conducted the melody while the assistant interjected the little touches without which the music would be lifeless. It reminded me of Rudy Molinaro and his accordion orchestra—all precision and perfection.

Creating a pouch in the cheek large enough to insert the surgical scissors, Hank forcefully opened the handles and separated the fascia from the underlying muscles.

"Whenever you can, do blunt dissection without a knife," Hank said, "It's safer."

I'd encountered fascia in my Georgetown cadaver—which I'd coincidentally nicknamed "Hank"—but that fascia had been lifeless and devoid of bleeding. Nonetheless, it retained the characteristics of the cobweb-like fuzz that attaches skin to muscle. Next, Hank released the entire skin on the right side of the face—from just lateral to the eye, to below and behind the ear— and pulled it taught, making it wrinkle-free. Before the surgery, the skin had resembled a dried prune. The patient was a tennis player who'd spent many hours in the sun, which causes ultraviolet radiation to break down the subepidermal connective tissues. Continuing to stretch the skin with his left hand, Hank drew a new line to mark the excess tissue and then, with surgical scissors, cut along the line. Finally, he closed the skin while explaining his suturing technique.

Hank rotated the patient's head, and we went to the other side of the table to administer a local anesthetic and repeat the procedure. "I'll mark the incision, and you make the cut," he said, switching places with me. "Bevel your incision to 45 degrees in the area of the hairline. That will promote hair growth through the scar."

With Hank close by, at times barking instructions, I performed the entire left side facelift, except for the suturing. When I finished, Hank rotated the head, her nose pointing to the ceiling. "Nice job!" he said. "I can't tell the difference."

I swelled with pride—not such a bad thing, after all. A surgeon must possess self-confidence, decisiveness, and perseverance to do the job.

The next morning, when we entered the operating room in the same fashion, the patient was draped except for her face and chest. "She's a thirty-two," Hank said. "But she'll soon be a thirty-six."

Compared to a facelift, a breast augmentation is simple. I remember how Hank placed the silicone implants in the exact position for symmetry. Before suturing, he had me join him at the foot of the operating table, where he made a fist with his right hand, raised his thumb, closed one eye, and superimposed the upper edge of his thumb onto the contour of the left breast. Then, without moving the finger, he moved his head laterally four inches to the right so that the finger outlined the superior aspect of the right breast. "Perfect!" he said. "You try it."

I did. "Perfect," I repeated. "In more ways than one." Hank chuckled.

Chapter 10   Storm Clouds

I THOUGHT I'D SEEN it all when Richard Lipman and I encountered that lovebug storm on our way to Mexico, but I was wrong. Several weeks earlier, tens of thousands of cicada nymphs had emerged from the Biloxi soil, climbing the trees, shedding their skins, and exposing new bodies. An inch or two long, they were multicolored, with beady eyes and membranous wings. They sucked sap and vibrated their tymbals—their protective external skeletons—while emitting a relentless, high-pitched, pulsating sound, competing with the roar of the wind that had suddenly begun buffeting the needles and cones of the short-leaf pines.

But there was something different about the sky now. The clouds were ominous—as dark and threatening as a shark's dorsal fin, expanding to fill the southern sky and blot out the sun. The mating call of the cicadas created a sense of eeriness I'd never quite experienced before. My neighbor, Lieutenant David Bigby, was pacing in front of his home. "John!" he called. "Did you tape your windows and fill your bathtub?"

"Yeah"—I knew the drill—"but I'm more worried about these pines. They must be eighty feet tall. They could do serious damage. Camille's now a Cat-5!"

"Hate to disagree with you, Captain, but these pines have survived many hurricanes. So don't sweat 'em!"

For some reason, I couldn't let this go. I wanted to argue. Who did Lt. Bigby think he was—a hurricane expert? He'd grown up in New Jersey! I was older and wiser and had seen hurricanes damage the Connecticut coast.

Hurricane Camille struck on Sunday, August 17, 1969, with the largest storm surge on record, almost twenty-five feet, surpassed only thirty-five years later by Hurricane Katrina. Margaret and I had been attending church on Sundays since our arrival—she attentive, I daydreaming—and during one Mass, the priest had said, "Father, we pray for your protection during this hurricane season."

That surprised and puzzled me. With so many things to pray for, why was there such an emphasis on hurricanes? There hadn't been a major hurricane in Mississippi since 1947, when fifty-one people died. I was on active military duty in the land of milk and honey, unaware of any downside except, perhaps, for the heat and humidity.

I was still bantering with Lt. Bigby about the threatening storm when Margaret, seven months pregnant with our first child, yelled through the screen, "Honey, someone from the hospital's calling. It sounds urgent." Ducking inside, I took the phone and rummaged for a pencil and paper. "Yes, sir," I said. "I'll be there . . . Give me that address again for my wife."

Hurricane Camille was over the Gulf, with winds up to one hundred eighty miles per hour. "We've got to separate," I told Margaret. "You're going inland. I've got to report to the hospital."

Keesler is one of the largest Air Force medical centers. The hospital has two wings, each five stories tall, with an impressive entrance at their junction. It offers internships and residency programs in all medical and dental specialties.

"Captain Sottosanti," the commanding officer said as I entered the glass doors, "I have you stationed in the lobby by the reception area. You're to help with arriving patients. You'll be part of the triage team. Assess the severity of the injuries and send them for treatment as needed. It may be a while before you see any action, as water and debris will block the roads. We expect a large number of patients this evening."

What in the world am I doing here? I asked myself. *I wanted palm trees, not a life-threatening hurricane!* Now I was separated from my pregnant wife.

Dressed in scrubs, I sat on the floor, back to the wall, in the quiet corridor adjacent to the noisy reception room, a transistor radio to my ear, listening to weather updates. "Camille's eye will arrive within the hour," one broadcaster said. Then multiple stations sequentially went silent as power outages hit the hospital and surrounding areas. The emergency lights and eerie silence cast a somber mood on those near the entrance. An older man in a hospital gown eventually broke the silence, running into the corridor from a nearby stairwell. "Fire!" he screamed. "The hospital's on fire!"

"How d'ya know?" I yelled. I didn't smell any smoke—I was no expert, despite my rec-room fiasco in Stratford.

The patient was running in circles, screaming, unembarrassed by the slit in the back of his skimpy gown. "I saw flames from my room! On the roof of the other wing! Y'all gotta do something! We gotta get outa here!"

I couldn't tell if he was delusional. Even though the storm had struck, I needed to see the flames for myself. Which meant I had to brave one hundred eighty miles per hour winds and torrential rain. All these people couldn't leave the hospital during a hurricane. Peering out the glass doors, I couldn't see the roof of the adjacent wing. An overhang above the entrance was blocking my vision. I pushed on the heavy doors as I'd pushed on the cellar hatchway at home. But, as in Stratford, they didn't budge. Bracing myself, I pressed against just one of the doors, and it opened just enough to squeeze through. But the moment I stepped out, the wind shoved me flat against the other door, and I slid to the concrete beneath the overhang. Rain and pinecones pummeled me. Distant palms, enshrouded in heavy fog, rippled like waves. I crawled forward, struggling to keep from scraping my chin on the concrete.

At the end of the overhang was a metal railing on my right. Grabbing it, I pulled myself up enough to see the roof of the adjacent wing. The screaming patient was right—tall flames danced in the relentless wind. But there was no smoke. And those flames were strangely unchanging. Instead, they were thick pieces of plastic, loosened by the wind, put there to protect a leaking roof, now lit by red warning lights for airplanes at the nearby landing strip.

Crawling back, I squeezed through the door into the warmth of the reception room and collapsed on a couch, soaked to the bone. Everyone fell quiet as I told the group what I'd learned. A half hour later, when the howling wind suddenly stopped, breaking off like a pack of wolves in the night, I asked, "Is it over?"

An enlisted corpsman, a Keesler veteran, responded, "No way, sir! The eye is passing through, and the worst is yet to come!"

* * *

It was 3:45 a.m. Two police cars were outside. Six people in drenched, torn clothing were staggering into the reception area. The triage commander yelled in my direction. "Get these two to Room 114! Get them warm clothing, take their histories and vitals, and check for injuries." The couple was in their late twenties, anxious and wet but uninjured except for minor bruising. The husband, Paul, spoke first.

"We were in our apartment on the second floor. The wind was rattling the window, and rain was blocking our visibility. Our landlord slammed the door and left the building—in a Category 5 hurricane! I forced the window open to call him back, but all I saw was rising water. He got washed away. Seconds later, a turbulent river came up through the flooring."

Mary, Paul's wife, took over. "We climbed through the window and swam from the house, which exploded behind us. I thought we would drown, but Paul helped me onto the roof. We grabbed the chimney and some pipes, floated for hours, then ran aground. We jumped to land, found a road, and a cop brought us here. We've lost everything, but we're alive! Our landlord—wasn't so lucky." Then she broke down and cried, her husband cried, and I cried, too. I gave them dry clothes and hot soup, and they were fine, except for their deep emotional distress. As the storm moved inland, other victims arrived and were seen by various personnel, but Paul and Mary were my only patients.

In the morning, I fetched Margaret. Back home, I found our neighbors, Lt. Bigby and his wife, in their front yard. Two tall pines in front of our house had crashed through their kitchen and living room roofs. I was elated that none of us had been injured. But, at the same time, I was proud that I had been right and David had been wrong about those pines. *So where's this attitude coming from?* I wondered. Just the morning before— which seemed years ago now—the priest at Sunday Mass had addressed the sin of pride, quoting Thomas Merton's famous book, *No Man Is an Island*: "Pride makes us artificial. Humility makes us real." I found myself pondering that message and how it might apply to me. In certain respects, I realized I had lots to learn.

In the following weeks, TV, radio, and newspapers detailed the devastation wrought by Hurricane Camille—from the Mississippi coast to the Appalachian Mountains of Virginia. According to one source, 259 had died, 8,931 were injured, and 19,577 homes had been destroyed or sustained major damage, the Bigbys among them. At the height of the storm, winds had averaged one hundred seventy-five miles per hour along the coast, but an embedded tornado had caused a Keesler runway wind gauge to freeze at two hundred thirty miles per hour. The flood surge had swept huge ocean-going ships inland, necessitating their dismantling to remove them. A large, diesel-fuel barge had ended up on the median strip on US Highway 90 in Biloxi, the main east-west thoroughfare, and traffic had to be rerouted for months.

But the single worst tragedy happened at the nearby Richelieu Manor Apartments, where twenty-three people had decided to have a hurricane party and ride out the storm. Margaret and I watched the evening news as Walter Cronkite dramatized the incident with a photo of the large apartment complex before the storm. A camera panned the demolished building—only the slab was intact—as Cronkite noted, *"This is the place where twenty-three people laughed in the face of death. And where twenty-three people died."* These fun-loving human beings had toyed with death, flaunting their imagined immortality, and lost. Death, I remember thinking, always wins.

* * *

After my rotation in plastic surgery, everything else was anticlimactic. The only dental specialty I really enjoyed was periodontics, which treated unhealthy gums. I learned to save teeth by doing surgery to regenerate bone lost to chronic disease. My mentor was Major Jim Hardeman, one of the kindest people I'd ever met. What made him different was that he was a nine-fingered surgeon.

"I see you're wearing a wedding ring," Jim said. "I suggest you take it off." He held up his left hand, and I saw he was missing the fourth digit. "I was working on my car," he explained, "and I got too close to the fan. The blade caught the edge of my ring and tore off my finger. Fortunately, it was my left hand."

"You should meet my father," I said. "He's lost several fingertips to a table saw."

With two months to go in my internship, I was asked to fill out a "dream sheet," informing the Air Force of the top three bases at which I would like to spend the next two years. Yet—as it was made clear—nothing was promised. I only knew I wanted palm trees, just not in Southeast Asia. So one choice was Homestead in Miami, Florida. Another was Vandenberg on the California coast, one hundred fifty miles north of Los Angeles. A third was Nellis in Las Vegas.

Margaret had given birth to a healthy baby boy in October, so wherever we were assigned, we'd travel with an eight-month-old in a car stuffed with luggage and diapers. At least the Air Force would pay for shipping the furniture.

I was assigned to Las Vegas— the original "Sin City"—and couldn't believe my luck. Newspapers were filled with tragic stories from Vietnam, and we were going to Las Vegas!

Chapter 11   What Happens in Vegas

RODEHEAVER HICKS, A MAN on a mission, was born in 1921 in Atkins, a small town in southwest Virginia with a population of less than two thousand and a median income half that of the rest of the state. He was one of seven children. Atkins' main claim to fame was the Old Stone Tavern, a historic inn built in 1815. "Rody," as family and friends called Hicks, had known poverty similar to my dad's. After graduating from a local college, he served as a gunnery officer in the Navy in the South Pacific during World War II. After the war, he went to dental school at Northwestern and became a dental officer in the Air Force in the early fifties.

There was a subtle but rough edge to Hicks, perhaps a remnant of his early privation and fight to excel—again, not unlike that of my own father. Telling incidents had punctuated his career, including a fist fight with a junior officer early on, a black mark rumored to be concealed in the depths of his Officer Evaluation Reports. These documents assessed the work ethic, mentorship ability, job competency, and personal character used to determine if an officer advances to a higher rank. When he took command of the Nellis Air Force Base dental clinic, Hicks had been a lieutenant colonel for more than ten years and had twice been turned down for promotion. According to several career dental officers, he was determined to gain the rank of full colonel before retiring at age fifty-two, enhancing his prestige and retirement pay.

Escorted by Doris, a middle-aged civilian secretary, I entered Lieutenant Colonel Hicks' office. Doris pointed to a chair in front of an empty desk and left. The surface of Hicks' desk was strewn with papers—large piles sliding into smaller ones—along with a few issues of *Road & Track*. An empty white coffee cup was stained with light brown rivulets.

The door opened, and a stocky man of medium height with a thick neck and short blond hair greeted me with half a smile. "You must be Captain

Sottosanti. I'm Lieutenant Colonel Hicks." Without extending a hand, he sat down behind his desk, picked up the thin manila folder holding my file, and said, "Welcome to Nellis. I see you're one of those interns the Air Force is grooming for a possible military career. You've got an impressive record from Keesler. I know they promised you a choice duty in a specialty department, probably doing surgery. But things are different here at Nellis."

Hicks then told me that all new dentists at Nellis must prove their loyalty to him for the first year by performing well on the "amalgam line," which meant doing silver fillings all day. He was strictly a *drill 'em and fill 'em guy*, and if I did well, I might be cleared for surgery in my second year. This, however, contradicted my Air Force acceptance letter . . . *"transfer to a clinic lacking a dental specialist in one or more of those disciplines. Your training will allow you to fill this role."* Nellis had no board-trained specialists. Before I departed, Hicks had words of advice. "Stay away from Captain Grossman. He's a troublemaker."

Later, I joined some familiar faces at lunch in the hospital cafeteria. After greetings and introductions, I asked, "Who's this guy Grossman, anyway, and what does Hicks have against him?" Simultaneously, fingers pointed to a table in the far corner, where Grossman sat with several enlisted corpsmen. Alan Gibbs, a young dental officer from Philadelphia who'd arrived with Grossman, said, "We're ordered not to sit with him or talk to him. The Hoover and Wally are like oil and water."

"The *Hoover?*"

"Wally gave him that name. Because he sucks!"

How appropriate. The Hoover had been the most popular vacuum cleaner for fifty years. Mom had one.

The guys told me that Grossman was an idealist. He cared deeply for his patients and wanted to do everything he could to save their teeth. That word— "idealist"—brought Margaret and her commitment to the Catholic faith to mind. Later, when I learned Grossman attended Mass weekly, I mused about the possible connection.

"The Hoover only cares about one thing," Gibbs added. "Getting promoted to a full bird colonel." Evidently, the Air Force had developed a numerical point system to distinguish the most productive clinics from the laggards. Each procedure was assigned a number of points, and Hicks realized that some—like root canals to save back teeth—required too much time for the number of points they received. Hicks wanted to show that he ran the most efficient dental clinic in the Air Force, which meant piling up points—even if it meant extracting teeth that could be saved. Extractions were quick, but gum surgery took time.

Back in Biloxi, Major Hardeman had taught me that periodontal surgery was very effective in preventing tooth loss. It was my favorite type of oral surgery. But, listening to Gibbs, I sensed a cloud descending, not as dark and turbulent as those brought by Camille, but still disheartening—I wouldn't be able to use my training. But I felt empathy for the patients who were losing their teeth due to the pride and greed of a single man.

"But that's malpractice," I said. "He's ordering us to commit *malpractice?*" Gibbs nodded.

It wasn't long before I realized that Grossman was an honorable man, a man with the nerve to confront the Hoover. As a result, he suffered isolation, extra work hours, refusal of leave requests, and any other humiliation Hicks could create for him. I couldn't believe it. Everyone was told not to even talk to him. So, there we were—stuck in the middle of the desert, with no one in the Air Force hierarchy to give a damn about our little clinic. If anyone tried, the Hoover punished him. Only Wally Grossman had the guts to fight every step of the way.

After discussing the situation with Margaret, I made a difficult decision. I decided to relinquish the ways of my dad's family—always looking out for myself and my family—and meet with Grossman. In retrospect, religion played no role in this decision, although perhaps my grandfather—Charlie Russo, back in Greenwich, Connecticut—had influenced me. Despite being a poor man, he sent small checks to every Catholic charity that supported the disadvantaged.

"Wally," I said when we finally sat down together, "I just learned from my wife that my father-in-law—the highest-ranking colonel in the entire Air Force Medical Service—taught Internal Medicine to our hospital commander, Colonel Antonelli. I think I can pull rank on the Hoover!"

"No harm in trying," Wally said. "Keep me posted."

A few days later, Colonel Antonelli rose to greet me. "A pleasure to meet you, Dr. Sottosanti. I understand you're Phil Keil's son-in-law. What a great doctor and teacher! He taught me so much about medicine. I've the utmost respect for him. Sit down and tell me what's going on in the clinic." So I did.

"I had no idea!" he replied. "Colonel Hicks said Grossman was a no-good troublemaker. I'll explain the situation to Colonel Oliver Knoll. He's the Tactical Air Command Dental Surgeon at Langley Air Force Base in Virginia. Lieutenant Colonel Hicks has to report directly to him." Then he asked for the names of the others who agreed with Grossman and me—Captains Mackie, Goldner, Comeau, and Gibbs—and promised not to reveal their names. He requested that we list our complaints in an unsigned letter, and he would forward it to Langley.

Two days later, Lieutenant Colonel Bill Clark, second in command to the Hoover, called Wally into his office to take a call from Colonel Knoll. Wally described that call to me later in the day. An angry voice on the phone had said, "Grossman, I received the letter from you and the other five junior officers! I need their names before taking action. I know Sottosanti's involved. Who else?" Wally gave the names. Knoll would be coming to Nellis for "an investigation." We learned from an overheard phone conversation that Colonel Knoll would stay at the Hoover's home since they were old friends.

When he arrived, Colonel Knoll interviewed us individually, always defending Hicks with phrases like "he didn't mean that . . . you must've misunderstood . . . I know he wouldn't do that . . . you must be mistaken." Now that he had our names, Hicks punished us in various ways, and patient care suffered. I called my father-in-law and told him what was happening.

Margaret's father was hardly optimistic. "I tried to go over Knoll's head, but he's got a friend in the Corps—a general—so my hands are tied." He paused. "But there's one thing you can do. See the base Inspector General, who settles disputes involving senior officers."

The Inspector General at Nellis was Colonel Paul Ackerman. A few days later, he greeted our defiant group in his dress blues, the eagles on his shoulders sparkling in the fluorescent lighting. His neatly groomed gray hair and winsome smile projected a grandfatherly image of kindness and authority that encouraged me. He, too, met with us individually, hearing the same story repeatedly.

"I know nothing about dentistry," he told us, "but I know much about people. I can tell you're all telling the truth. I'll investigate on Monday. I'll come to your clinic, rattle some cages, and get to the bottom of this."

But Colonel Ackerman did not appear on Monday. Weeks passed, and nothing improved. Meanwhile, the Hoover vented his anger on Grossman and me, the perceived ringleaders. Finally, Colonel Antonelli called a conference on a Wednesday morning in early November of 1970. Standing at the end of a long table, clutching a letter with both hands, he quieted the room, and despite his best efforts to keep that paper from rattling, we could sense his discomfort. He appeared tormented by the inability to right a wrong. He read nervously:

From the Tactical Air Command Surgeon General, Langley Air Force Base. To Captains Grossman, Sottosanti, Gibbs, Comeau, Goldner, and Mackie. I have learned that the six of you refuse to follow the direct orders of Lieutenant Colonel Rodeheaver Hicks in his efforts to provide dental care at the Nellis Air Force Base Dental Clinic. Unless this intolerable behavior ceases immediately, you will face one of two penalties: One . . . Article 15, with the possibility of loss of rank, reduction in salary, extra duty, and other compensatory penalties for your actions. Two . . . face a court-martial, possibly resulting in one year of imprisonment, a dishonorable discharge, or both.

I looked at Antonelli, but he was gazing at the floor, gripping that letter. Then he quickly left the room. My heart was thudding. I felt conflicting emotions of shame, fortitude, and determination. I looked at my cohorts, who were staring into space, until I broke the silence. "My place tonight? Seven sharp?" Everyone nodded affirmatively.

That evening, I was resolute. "If we're to proceed, we've got to commit to each other that we'll only act in unison, no matter what bribes or threats are made. I discussed everything with my father-in-law, and we have but one choice—to ask Congress for help." I spoke confidently, wondering where such confidence came from. For once, my efforts were altruistic.

We were all from different states—each with two United States Senators and one Congressman representing us in Washington. "We need eighteen different letters," I said, "three from each of us, stating the same grievances." I handed out a list of names and addresses. Margaret mailed the letters the next day.

It didn't take long for a response. During lunch the following Monday, Lieutenant Colonel Clark interrupted us in the cafeteria, a grimace on his face. "What in the world did you guys do?" he exclaimed. "The Surgeon General of the United States Air Force just called. His phone's been ringing all morning. He's never seen anything like this!" He shook his head. "How many Congressmen did you contact? I can't believe it! This is the largest request for a Congressional investigation the General has ever seen, and he's been in for thirty years!"

They arrived the day after Thanksgiving—Colonel Bob Thompson, the Deputy Assistant Surgeon General for Air Force Dental Services, soon to be promoted to General, and Colonel Kenneth Dill, both attired in Air Force dress blues; and a civilian, Dr. William Hiatt, in gray slacks, white shirt, blue blazer, and red-white-and-blue striped tie. A three-day meeting ensued. It grew tense at times, but Colonel Hicks became unhinged under the weight of his own lies. At one point, he was asked to be quiet when others spoke. Finally, Colonel Thompson had to order him "to leave the courtroom," the same conference room where Colonel Antonelli had read us the threatening letter.

I'd heard of the immutability of truth—that it would eventually prevail—although from experience, I knew it often took forever. In a history class at Penn, I'd encountered a statement from Winston Churchill: "The truth is incontrovertible. Malice may attack it, ignorance may deride it, but in the end, there it is." Personally, I didn't always tell the truth because

I'd learned from my father that lies could get you out of trouble unless they're revealed for what they are.

The verdict came several weeks later. Hicks was relieved of his command and confined to his office, his *Road & Track* magazines now the only clutter on his desk. The paperwork had been transferred to his subordinate, Lieutenant Colonel Clark. Further, the investigating team recommended that I function as the base periodontist. Bernie Comeau became the base endodontist, and we headed up departments that previously hadn't existed.

But the victory was bittersweet. The Air Force transferred Hicks to Luke Air Force Base in Arizona, the top choice on his dream sheet, and promoted him to full colonel. He retired in 1974 and died in 2009 at the age of eighty-eight. His tombstone in Phoenix, Arizona, reads: "Honest and true, a friend to all."

No doubt Grossman would contest that statement. But when we depart this world, I think we'd all like to be remembered that way.

Chapter 12   The Seven Deadlies

THROUGHOUT THE EARLY YEARS of our marriage Margaret was a supportive wife to me and a devoted mother to our son. She prepared nutritious dinners, cleaned the house, made the beds, did the dishes, and shopped at the exchange on the base. I brought home a paycheck, watched TV, and planned trips to the National Parks—trips we took in our Chevy Malibu and pop-up tent trailer. I did attend weekly Mass—my only non-negotiable duty—and helped to keep Wayne quiet during the service, taking him outside when necessary.

With the dramatic Hoover conflict behind me, I began to enjoy the Las Vegas shows, gambling, and buffets while slowly growing aware of my susceptibility to Sin City. But I didn't care. The priest at Guardian Angel Cathedral, only blocks from the Strip, accepted casino chips in the collection basket while he preached on the Seven Deadly Sins—pride, greed, lust, envy, gluttony, wrath, and sloth. This well-known list had been compiled by the Desert Fathers, monks and hermits from the second to fourth centuries after the dawn of Christianity, as they lived in the Egyptian desert in an attempt to conquer temptation.

Despite listening to these Sunday sermons with Margaret and Wayne at my side, I made no effort to control my behavior towards things that some might consider sinful. If no harm was done to others, I figured, *who cares?* I'd become a moral relativist, a stance popular in the early twentieth century, long before that term became fashionable.

In *Mere Christianity*, C.S. Lewis denounces pride as "the great sin." I could now recall instances when my own feelings of pride and self-righteousness—aroused, for example, by the disagreement with Lieutenant Rigby over the pine trees at Keesler—had overtaken my common sense, placing me, in my own estimation, above others. In March of 1971, the first of several similar instances occurred when Colonel Antonelli called the dental clinic and asked for me. Having had no contact with him since the letter incident, I was surprised.

He heard I had discovered a special liquid treatment for difficult canker sores and explained that Colonel Ackerman's wife had a persistent one he had been treating unsuccessfully for months. I asked to see her as I knew an individual lesion should disappear within fourteen days. Examining her, I suggested the lesion be biopsied. It was, and the diagnosis was squamous cell carcinoma of the tongue—with a dire prognosis. Subsequently, she flew to have treatment at a major Air Force hospital in Texas.

Upon learning of her situation, a more sinister thought entered my mind. Her husband shouldn't have made promises he couldn't keep.

* * *

A month later, Colonel Brest, the Hoover's replacement, called a quick staff meeting in the lounge. "Anyone want tickets tonight for Robert Goulet? The Desert Inn's offering them for free."

A famous singer, Grammy winner, and star of Broadway and television, Goulet was "tall, dark, and handsome" with a rich baritone voice. When performing, he loved to interact with his audience. I accepted two tickets, knowing Margaret would enjoy a night out.

That evening, we found ourselves in a booth facing the stage, at eye level with Robert Goulet. Between songs, he told some one-liners, and at one point, looking directly at Margaret, he said, "The first thing I notice about a woman is her eyes." Then he paused. "And when her eyes don't look back, I notice her breasts." The audience laughed, and Margaret managed a smile.

At least twenty women were in the theater's lower section, but Robert Goulet had chosen Margaret—beautiful, tall, and slender. Margaret was not buxom but camouflaged by a pink ruffled blouse, she fit the bill. Rather than being offended, I beamed with pride. I knew she was beautiful, but I also needed to know that others did.

In Vegas, occasions for lust were everywhere. Ivan and Romola Goldner, Bernie and Peggy Comeau, and Bob and Punkin Mackie were all good friends who'd experienced the Nellis dental clinic investigation with Margaret and me. (Wally Grossman and Alan Gibbs had since finished their military careers.) One day at work, we decided to convince our wives to take in the 9:00 p.m. cocktail show at the Tropicana, rather than the family-dinner show, to see the Folies Bergere, whose showgirls had been entertaining Vegas audiences for the past decade. They patterned the show after the one in the famous theater in Paris, which had opened in 1869, and as the Victorian era ended, it was the first venue to feature a nude showgirl. Neglecting to tell our wives that in the late show all the girls would be topless, we tipped the maitre d' for a stage-side table.

The Folies was an extravaganza. Horses and riders charged the audience on treadmills, motor scooters circled the stage, and a variety of acrobats, jugglers, and singers performed. The gorgeous and perpetually smiling, bare-breasted showgirls wore skimpy costumes, and for me—a kid from a small Connecticut town that still observed the blue laws—they were the main attraction.

The curtains had opened on an empty stage, except for an elegant, spiraling, gold staircase, wide enough for thirty showgirls to descend in pairs. The backdrop, illuminated by crisscrossing and flashing neon lights, featured broad red and black stripes. Then the smiling girls came down, arms straight out to the side, heads held high as if balancing a book. Their white sequined hats contained V-shaped, red, and black plumes. They wore metal neck collars spelling CASINO in a vertical chain of letters that fell between their naked breasts, all the way to their sequined bikini bottoms. Dancing to lively show-tune music, they came to the edge of the stage—just feet from our faces—twirled in unison and then retreated, joined midway by ten fully-clothed, trim, and athletic young men in white jackets, trousers, and top hats.

Leaning towards Ivan, I whispered, "Having done a breast augmentation, I've been looking for scars but haven't seen any!" Ivan smiled, then turned back to the stage.

As we left the showroom that night, Margaret was quiet and non-judgmental.

When my colleagues and I had first considered the Folies, we'd asked Lieutenant Colonel Rank, a man we admired for his gentleness, kindness, and professionalism, if he'd like to join us.

"I can't," he'd replied. "My faith teaches me to avoid temptation. Being married precludes accepting your invitation." I've never forgotten that moment, while at the time, I'd thought: *He's a nice guy, but his religious beliefs are a bit rigid.* Then I began to wonder if his strong moral convictions were in any way related to our admiration for him.

So much, then, for lust in Las Vegas. But what about greed and envy?

Having read a book on card counting, which is illegal at Blackjack tables, I told Margaret that I wanted to spend one night a week playing at the Mint Hotel. As usual, she deferred to my wishes. The Mint was in the downtown area known as Glitter Gulch, where the number of light bulbs made the evening appear as day, and the dealers used a single deck, dealing it down to the last card. Margaret was concerned about losing money, so I promised to take no more than ten dollars, and if I doubled my money, I'd come right home and put it in a large mayonnaise jar, using it as seed money for the next week. This assured her that I wouldn't gamble away our food money.

On my first night out, I handed a ten-dollar bill to the dealer, who gave me ten chips in return. Then the pit boss, bored on a slow Tuesday night, came over and started a conversation.

"Haven't-a seen you here before . . . where ya work?"

"I'm a dentist out at Nellis."

"Hey, Doc. What's-a ya name?" His tone took on a level of respect. I told him, affecting an Italian accent like his own.

"Giovanni Sottosanti," he repeated slowly and phonetically. Then he paused. "A good Italian name. Look, *paisan*, we Italians gotta stick together. You play atta my table—I take-a care a-you." He put out his hand, "I'm-a Frankie Gambini. You a-wanna a drink on da house?" Then, without waiting for an answer, he called out to a cocktail waitress, a comely young woman in high heels and a short black dress with a plunging neckline. "Jeannie, get da doc a drink. What-ta ever he wants." Soon she returned with a scotch on the rocks and bent forward as she placed it near my pile of chips—which now totaled twenty, meaning it was time to leave after I downed my drink.

I made weekly trips to The Mint, always to the same Blackjack table. Often, Frankie would greet me. "Hey, Doc. Ya hungry? Go to da restaurant upstairs before ya play. Order a steak on me, and if you like-a any waitress, let me know. Dey available for you causa me."

I never accepted either offer. This was indeed Sin City. I relished taking the Casino's cash, meager as it was, but I envied the men playing with twenty-five dollar chips, often betting four or more at a time. Within months, my mathematical card-counting skills resulted in a full mayonnaise jar—if Mr. Hathaway could only see me now! We jointly agreed to purchase some needed appliances with that money before we left Sin City for good.

I certainly understood that I had weaknesses—that there were things that I simply shouldn't do—but I lacked a strict moral code. So leaving Las Vegas was a good thing.

* * *

Our second child, Mark, was born on October 30 in the middle of the night after we had dined at Battista's Hole in the Wall. Tipsy from too much wine, I'd slept well until Margaret awoke me at 3:00 a.m. "We need to go to the hospital."

Three weeks later, after Margaret had cleaned up Wayne's spilled milk and changed Mark's diaper—I still had never changed one—I announced, "Chet Dissinger and I are going on a ten-day trip to Japan on an Air Force transport. It's free. We're leaving on the fifth of December."

But Margaret, who'd always been more than tolerant of my whims, had had enough. "You're going to Japan and leaving me with the kids? No way! You're not going!"

"Oh yes, I am!" I screamed. "Try and stop me!"

She couldn't, of course, because I was stubborn. And I was angry. She wanted to prevent me from taking advantage of free travel to Asia, a program scheduled to end on the first of the year. I could buy expensive cameras, lenses, and stereo equipment in Japan at a fraction of what they'd cost in the States. These were hardly the appliances we'd agreed on, but why squander the opportunity? I didn't realize that my anger—my *wrath*—was another of the Seven Deadly Sins.

And so, I went.

* * *

"Education, education, and more education."

My father's words echoed in my brain when I returned from Japan. Remembering his sound advice, I decided to take advantage of another opportunity as my two years of Air Force duty came to a close. I would become an actual periodontal surgeon—a specialist—not one partially trained in the Air Force internship program. The government would finance much of my education under the 1966 Veteran's Readjustment Benefits Act, a "GI Bill" for Veterans of the Vietnam era, providing me with a generous stipend. To that end, I accepted a residency in periodontics in Los Angeles, a joint program at the Wadsworth Veterans Administration Hospital and the University of Southern California.

Two weeks before my discharge from active duty, Colonel Antonelli hosted a party for the departing physicians and dentists. Across the room, I spied Colonel Ackerman. It was impossible to miss his full head of white hair. He was conversing with the base commanding officer, a two-star general, in what appeared to be a lively conversation, and as I headed to the bar, I was surprised to hear him call my name.

"Dr. Sottosanti," Ackerman said, "may I have a word?" He'd left the general standing there, timing his trip to the bar to intercept me. "I must apologize to you and your friends for letting you down. It's been weighing on my conscience. I was outranked," he continued. "Lieutenant Colonel Hicks and General Ruffin, the base commander, are friends."

"I understand," I said. "It's OK." I turned to leave.

"There's more, Dr. Sottosanti. I can't . . . I can *never* . . . thank you enough for saving my wife's life. I'm so grateful that Colonel Antonelli asked for your opinion. Louise almost didn't make it." His piercing blue eyes looked deeply into mine, and he appeared to be struggling to hold back tears. I was touched by the moment, and the words—*saving my wife's life*—would stay with me forever.

* * *

Our Chevy Malibu headed south across the desert. It was June of 1972, and the terrain was hot, brown, and boring. The only color was the pale green of roadside scrub, insufficient for Wayne, now two-and-a-half, who was only interested in stopping for ice cream in Yermo, just north of Barstow. As Wayne drank his chocolate milkshake, he asked, "Daddy, why are we moving?"

My answer confused him. "To fulfill a dream of your Grandpa Sottosanti."

But it was a lie. The truth was my ego and personal drive were propelling me far beyond what my father had expected. How could I tell little Wayne that I'd stopped keeping track of the Seven Deadly Sins?

Chapter 13   Saint Mafia

DAD HAD CHANGED. HE was no longer the skeptic who challenged my mother on her religious beliefs. According to Mom, however, he still had two beers a day, maybe three in hot weather, and told off-color jokes to anyone who'd listen. He'd become a bit chubby for someone only five-eight, and his wavy dark-brown hair was graying at the temples. He had a slight double chin, and thick eyeglasses dented his chubby cheeks when he smiled. Yet he seemed more peaceful than I ever remembered—if a Sicilian male could be described that way.

Margaret and I were in Stratford with our boys for a week-long vacation before my residency began, having arrived late on a Friday. After breakfast on Saturday, while the kids took a mid-morning nap, Margaret and I entered the living room, and I sat beside her on my mother's new shell-pink sofa—tufted velour in rococo style, with gilded trim of tiny flowers, leaves, and fruits. The night before, when Dad referred to it as Mom's "bawdy-house couch," Mom had given him the *occhio malocchio*—the "evil eye"—her version of a silent curse. She was too proper to respond with what in Southern Italy is known as "the horns"—by extending her second and fifth fingers, with the others folded down—the ultimate insult.

Content with breakfast in his belly, Dad pulled the handle of his Barcalounger, raised the footrest, and reclined at a forty-five-degree angle as I gazed into the dining room through a wide archway framed in wrought-iron vines and gold-tipped leaves. Beyond the floral wallpaper and massive china cabinet, I could see through the picture window into the backyard. All was lush from the Connecticut spring rains. Mom was cleaning up in the kitchen.

"You've built something," I said. "What's all that raised stone beside the dogwood? Is that a statue in there?"

"Have a look," Dad said. "Then come back, and I'll tell you a story."

Margaret rose with me, and as we walked through the dining room, the elaborate structure out back became clear. It was a six-foot-wide Romanesque arch of perfectly hewn gray granite blocks, held in place by a trapezoidal touchstone, the product of a talented civil engineer with exquisite masonry skills. On either side, supporting columns rested on a base constructed of irregular river rocks and concrete. Below was a semicircular pool—a miniature version of the Trevi Fountain in Rome—with a circulating waterfall. In a niche under the arch, a blue background contrasted with a pure white, four-foot statue of the Virgin Mary.

"It's beautiful," Margaret said.

"Why'd you make it?" I said. "The stone must've cost a fortune. It looks like something from Ireland or Italy."

"Sit down," Dad said in a serious tone. "This'll take a while. And you may have a hard time believing it."

Margaret and I settled back into the sofa.

"I got a good friend," Dad began. "His name is Andy Brose, and he had severe asthma as a kid. When he was twelve, his doctor told his mother he didn't think Andy would survive his teens. His medications were no longer working. So his mother took him to a shrine in Quebec—Sainte-Anne-de-Beaupré, in honor of Saint Anne."

"The mother of the Virgin Mary," Margaret said.

"Exactly. People have been healed at that place for three hundred years."

"Don't tell me Andy was cured," I said.

"Shush," Margaret said. "I want to hear this." Though she'd been trained as a nurse, she took many of the same basic courses as I had. Yet, strong in her faith, she believed in miracles—especially the resurrection of Jesus.

"Andy prayed at the basilica all day," Dad went on, "in a chapel next to fragments of bone taken from Saint Anne—two from her arm and one from a finger. He said that hundreds of crutches, canes, and braces were hanging on the walls, left by cripples who went home without further need of them. At the motel that night, Andy prayed to the Virgin Mary. 'If you heal my asthma,' he said, 'I'll go to church every day for the rest of my life.'"

Margaret's eyes brightened. "Wow."

"Andy woke the next morning without any asthma symptoms, went home, and his doctor confirmed there were no signs of the illness. Andy hasn't missed daily Mass for the past forty years, except when he's been too sick, or the weather's prevented him."

"Maybe his condition was misdiagnosed," I said. This was the doctor and scientist in me speaking. "Maybe he didn't have asthma. Maybe his condition was triggered by a psychosomatic condition." I paused, gazing out the picture window at the distant shrine to avoid looking at my father. "I know for a fact that stress can make someone susceptible to asthma. I don't believe there was a miracle involved."

"John," Margaret said, "will you just listen?" She usually avoided challenging my lack of faith, but my disrespect—I'd interrupted my father—was something she couldn't tolerate.

"Last year," Dad continued, "Andy and his wife Adeline invited us to visit on the Fourth of July, and your mother started berating me as I drove home on the Merritt Parkway. 'Slow down . . . you're too close . . . you're weaving . . . close your window!'"

"Don't you tell them any of your lies," Mom yelled from the doorway to the kitchen. "You drank too much that night! You embarrassed me in front of Andy and Adeline! Andy's such a good man. A holy man. He doesn't drink, use bad language, or tell dirty stories! Why can't you be like him? Oh, Mother Mary, please help me!" Then, looking out the window at the statue, she made the sign of the cross.

"*Ah, fanabla!*" Dad shouted. "Shutta your mouth!"

I was accustomed to these verbal battles, but Margaret wasn't. And the last thing we needed was for the kids to wake up. So, I played the peacemaker. "Tell us more, Dad. And Mom, please go back into the kitchen. Mark and Wayne are sleeping." Then, having made her point, Mom disappeared quietly.

"When Andy was twenty-eight," Dad said, "jobs were hard to find. It was in winter, about 1946, and he worked as a carpenter. Adeline was eight months pregnant with their first child, and they had no medical insurance. So, he decided to play the numbers, hoping to win money for the hospital and doctor bills. He knew the odds were slim."

In Connecticut, as I'd known for years, the Mafia ran the numbers racket, often called the "Italian lottery." It was popular among the poor because a "win" could mean a six-hundred-times return. You placed a bet with a "runner"—not a bookie, as many think; bookies take bets on horses—and tried to guess the winning number for the next day, usually the last three digits of the daily balance of the United States Treasury, as published in the morning papers.

"Andy had to choose a three-digit number from 000 to 999," Dad said, "and since he'd been saying the Rosary every day before Mass since he was twelve, he knew there were six Our Fathers and fifty-three Hail Marys in the entire set of beads. So he bet a dollar—a lot of money then, as gas was only twenty cents a gallon—on number 653. And the number came up."

I couldn't contain my disbelief. "He was lucky."

Dad ignored me. "He told the bookie he wanted his winnings in one-dollar bills and brought those bills home in several grocery bags. Then sitting behind the wheel of his car in the driveway in his long carpenter's apron, he dumped the bills onto his lap. Then he folded the apron to his chest, squeezed the corners in one hand, left the car, and rang the doorbell. 'Why didn't you use your key?' Adeline said as she opened the door. 'I'm mopping the floor!' Andy threw the apron towards her, showering her with dollar bills, and Adeline hugged and kissed him. He was pleased. After all, an Italian man must provide for his family."

Mom was in the kitchen doorway again, listening, but now she was smiling. "It's true, Johnny," she said. "I heard Andy tell that story at dinner, and Adeline agreed with everything he said. They wouldn't lie."

"Alright," I said. "I know you're telling us what you heard. But it had to have been a coincidence. The odds were one in a thousand. Andy was simply lucky. So why, twenty-five years later, did you build a shrine to the Virgin Mary just because your friend Andy won the lottery way back when?"

It was mid-morning, so Dad hadn't been drinking, but he became visibly excited. His face was flushed, and he began flailing his arms, nearly knocking over the adjacent floor lamp.

"After returning from Andy's, I lay back in bed. I was restless and prayed to the Virgin Mary for the first time in my life. I said, 'Mother Mary, Frances wants me to be more like Andy, but Andy experienced two miracles. I've never had a miracle, but if I did, I'd become religious and go to Mass every day for the rest of my life.' Then I drifted off to sleep."

Dad seemed sincere, but I, personally, had no time for religion. Instead, I was concerned with our move to Los Angeles—with my family, career, and upcoming residency. Still, Andy's story puzzled me. And Dad's excitement didn't wane, a sign he believed what he was saying was true. He spread his hands and threw his arms in the air.

"Next morning, I go to work. I'm at my desk, and I get a call from Tony Mancini at the high school construction job. He asks me to clarify something on the building plans. I did and said goodbye. But I hear him saying. 'Don't hang up, John . . . I wanna ask you something. The runner will be here in a few minutes. You wanna play a number?' So I said, 'Listen, Tony. We talk every day, and you've never asked me to play before.' So Tony says, 'I dunno. The idea just came to me. I never thought about it. You went to college—I thought maybe you're above betting da numbers.' So I said, 'OK, what the hell. Put two dollars for me on 653.'"

"Dad"—I was interrupting again —"I . . . don't . . . believe . . . this."

Margaret frowned. "Let him continue, John. This is fascinating."

"So Tony says, 'You never wanna put two dollars on one number. That hardly ever wins. Most guys play dimes and quarters. Pick another one. Play *two* numbers and double your chances. Or if you really like that number, put a dollar on it today and again tomorrow to improve the odds.' So I said, 'OK. A dollar today and a dollar tomorrow.'"

Mom reappeared in the doorway, saw the expression on my face, and said, "Johnny, he's telling the truth. This happened. Look what he's built!" She turned to look at Mary in the backyard shrine and smiled.

"Next morning, Tony calls and says, 'Where'd you get that number? You won!' Well, I come home with all this money in big bills, and your mother says, 'You can't spend that on yourself. It was a miracle. You either give it to the Church or build a shrine to the Virgin Mary—she made you win!'"

I shook my head. "Looks like you spent more than just your winnings. That's expensive stone. Something must have motivated you to spend a lot of money and do all that work. It's beautiful!" I didn't mention the statue. I didn't want any of my friends who might see it to think we were a family of religious fanatics. Sensing that Margaret was anxious to hear the rest of the story, I asked—quite facetiously—"So what happened next? Did you win again?"

"I lay in bed that night and prayed again," Dad said. "Mother Mary, I don't know if it was a miracle or not. It just might have been one helluva coincidence. I've never heard of the same number coming up two days in a row. If you make 653 win tomorrow, I'll know for sure it's a miracle, and I'll go to church every day for the rest of my life. But it's OK if you don't since I really don't wanna do that."

I shook my head again. What a curious bit of negotiating!

"A different number appeared the next day," Dad said. "Yet when I thought of everything that had to happen for me to win that first day—Andy had to win, he had to tell me about it, and I had to pray for a miracle that same night—I had to wonder. I talked to Tony almost every workday for five years, and he never asked me to play the numbers. Then I hit the number with my very first bet. I think it was a miracle!"

I knew the odds of dad winning on the first day were one in one thousand, but the odds of the same number coming up two days in a row were astronomical. Still, the other coincidences were disconcerting. But I didn't give it much thought. My head was in Los Angeles.

That afternoon Mom and Dad invited our local family to a meal in honor of our visit. A photo of the event in our album shows thirteen of us at the dining room table—ironically, the same number as at the Last Supper. Dinner consisted of lasagna, roast beef, sausages, and veggies, with the Virgin Mary prominent in the background, whiter than white against a blue backdrop, amid extensive green foliage, looking serenely from her stony abode, financed by money from Italian racketeers. I wondered: *Would God use the Mafia to perform a miracle?*

The next day, when Mom, Dad, Margaret, Wayne, Mark, and I went to Mass at St. James —where Margaret and I had been married—I was surprised to see Dad take out rosary beads and pray before the service began.

Afterward, as we walked to his big white Chrysler, which was parked, as usual, along the sidewalk in front of the church, I noticed his new license plates: JMJ653.

"I get the 653," I said to Dad, "but JMJ?"

Margaret answered for him: "Jesus, Mary, and Joseph."

Dad was so proud of those plates and pleased that his daughter-in-law understood their full meaning.

Back at the house, however, I—a periodontist-in-training and a scientist—couldn't drop the subject. "I'm not so sure miracles were involved, Dad. If you can't measure it or reproduce it, it doesn't exist."

Margaret frowned at me, and Dad said, "If that's what you learned at school, Johnny Boy, you went to the wrong schools. And don't forget who paid for them!"

I decided to keep silent.

Chapter 14   L.A. Confidential

WE SETTLED INTO OUR Los Angeles rental home in Westchester, just north-east of the Los Angeles International Airport. It would be my home base for clinical work at the Wadsworth V.A. Hospital in West Los Angeles and science-based courses at the University of Southern California.

During one of my first days at the VA clinic, Mary Suzuki, the receptionist at the front desk, announced a special patient. "It's William Lundigan," she said. "The movie star."

I was fascinated with the number of Hollywood celebrities in the LA area. Occasionally we'd see one at a distance in a restaurant, but I never expected to find any in my office. Many lived in West LA, the most glamorous section of the city. Expensive neighborhoods such as Beverly Hills, Bel Air, and Brentwood surrounded the hospital because the major studios were nearby. It was just four miles to MGM, sixteen to Universal, and seventeen to Warner Brothers.

Mary quickly told me everything she knew about the fading star. With over a hundred films to his credit, mainly from the forties and fifties, Lundigan had been known for his handsome face, trim six-foot-two-inch frame, and deep voice. He'd appeared opposite Susan Hayward, a five-time Academy Award nominee, in the 1951 movie *I'd Climb the Highest Mountain*. In 1953, he starred in *Inferno* with Rhonda Fleming, a leading lady with male legends such as Gregory Peck, Robert Mitchum, Charlton Heston, and Burt Lancaster.

Lundigan's name had been listed above Marilyn Monroe's in the credits to *Love Nest*, a 1951 comedy-drama film, and that top billing impressed me. As a teenager, I'd believed that Marilyn Monroe, with her beautiful face, gorgeous figure, and tight sweaters and skirts, was the sexiest woman alive. Someone described walking behind her as "like watching two boys under a blanket having a pillow fight." So I was deeply disheartened in 1962 when

Monroe, only thirty-six years old, died of an overdose of barbiturates. Why would a wealthy young woman, a famous sex symbol in Hollywood and a close friend of President Kennedy, commit suicide? It was incomprehensible to me. At the time, I was a naïve twenty-year-old in college, not yet hardened to the realities of life.

"Mr. Lundigan," I said. "It's a pleasure to meet you."

"Call me Bill," he replied in a deep, friendly voice. "I hope you can save my teeth." He smiled. "If you do, Doc, I'll like you—even though you're a dentist."

I'd grown accustomed to such remarks early on in my career and learned not to take them personally. Only real doctors did the hard work, and dentists caused pain.

After several surgeries and a series of post-op visits, Bill Lundigan and I became friends. I admired him for having left his film career to enlist in World War II, even though he'd had a medical deferment. But, unfortunately, his selfless act cost him his contract with MGM since his enlistment infuriated Louis Mayer, who'd founded the studio with Sam Goldwyn and Marcus Loew just when they were promoting Lundigan as a star.

Once again, I found myself wondering: *Why was a movie star coming to a V.A. clinic for free dentistry?* Of course, he'd been in the service, but weren't all these guys *rich?*

"I was at the top of my game in the forties and fifties," Bill said, "but as the years passed, I accepted crummy parts in lousy movies. Damn it, Doc. I made some mistakes."

I liked this humble guy. I hadn't yet realized that humility is a virtue, in contrast to pride, one of the deadly sins, which I was beginning to know all too well.

A heavy smoker for years, Bill had made commercials for Chesterfield and Lucky Strike. Consequently, emphysema had ravaged his lungs. Just walking down the hall caused him to wheeze from shortness of breath. But the longer I knew him, the more I respected him. In 1945 he'd married Rena Morgan—a woman, as he described her, with a heart of gold and a strong will. And though he'd played opposite some of the most beautiful Hollywood actresses, as handsome as he was, he was still married to her twenty-seven years later and was a devoted father to their daughter, Anastacia.

As Corporal William Lundigan in the 3rd Brigade, 1st Marine regiment, Bill had been a combat photographer, filming action in the battle for Okinawa, which raged for five weeks and resulted in the highest number of casualties in the Pacific Theater. He cared deeply for his country, his family, and kids with cystic fibrosis—an inherited disorder that caused severe, progressive lung damage, which triggered coughing and wheezing, and shortened lives. Bill understood the condition better than anyone.

"Would you like to see Rosemary Clooney?" Bill asked one day. "She's performing with me at a live benefit for cystic fibrosis."

"Sure!" I knew who Rosemary Clooney was. Every year, at Christmas time, my parents watched *White Christmas*—possibly the most popular holiday movie of all time—starring Rosemary Clooney, Bing Crosby, and Danny Kaye.

"I'll get you seats up front," he said. "Rosemary's a sweet lady. She went through some hard times five years ago, but she's starting a comeback. So you'll be among the first to see her."

Bill explained that Clooney's messy divorce, hard work, and constant travel had taken their toll. The breaking point had come after her good friend Bobby Kennedy was assassinated in LA—on June 5, 1968—at the Ambassador Hotel. Rosemary and several of her children stood only feet away when Sirhan Sirhan pulled the trigger. Rosemary's mental break-down, following a period of drug and alcohol abuse, came on stage in Reno soon after.

Those damn addictions, I thought. *Bill ruined his lungs with cigarettes, and Rosemary sacrificed peace of mind for fame and money. When the castles she built began to crumble, she smoked heavily to ease her stress. Marilyn Monroe, Rosemary Clooney, and others. It was all too common.*

"What do you think, Doc?" Bill said a few nights later. "Best seats in the house!" He appeared winded after rushing from table to table, greeting old friends.

"I'd like you to meet my wife, Margaret," I said.

"A pleasure." Bill smiled as he shook Margaret's hand and looked into her eyes —not elsewhere, like Robert Goulet in Las Vegas. Margaret appreciated the gesture as much as the opportunity to see Rosemary Clooney. Despite the strident air of feminism in the country, Margaret was content with her role as a homemaker. A devoted mother to Wayne and Mark, she provided constancy and love to our family at a time when I was obsessed with my career. And she thoroughly enjoyed these evenings we shared, breaks from our routine that my schedule occasionally provided. She hadn't mentioned my selfish junket to Japan for a while, although I'm not sure she'd forgiven me, especially since I'd never demonstrated any remorse. But at times, I could sense her resentment simmering beneath the surface.

Bill checked his watch. "Hey—we've got ten minutes. Let's go meet Rosemary."

Backstage, he knocked on a closed door. "Rosemary, it's Bill."

"Come in." The voice was deeper than I remembered it from television.

As a teenager, I'd watched *The Rosemary Clooney Show,* and I'd seen Rosemary as an occasional guest on *Your Hit Parade,* my mother's favorite program. In those days, she'd worn her blonde hair in a pageboy with the ends rolled under. She'd been charming and attractive—not gorgeous or sensual like Marilyn Monroe—more like the nice lady next door. Her rich, smooth, and comforting voice caused some to call her the female Bing Crosby.

As I trailed Bill and Margaret into the dressing room, past images of Rosemary Clooney filled my mind. Then I was shocked—*This couldn't be her!* She was only in her mid-forties but had gained fifty pounds. Dark circles underscored her eyes, hardly concealed by makeup. Her face was round, and her diminutive chin was lost in the heaviness below. Simple pearl earrings encircled her neck beneath her blond hair, now worn in a bouffant with loose curls. Rosemary Clooney was warm, friendly, and vivacious, but her weight and labored breathing—and the cigarette trembling in her chubby hand— made me wonder if she'd even be able to perform.

Back out front, Bill Lundigan climbed the steps of the stage to M.C. the show that featured half a dozen performers, but Rosemary Clooney was the only name I recognized. I was concerned about his emphysema. Bill was a friend, and I didn't want to see him embarrass himself onstage.

But Bill Lundigan was a pro who knew the meaning of *"Showtime!"* Applause greeted him as he approached the microphone with a slight smile on his lips, and as it continued, his smile grew wider, and the corners of his mouth turned up. Dressed in a stylish light-gray suit with a white pocket square and a blue-and-white striped tie, he stood tall, smiled, and looked the audience in the eye. Then, nodding in acknowledgment of the warm welcome, he bowed, straightened, and began. "Good evening, ladies and gentlemen, and welcome to the 1974 version of the *Shower of Stars!*"

Bill spoke with strength and confidence, sparking memories of the person I'd seen on the mid-fifties TV show, *Shower of Stars,* another of my parents' favorites—a celebrity-studded variety program on CBS, hosted by Lundigan and sponsored by Chrysler, the manufacturer of my father's favorite automobile.

"Tonight we have with us a star," Bill said, "one of the most famous in all of show business, the first female singer ever to grace the cover of *Time* magazine." Bill's liquid baritone held everyone's attention. "I know you're all looking forward to hearing Rosemary Clooney." He clasped his hands in front of him as if in anticipation. "Tonight, Rosemary will thrill us with sixteen of her greatest hits, interspersed among our other fine performers."

Looking over his right shoulder to the side curtains, he said, "Ya know, I think I see her now. So without further ado, let's welcome the incomparable Rosemary Clooney!"

The main curtains parted, revealing four musicians—piano, bass, sax, and drums—and Rosemary strolled to center stage with a microphone in her left hand, a burst of energy, and a big smile. Then, resting her right hand on the piano, she smiled broadly and began singing: *"Hey there, you with the stars in your eyes."* She was relaxed and moved rhythmically to the music, although her voice still struck me as deeper than I remembered. But she had energy and immediately charmed the audience with her beautiful voice and charming personality.

Following that evening in 1974, Rosemary Clooney resumed a full career on television and in the recording studio until her death from lung cancer in 2002. By the time she was diagnosed in December 2001, she'd been a regular smoker for many years. Months later, her famous nephew, the actor George Clooney, was a pallbearer at her funeral.

What did I learn from Bill Lundigan and Rosemary Clooney? Regardless of success, we all face difficulties in life precipitated by addictions, misfortunes, illness, and, ultimately, age. In 1975, a year after the cystic fibrosis variety show, Bill died of heart failure, a condition related to chronic obstructive pulmonary disease precipitated by his many years of heavy smoking. Thinking of Bill and Rosemary reminded me of my pathology professor back at Georgetown University, the expert on smoking-induced lung cancer who'd turned to answer my question after class with a cigarette in his hand. *Addictions are powerful detriments to a fulfilling life. They adhere to us steadfastly, regardless of our understanding of their toxicity to body and mind.*

* * *

During my residency, I became obsessed with bone regeneration because the loss of bone from periodontal disease is the primary reason for adult tooth loss. This, in turn, begets the need for dentures, resulting in the diminution of taste, comfort, esthetics, and self-esteem. In *Reuben, Reuben*, a later film, an unscrupulous Scottish poet loses his teeth when a cuckolded dentist seeks revenge for his wife's infidelity. In a final monologue, just before a successful suicide attempt, the melancholy poet ruminates on getting dentures as the precursor to his inevitable deterioration and death, which he could not handle. *Suicide is serious stuff!* I thought.

Could my obsession with bone be related to an accident at my eighth birthday party? I'd tripped while playing tag, and one of the neighborhood kids, running close behind, had fallen on me, breaking my arm. When the doctor showed Mom and me the x-ray, he pointed to a black line on my radius and said, "If we protect it with a cast, the body will grow new bone and heal itself." Six weeks later, when he removed the heavy cast, a new x-ray proved him right. I was amazed and never forgot the body's efforts at healing itself.

While I was in LA, Dr. Marshall Urist at UCLA discovered the secret of transforming stem cells into osteoblasts—cells responsible for bone formation—an essential consideration for repairing complex fractures, spinal fusions, joint replacements, and treating periodontal disease. Urist had earlier identified an inductive substance known as *bone morphogenetic protein*, commonly called BMP, which is present in bone but masked by its hard mineral structure. He'd developed a demineralization protocol that used weak hydrochloric acid to extract the mineral content and expose the BMP. In animal studies, he took the femur bone from one rat, demineralized it, and placed small particles of it in the belly of a second rat, growing bone there— an amazing experiment with an astonishing result.

Soon after, he'd begun using the technique in humans. Dr. Alton Register, my mentor at the V.A., introduced me to Dr. Urist in his orthopedic research laboratory at the UCLA Medical School, a few miles from our hospital.

"Dr. Sottosanti," Urist said, "if you want to grow bone in your dental patients, you've come to the right place."

I followed Urist into a closet containing shelves of large jars like the one I'd used for my Las Vegas gambling money. Labels identified the deceased donor's name, age, and cause of death. Each jar had a short section of human femur in it. Selecting a jar, Urist stared at the label, returned it, took another, and handed it to me. "This will grow lots of bone. Take it to your clinic and grind as much as you need into small particles. But grind it slowly as heat from rapid grinding will denature the BMP."

That evening I followed Urist's instructions. Two hours later, I had an amount I believed would be sufficient to treat a patient needing a bone graft the following day.

I began the surgery alone—there were not enough assistants available—pausing to suction and blot until I exposed the defect in the bone, which turned out to be larger than the x-ray indicated. Sticking my head into the corridor, I yelled, "Carol, I need you!" I'd just placed the BMP-laden bone particles on a sterile gauze pad when Carol, one of the busy assistants, rushed in, swinging the doors inward and creating a breeze that sent two-thirds of the bone particles onto the floor, leaving an insufficient amount for the surgery.

"Sorry," Carol said. Then, no longer needed, she backed into the corridor.

What now? I asked myself. My precious particles lay on the floor, blending with the pale yellow tiles. Then I remembered that there was calcium sulfate hemihydrate—plaster of Paris—in a sterile jar in the cabinet above. This common substance had been employed in orthopedic and oral surgery since 1892, when a German surgeon used it to fill bone cavities in tuberculosis patients. Since it could not stimulate bone growth by itself, it had fallen into disuse. But no one had explored combining it with other materials to form a composite graft.

I quickly mixed equal amounts of plaster and BMP bone particles to fill my patient's defect, which was so severe that, a year earlier, it had failed to respond to "osseous coagulum," a grafting material made of chips from the patient's own bone and blood. Now, moistening my composite graft with sterile water, I packed it into the bone deformity. Then, mindful of the protective cast placed on my fractured arm years ago, I added a thin layer of wet plaster, which would harden in minutes. I used it to prevent graft particle dislodgment and invasion of the site by epithelial and fibroblast cells—which do not form bone—allowing the stem cell-derived osteoblasts to do their work.

Three months later, a postoperative x-ray on my patient revealed that much of the defect had filled with new bone, and he was delighted to keep his tooth. Subsequently, treating other patients with the same technique, I achieved similar results. The experience mirrored my fortunate discovery years ago at Huyck Manufacturing in Connecticut when I separated metal fibers from sand. Now, I began to think about the nature of all such discoveries.

In fifth grade, I'd seen a movie about George Crum, a chef at the Moon Lake Lodge in Saratoga Springs, New York. In 1853, responding to a customer's complaint that his French-fried potatoes were too thick and soggy, he sliced fresh potatoes as thin as possible and fried them until they were hard and crunchy, delighting that diner and, later, a multitude of others. I never forgot that film or my love for potato chips.

In LA, my friends and professional colleagues thought I was just "lucky." It was a term I preferred to the ones attributed to me as a boy in Stratford—by my parents and kids in the neighborhood—lazy, stupid, and clumsy. In turn, I began to ponder the concepts of luck, chance, coincidence . . . and miracles.

Could luck be related to intelligence, mental toughness, optimism, diligence, and tenacity? Did luck need only to await an opportunity to present itself? Is coincidence simply cosmic chance, in which "the odds" must be calculated in sophisticated ways that Mr. Hathaway would appreciate? Could miracles, not explainable by scientific or natural laws, be mediated by some other means?

My father had been born on October 8, his father, Biagio, on October 9, and his mother, Vincenza, on October 10— the same day as my oldest son. Was this a miracle? Not at all. Highly improbable events occur more often than statistics would have us believe. Yet the chain of events related to my father's encounter with the number 653 had challenged my belief that it's possible to explain all related events by science, coincidence, or chance.

Under the tutelage of Mr. Hathaway in high school, I'd studied probability theory. Playing the numbers game, Andy Brose had to choose a number from zero to 999. The chance of it coming up on any given day was one in a thousand. He selected 653 and won the first time he played it. He then told my father, and two days later, Dad won—the first time *he* played that number. The chance of dad winning that day was one in a thousand. Now, the probability of two independent events occurring together can be determined by multiplying the individual odds. So, one in a thousand times one in a thousand is one in a million. One in a million! Amazing! The implications intrigued me.

It is possible to explain all related events by science, coincidence, or chance. That's what I believed, and that's what Dad believed—*until he didn't.* The occurrence of the "one in a million" event did not spark a religious conversion in me, but it sure captured my attention.

Chapter 15   With Stars in My Eyes

WHEN I COMPLETED MY graduate program and residency in LA, I planned to call home and tell my parents that I wouldn't be returning to live in Connecticut. I'd been offered, and had accepted, a position in the largest periodontal practice in San Diego. To assuage my folks' disappointment, I planned to tell them of my recent accomplishments, hoping they'd be pleased. I rehearsed that phone call in my mind, then talked to Dad, with Mom on the extension:

I discovered a new way to regenerate bone, using common plaster. I conceived and planned the first annual periodontal symposium at the University of Southern California. I had three articles this year accepted for publication in the Journal of Periodontology.

But Dad didn't seem impressed. In his opinion, these achievements didn't deserve praise until they'd produced a financial gain. Which would come, only twenty years later, when I parlayed the breeze that Carol generated in my surgery into a source of wealth and fame

I admired my father. He had a strong influence on me because he'd transformed his own life through the strength of his intellect, ambition, and cunning, progressing from an impoverished Sicilian kid in Greenwich, Connecticut, to the king of Park Street in Stratford. He'd built a home for his family with his own hands, on a double lot, at the top of Park Street hill—a home I'd nearly burned to the ground. And Mom believed it was protected by a four-foot statue in a stone grotto, above a pool of clear water.

* * *

Long, sleek and stunning, the red Maserati convertible departed downtown San Diego with its top down, slicing through the wind and speeding north on I-5—ten miles-per-hour over the speed limit— hugging the median and heading for Los Angeles. I was riding shotgun, and the fierce breeze whipped back my medium-length blond hair, making me all too conscious of my receding hairline. *What?* I thought. *I'm only thirty-two!* And for a brief moment, I realized I was aging, a thought I'd previously barred from consciousness.

Whizzing by a tractor-trailer, Dr. Arnold Ariaudo, the senior member of our periodontal practice, raised his voice, his left hand on the wheel, his right moving in mid-air in a manner reminiscent of my father. He was four years older than Dad, and this day, Monday, September 16, 1974, was his sixty-fifth birthday.

We descended a hill beyond the Del Mar Heights exit. "The Del Mar Racetrack's off in the distance," Arnold hollered into the buffeting breeze. Then he broke into the Bing Crosby classic, "*Where the turf meets the surf down at old Del Mar . . . take a plane . . . take a train . . . take a car.*"

I could see the grandstands of the race track far off, regal in their Spanish Colonial Revival style. The oval racetrack had been the playground of post-World War II Hollywood stars from Bing Crosby and Ava Gardner to Red Skelton.

Arnold was one of the most respected periodontists in the nation, the author of many articles on innovative surgical techniques in peer-reviewed publications. With an affable and assertive personality, he could charm anyone, yet he had always remained faithful to Belva, his loving and beautiful wife, and the best office manager any doctor could want. Belva was delightful—the brain behind his thriving periodontal practice. She kept Arnold in line but gave him the freedom to express the features of his unique personality.

"Did you meet Burt Bacharach last week?" he said. "When he was in for a cleaning?"

"I did. You were running late, so Sally pulled me in and introduced me."

I certainly remembered Bacharach, composer of countless hits, and the greatest songwriter of the day, with Grammys and Academy Awards for his music. Who could forget Paul Newman and Katharine Ross in *Butch Cassidy and the Sundance Kid*, riding a bicycle to Bacharach's *"Raindrops Keep Falling On My Head"*? "He was telling dirty jokes to the girls," I said, "and making them blush."

Arnold switched hands, grasping the steering wheel with his right and gesturing left toward the racetrack. "That's where I met Burt." He kept his eyes on the road. "We both own racehorses. They don't make me money, but it's a great tax write-off. I have fun meeting all the celebrities. Having a celebrity like Burt in the office is great," Arnold said, "but the best part is that he introduced me to Angie Dickinson, his gorgeous wife."

Once again, he pointed. "Look beyond the bridge of the Pacific Coast Highway, and you can glimpse the ocean. They have a beach house over there. They're always there during the summer racing season."

Arnold knows Angie Dickinson! This revelation piqued my interest, the same interest that had taken me to the front row of the Folies Bergere. In my mind, Angie Dickinson had replaced Marilyn Monroe as the new sex symbol. I'd seen John Wayne in *Rio Bravo*, where Angie played Feathers, an audacious gambler. In one scene, she wore nothing but an ink black teddy, with black heels supporting her shapely legs in sheer black nylon. Back home in Stratford, Shakespearean actresses like Katherine Hepburn had done little to arouse my prurient interest. But Angie Dickinson—that was another story.

By 1974, Angie Dickinson had appeared in thirty-seven movies—the majority as the female lead. *Rio Bravo* had brought her the 1960 Golden Globe Award for New Star of the Year. As she aged, she accepted roles with nudity, such as the 1971 sexual thriller *Pretty Maids All in a Row*, directed by Roger Vadim, the acclaimed master of eroticism who'd introduced Brigitte Bardot as a sex kitten in the 1956 movie *And God Created Woman*. Later, in 1968, he cast Jane Fonda in *Barbarella*, which opened with the star performing a floating, zero-gravity striptease. And now he'd turned his attention to Angie Dickinson.

"Arnold," I said, "just before graduation last June, the USC and VA residents were drinking at the 901 Bar and Grill. Howie Smith said he'd seen Angie's latest movie, *Big Bad Mama*, in which she lets it all hang out—full frontal nudity." I paused. "She a friend of yours?"

"And a patient, too. You're going to meet her today. Angie's complex," Arnold continued, turning to look at me. It was a habit I hated because Dad did the same thing on the Connecticut Turnpike when absorbed in the conversation. But the speed limits here were higher than at home. "She's sweet and talented, but she made some wrong choices. She tells me personal things. She lost her dad eight years ago, and I remind her of him."

Born Angeline Brown in Kulm, North Dakota, Angie had been raised as a Catholic by loving German-American parents. When she was ten, the family moved to Glendale, California. Later, for a while at least, she attended Immaculate Heart College near Hollywood.

I didn't know if Arnold was Catholic but presumed so because of his Italian heritage. But my thoughts were on Angie Dickinson. *How could a South Dakota girl, born to staid Midwestern parents, go from a Catholic girls' college to nude roles in Hollywood movies?*

Arnold returned his eyes to the road. "Things changed when she developed into a real beauty. She met Gene Dickinson, a pro football player, and they married in '52. Then, someone told her to enter the local Miss America contest, and even though she finished second, she garnered attention. A role on *The Jimmy Durante Show* followed—she was one of his six long-legged dancers."

I certainly knew Jimmy Durante. The actor, comedian, singer, and pianist, with a low, rough, gravelly voice, was best known for his enormous nose, earning him his nickname, "The Great Schnozzle." I'd always been a bit concerned about my own larger-than-average nose, once telling a friend it was a "Roman nose"—because it roamed all over my face, and I wished I could make light of it, like "the Schnoz" did. In that respect, Jimmy Durante had a measure of confidence that I lacked.

An Italian-American Catholic, Durante was a beloved national icon. His first wife had died young of a heart ailment. He'd married his second wife in St. Malachy Roman Catholic Church in New York City, and together they raised over twenty million dollars for disabled and abused children. The street leading to the Del Mar racetrack is Jimmy Durante Boulevard. Like Danny Thomas, he had put his faith into action for the betterment of humanity. *How to become that kind of person?* It was a thought I couldn't shake. I'd asked myself the same question after selling my defective Austin Healey Sprite to Tom Pritchard and his son in Stratford years ago.

Arnold continued yelling. "One thing led to another. Someone saw Angie on the Durante show and suggested she consider acting. She took lessons, then appeared on the *Colgate Comedy Hour*, where she met Frank Sinatra in 1953. Then the trouble began. Angie attracted Sinatra, and "Old Blue Eyes" wanted to meet her." Arnold's loud voice took on a somber edge. "She couldn't resist. She accepted his invitation, which led to an affair ending her marriage to Dickinson in 1960. Meeting Sinatra began the wild part of Angie's life. He was irresistible. Talk about charisma! There was Dean Martin as well, and some even say JFK, though Angie's never admitted it. She married Burt in 1965."

Arnold looked at me briefly. "Has it been a happy marriage?" I shouted.

"No. She said Burt had two affairs in their first year." So there it was again, the law of cause and effect. *What goes around comes around*—the principle of Karma. We reap the fruits of our actions. Which always left me wondering, *could an element of Divine justice be at work?*

"I think they're going to separate," Arnold said. "Too bad. I like them both. She really loves Burt. But he doesn't seem to feel the same about her."

My mood turned melancholy. I thought of Margaret and the similarities to Angie Dickinson. Both were descended from German heritage and had been born in the Midwest—Angie in South Dakota, and Margaret in Iowa, just hundreds of miles apart. Each attended Catholic schools. Both were blonde and beautiful. But that's where the similarities ended. Margaret was five inches taller. And she'd remained close to her faith.

I recalled her words on our wedding day: "I, Margaret, take you, John, to be my husband. I promise to be true to you in good times and in bad, in sickness and in health. I will love you and honor you all the days of my life." *And she really meant it!* Margaret's faith ran deep. The Ten Commandments and Seven Deadly Sins held meaning for her. And as Arnold's Maserati zipped along, these thoughts of her warmed me, soothing my body and calming my mind. I felt grateful—the perfect antidote for melancholy.

* * *

A few raindrops hit me as we pulled into the faculty parking lot at the dental school. Burt Bacharach again—*Raindrops keep falling on my head.* Jumping out, I helped Arnold put the top on his Maserati.

We spent the next thirty minutes in the second-floor office of Dr. Alex Koper, the Director of Continuing Education. A slightly built man with neatly groomed black hair, he had dark eyes and an engaging smile.

"John," he said, "I thought your idea for a symposium on bone regeneration would never fly—way too expensive." His smile broadened. "But with almost four months to go, it looks like a sell-out. I should've booked a larger auditorium!"

I was thrilled. After discussing the symposium logistics with Alex, Arnold and I walked the long corridor to the open bay dental clinic, where three rows of fifteen dental chairs, lights, and stools, spaced ten feet apart, were attended by forty-five eager students. Continuous windows afforded a view of the tops of several carob trees and the still-ominous dark sky. With Angie Dickinson expected in ten minutes, we entered a private examination room adjacent to the open clinic to discuss her dental situation.

Then came a knock at the door, and there she stood—Angie Dickinson—a long, double-breasted trench coat, its belt neatly tied in a bow. She appeared to be about five-seven in heels. And she was stunning. Crescent eyebrows and dark lashes roofed her light brown eyes. Her hair, dramatically lighter than in *Rio Bravo*, looked golden. Parted right of center, it was styled in a bouffant, full and smooth—hanging down on the right while exploding up on the left. Every part of her—hair, clothes, makeup, lips—exuded beauty and sensuality.

She greeted Arnold warmly, hugged him, wished him a happy birthday, and smiled widely at me, her perfect teeth resting on her bottom lip. Arnold introduced me as a "rising star in periodontics" and his "new associate in San Diego." Angie folded her cougar-print umbrella, wet from the rain, and tucked it in the corner. Then she removed her coat, hung it with her shoulder bag on a hook on the closed door, and slipped into the chair.

After a few minutes of examining her teeth, Arnold said—for my benefit—"John, I'd like your opinion. Take a look," and handed me a dental mirror. It was a kind gesture. I could now tell my buddies that I'd treated Angie Dickinson, and would they be impressed!

When we completed the examination, Angie asked for a mirror with a twinkle in her eye and a tone of artificial annoyance. "You guys are really messy. No way I'm going to walk by those handsome dental students out there looking this disheveled!" Smiling, she wiped a pink stain from her teeth with a tissue, removing the lipstick we'd inadvertently smeared. "And look what you've done to my hair! Please hand me my purse!" Then, she teased the errant strands into place with a small brush.

She walked out, leaving me with this singular thought: One of the hot-test women on the planet was worried about appearing less-than-perfect before our male students, ardent admirers who've seen her movies and watched her on TV in *Police Woman*. Was her self-esteem really that fragile? Was being a Hollywood star worth it?

Dad would undoubtedly say the money was.

Chapter 16   Ego Encounter

MARGARET GREETED ME AT the door with a warm kiss. Wayne and Mark stood right behind her, reaching up to hug me before retreating to their rooms to argue about who had the best truck. I held Margaret close a bit longer than usual, cherishing, for the moment at least, the goodness of my attractive wife. *How could I hold her this tight,* I wondered, *if she or I were in an adulterous relationship, or even suspected one? How would we hide the underlying anger and resentment, or profess our love, without a hint of duplicity?*

Throughout the ages, the Seventh Commandment, and society at large, have condemned adultery, a sin that destroys marriages and wreaks havoc on children. As Margaret firmly believed, adultery is a scarlet thread, deceitfully woven into the white fabric of matrimony—a sacrament that should be laced with enduring love and commitment.

"Honey," Margaret said after supper—she'd prepared veal parmesan, my favorite—"your dad called. He's thinking of selling the house in Stratford and moving out here, but I doubt he'll do it."

My mind leaped. "If he does, he could build me an office!" The possibilities intrigued me. Dad could build my office, Mom could be my receptionist, and Margaret could be my business manager. But could such self-centered thoughts ever be realized? As motivational speakers tell their audiences, *Go for it!* What did I have to lose?

* * *

Four months later, with the USC Norris Auditorium filled to capacity, I stood on the stage at the *First Annual USC Periodontal Symposium.* Titled, quite simply, "*The Symposium on Bone Regeneration,*" it was a two-day meeting with five speakers each day. My goal was to make the program controversial and exciting in its search for truth, which, as Wally

Grossman would have said, *is the unrealized desire of many people.* Wally still exerted a palpable influence on me, although I didn't always choose to be truthful. As Dad had taught me, it was just too difficult. "If it weren't for the toilet on that train," Dad had said, "I would've been too poor to get married. And you wouldn't be here."

Having finished his presentation, Marshall Urist planned to leave immediately for the airport, meaning he'd miss the important panel discussion the following afternoon. Moving center stage with a microphone, I said, "Dr. Urist, tomorrow, Dr. Gerald Bowers, director of post-graduate periodontics at the University of Maryland, will describe the use of a non-demineralized human allograft. Since you won't be here, I'd like to ask you, now, what you think of his material for osseous induction and regeneration?"

I handed the microphone to Marshall, who, unhesitatingly, said, in a deliberately demeaning tone, "It's worthless!"

Seated in the front row, the mild-mannered Dr. Bowers flushed, clenched his teeth, puffed his jowls, and exclaimed, "That's not true!" After a brief exchange, Dr. Urist left for the airport, but the tone of the annual symposium had been set for the next twenty-seven years—it would be a search for truth, a forum for confrontation, and, above all, the advancement of science. I was proud and delighted.

The next day, Dr. William Hiatt, a periodontist in private practice and an expert in bone regeneration at the University of Colorado, addressed the symposium at my invitation. A few years earlier, Hiatt had helped us at the Nellis Air Force Base dental clinic. Moderating the panel discussion he participated in, I thought: *What a small world! What goes around comes around.*

* * *

"That's not how you hammer a nail," Dad said. "Do it like this." He lightly tapped the head a few times. Then, taking a full swing from the elbow and flicking his wrist before contact, it took him just two blows to drive the three-inch nail into a two-by-four, one of many that would provide partitions in my new office. Several hours later, I matched this feat, leaving in the past dreadful memories of the nail I'd launched at the Cub Scout Jamboree in Stratford, Connecticut.

A month earlier, Mom and Dad had driven cross-country, arriving in San Diego in time to meet the moving van carrying all their possessions. Dad had called me from their new house when the van pulled up, asking for my help to direct the movers when placing things.

The long, ten-wheeled tractor-trailer stretched from one driveway to the next on Cloudcroft Drive, an upper-middle-class neighborhood of Poway, California, just five miles from our home in Rancho Bernardo.

I hugged Mom and Dad and said, "Where'd you put my Topps baseball cards?" I was especially concerned about three from 1952—Mickey Mantle's rookie year.

"Oh, you wanted those?" Mom said nonchalantly. "I threw them out. I couldn't ship everything." Those cards were worth thousands of dollars, but I remained calm, at least for the moment, stifling my wrath and greed, two of the Seven Deadly Sins. Two movers were bringing out the first item—a heavy, elongated cardboard box, about six feet by three feet and a foot and a half deep.

"Be careful!" Dad called. "That's fragile!" He led the pair with the box to the backyard, and I followed out of curiosity. Taking his pocketknife, Dad slit the packing tape, revealing a bulky item swaddled in bubble wrap. It was his statue of the Virgin Mary, which the movers placed on a short, flat stone wall that separated the lawn from a raised vegetable garden and a lone palm tree. Mom was indoors, directing the placement of her ornate couch. Looking up, I caught her gazing out the dining room window, marveling at the California version of their shrine. Within a week, Dad ordered California vanity plates: JMJ653.

* * *

Dad *did* build my office, Mom *did* become my receptionist, and Margaret *did* become my financial manager, overseeing collections and expenses. *My* job was to perform surgery and promote my practice to the general dentists in the surrounding area—a source of much-needed patient referrals. I also moderated staff meetings. But without any formal leadership training, I didn't always do this very well.

Mom was an outstanding receptionist, especially for someone who refused a salary. She often remained in the office until 7 p.m., ensuring all appointment slots were filled for the following day. Taking a cue from Bel Ariaudo, I sternly told her, "Make sure to address me as Dr. Sottosanti in the office. I don't want patients to know you're my mother. I want them to think you support me because you believe in my skills as a periodontist— not as your son."

This attitude aggravated Carol Gross, my post-op nurse, a highly valued employee with outstanding clinical and interpersonal skills. "How dare you talk to your mother like that!?" she said. "You're not even paying her!"

In this instance, I deserved her rebuke. On several occasions, I'd reprimanded Mom in front of the staff for calling me "Johnny" within earshot of a patient. Full of pride, I wanted to be a success at all costs. I feared my image would be tarnished if people knew my mother worked for me. Such moments were a throwback to the days when Mom attempted to drive me home from Garden School in the rain, when I'd escaped out a side door into that very rain—raindrops to a different tune than Burt Bacharach's.

Which reminded me of Angie Dickinson. *Did we have a similar problem?*

* * *

Margaret and I had purchased a modest starter home, with a maximum mortgage, on the western edge of Rancho Bernardo, in the young-family area where a small fraction of the local retirement community resided. To keep fit for her role as mother and the office's financial manager, Margaret had been reading *Aerobics* by Dr. Kenneth Cooper and applying what she'd learned. *Oh, to be descended from the disciplined Germans instead of the lazy Italians! Then I could do the same!* Instead, I soon gained a few pounds, while becoming obsessed with the success of my practice and my reputation in the local community. Then, due to speeches I'd been giving about my research performed in a part-time position at the Loma Linda University Medical Center, I became consumed with my national reputation. In the face of this, Margaret made a surprising announcement one day.

"Honey," she said. "I'm going to be on national TV tomorrow! On *The Today Show!*"

I said, "No way," but it was true. Art Ulene, the show's celebrity doctor, was doing a story on physical fitness in Rancho Bernardo, one of the healthiest communities in America, according to a recent study. He'd gone to the Westwood Club that morning and, from all the individuals playing tennis, swimming laps, and engaging in various athletic activities, he'd chosen to interview Margaret, who'd been playing paddleball.

It has been estimated that sixty million Americans watched Margaret play paddleball the next morning as she answered questions from Dr. Ulene in a voice-over. Margaret was pursuing health and fitness while I was seeking fame to reinforce my self-worth, but were such disparate goals compatible? Margaret was surprisingly oblivious as to why Robert Goulet had selected her from a Las Vegas audience, and now Art Ulene had chosen her for an interview to be aired on *The Today Show.* I knew why, but she didn't. It was her beauty, enhanced by a broad smile, emanating from a firm foundation of truth, warmth, and humility. And the fact that she was unaware of it was the source of her charm.

From a distance, one might think we had a perfect marriage, but in reality, we had problems. I was absorbed in my work and committed to my financial and professional goals. I sacrificed involvement with my family to add many speaking engagements to enrich my bank account and gain fame in my profession.

Margaret's dedication to Catholicism presented a different issue. Soon after our marriage, Margaret told me we would practice the rhythm method instead of using artificial birth control. Wasn't she aware of the old joke? *What do you call Catholics who use the rhythm method?* The answer to this is: *Parents!* I was unhappy with her unilateral decision. Every morning, Margaret would record her temperature before she left our king bed. A slight temperature rise would mean she'd most likely be ovulating. Therefore, we had to avoid sexual intimacy for several days. As Margaret had read, the technique could be 99% effective if practiced flawlessly. And Margaret was a perfectionist.

One night, after a stressful day at the office—a surgery had taken longer than anticipated, causing a logjam of disgruntled patients—I sat beside Margaret on our lumpy-comfy sofa and put my arm around her.

"You look pretty," I said, "Why not wear your pink babydoll tonight? With the spaghetti straps."

"We can't have sex tonight, John. My temperature's up. I'm ovulating." Margaret called me *John* instead of *honey* when she was going to say something very serious.

"I have condoms."

"Not possible. The Church teaches that we must avoid artificial contraception. So we can be open to life. Natural family planning ensures that."

I hesitated. "I'm not sure I want a church that's so rigid."

"Until 1930, John, *all* Christian denominations taught this. Then, swayed by growing pressure from its worshipers, the Anglican Church allowed contraception in *certain* circumstances. In the past forty-five years, it grew from there."

Could a prohibition that had been in place for all Christians for nearly two millennia have any substance to it? I wondered.

Margaret went on to explain the dogma of "natural law." The original purpose of sexual intercourse was procreation. The pleasure of the act was an additional blessing. Mutual respect for this belief—and the discipline necessary to achieve it—strengthens the love of the individuals involved. When conception follows, the loving environment provides the perfect setting for nurturing children.

"Our sons need to know that we love each other as well as them," Margaret said. "That we'll always work together for the benefit of the family."

Bill Lundigan had told me that Rosemary Clooney was a practicing Catholic when she married Jose Ferrer, the 1951 Academy Award winner for his role as Cyrano de Bergerac. Between 1955 and 1961, she'd had five children, resulting in Bob Hope's snarky remark on national TV that Rosemary had so many kids because she liked to play "Vatican Roulette." Evidently, Rosemary hadn't been a perfectionist. Or Jose Ferrer had been selfishly obstinate.

My total immersion in my career was causing resentment in Margaret. Despite her commitment to our marriage, our marriage was obviously in trouble. Sensing a problem, friends suggested we attend a Catholic-sponsored Marriage Encounter Weekend to improve our communication and bring God into the equation. Prior to this weekend retreat—held at the Mission San Luis Rey in nearby Oceanside—the first priority in my life had been my profession. My sons were second, Margaret third, and God was absent.

During the weekend, three couples—newlyweds, a couple married for ten years, and another for twenty-five—gave presentations discussing marital issues, including intimate and embarrassing situations. Returning to our room after each talk, we were to employ techniques we had learned to comfortably share our feelings about topics that had been previously taboo. Fr. Chuck Gallagher, the participating priest, explained that he was "married" to the Church and had dedicated his life to helping its members become closer to God and each other. He was a powerful speaker, and one particular message—about avoiding marital infidelity—would impact my life sooner than I could have imagined.

Through Marriage Encounter, God became more visible to me, though my actions didn't necessarily reflect it. My mind, like Dad's, still wandered during Mass. I seldom prayed. What *did* change, however, was that I began to see Margaret's love and support as the key to my success— both as a father and periodontist—although my avid pursuit of personal goals still diminished our family life.

And so, in the fall of 1977, when Wayne's soccer team lacked a coach—newly motivated as I was by the Marriage Encounter, and resolving to spend more time with our children—I volunteered. But I failed to admit—even to Margaret—that I feared my leadership in this new role would be insufficient. Moreover, I had little experience in organized sports. My greatest fear was that the team would go winless, negatively impacting my self-esteem. Yet, with the same grit and determination that had surfaced at Penn to defeat Mr. Hathaway's prediction of my failure there, I read a series of books on coaching youth soccer.

To my surprise, we went undefeated, winning fourteen straight games. Inspired, I coached for two more years, resulting in forty-two consecutive wins and a full-page article in the local newspaper—about me, my methods, and our victories—under the headline: "A Coach for All Seasons." Again, I experienced a surge of pleasure—lasting for weeks.

Margaret hated it when I became prideful. Pride is considered by many to be the deadliest of sins because it promulgates the belief that one is better than others. Pride is never satisfied, it craves power, and its belief in self-sufficiency moves us away from God. Margaret had subtle, but effective, ways to rein me in, but this newspaper article challenged her. Ultimately, her method proved flawless—she just changed the subject, refusing to listen when I bragged about our victories.

This left me wondering where my pride—the result of a subconscious idea that I wasn't good enough—would take me. As King Richard had said in *Richard II*, performed at the Shakespeare Theater back in Stratford, "Pride must have a fall."

But why listen to Shakespeare when I wasn't even listening to God?

Chapter 17   *Día de los Muertos*

A FEW MINUTES BEFORE 9:00 a.m. on Monday, September 25, 1978, I leaned against the window of a Boeing 727 as it reached its holding point on the tarmac at San Diego International Airport, the busiest single-runway airport in the United States. I was off to Los Angeles for a day of teaching at UCLA. I'd missed my 8 a.m. flight because I'd failed to set the alarm.

It was a typically beautiful San Diego day. Low-lying hills were clearly etched in the distance, and the flat skyline highlighted the Church of the Immaculata bell tower at the University of San Diego. USD, a small, prestigious Catholic university, was often confused with the immense UCSD, the University of California San Diego. Despite my religious skepticism, churches had always provided a certain serenity for me, and all seemed peaceful now that I'd rebooked my flight and was on the plane. I closed my eyes. LA was less than an hour away.

I was flying Pacific Southwest—"The World's Friendliest Airline"— known for its twenty-nine-year history without fatalities. Its beautiful flight attendants wore brightly colored miniskirts. Its planes, with a whimsical black nose cone and smiley face, were nicknamed "The Grinningbirds." The airline encouraged the stewardesses to be friendly and, when appropriate, humorous. I opened my eyes as an attractive flight attendant, who appeared to be in her late twenties, spoke up:

"This is a no-smoking, no-whining, no-complaining flight. In the unlikely event, this flight becomes a cruise, you have a life vest under your seat in the form of a yellow itsy-bitsy bikini. In case of a drop in cabin pressure, two masks will drop from above. Put yours on first, and then pick your child with the most potential and put on the other."

Minutes later, the plane took off and slipped out over the Pacific, and it wasn't long before the captain said, in a deeper voice than when he first welcomed us aboard, "Flight attendants, please prepare for landing." The same

darling stewardess was less jocular now. "Ladies and gentlemen, in preparation for landing, please secure your seatbelts, straighten your seatbacks, and
place your carry-on belongings under the seat in front of you." The plane
touched down, and her voice grew even more subdued as we approached the
gate. "On behalf of the entire flight crew"—she paused for several seconds—
"it has been our pleasure serving you. We know you have a choice of airlines,
and we thank you for choosing Pacific Southwest."

When the plane came to an abrupt halt, and the chime sounded, I stood
and edged my way past the two cabin attendants, looking at each of them in
turn. But they didn't look back. They were expressionless, with downturned
heads and moist eyes, nodding in response to passengers' goodbyes. The
crew's anguish was palpable, reminding me of creepy feelings I'd experienced
long ago listening to Long John Nebel's late-night readings of Edgar Allan Poe
on a transistor radio under my pillow. Something was amiss.

I bounded up the jet bridge into the LAX terminal. Minutes later, in
a rented Toyota, I tuned to KNX, radio 1070, the Los Angeles all-news station. It was 9:59. After a brief commercial for Lucky Strike cigarettes, a male
voice, serious and articulate, announced: "Tragedy has struck in San Diego.
I'm George Herman of CBS News. One hour ago, Pacific Southwest Airlines
Flight 182, originating in Sacramento with a stop in Los Angeles, collided
with a Cessna light aircraft twenty-six hundred feet above San Diego. At
least one hundred forty perished. There were no survivors."

Overwhelmed by sadness, I turned off the radio. I'd been sheltered
from death throughout my youth by my mother. Although I'd encountered
it *en masse* in the anatomy lab at Georgetown Medical School, most of the
corpses there had been of older people—obese, cancer-ridden, or artery-
clogged. The passengers headed to San Diego on Pacific Southwest early
that morning were gorgeous young flight attendants, experienced pilots,
and business executives coming to close a deal, visit family, or lecture at the
University of California San Diego. Their lives—or so they must have been
thinking, just as I was—lay ahead of them.

As I approached the UCLA School of Dentistry, I stopped for the light
at Wilshire Avenue and Westwood Boulevard and closed my eyes. I still
only knew three prayers, the ones I'd said before final exams in the Newman
Center Chapel at the University of Pennsylvania. "Our Father . . ." A horn
blared behind me and, startled, I drove ahead.

That evening, when I dropped off the Toyota and took the yellow-and-
black shuttle to the PSA departure terminal at LAX, all employees were
business-like and efficient. A few forced half-smiles. My Boeing 727, the
same model that had crashed, headed south and skirted the shoreline after
takeoff, flying east over Pacific Beach towards El Cajon before making a

slow U-turn toward the coastal airport. From my seat on the right side of the aircraft, I looked down at San Diego's North Park area. Dark smoke was still billowing from hotspots in the block-long crash site. Exiting, I looked into the reddened eyes of the flight attendants by the door. The captain was standing behind them in the cockpit doorway. "I'm sorry," I muttered—insufficient words, but I hoped their sincerity would suffice.

The Grim Reaper, that morbid Halloween figure, had made an early trip to San Diego. As Margaret had made me aware, multiple religious traditions mention an Angel of Death, or Angel of the Lord, or angelic beings who, on God's order, slay the guilty. "Angel of Death" was the name given to Josef Mengele, the notorious German officer and physician who'd performed inhumane experiments and selected Jews for the gas chambers in World War II. In July of 1955, when the American Shakespeare Festival Theatre opened in Stratford with *Julius Caesar*, I'd read the play in advance. In Act 3, Scene 1, Cassius, the ringleader of the conspirators, has a particularly provocative line:

> "He that cuts off twenty years of life
> Cuts off so many years of fearing death."

It seemed to me that, while most people believe in Heaven, they ignore the possibility of Hell—although, if Christianity is true, their destiny might be to end up there in the event of an unforeseen tragedy. Rather than fear death, as Cassius believed, the majority exclude it from their thoughts, filling their lives—like me—with possessions, sporting events, and work.

Back home that night, I hugged Margaret. "I hope you weren't worried."

"No. Your flight was at eight. You were probably at UCLA by nine." She hadn't realized that I had missed my original flight and was on a PSA flight at the airport at the time of the crash.

In the next few days, the *San Diego Union* published photographs and stories about the crash victims—one hundred forty-four of them, many so young. Thirty-seven PSA employees had been aboard. Seven were actively working on Flight 182. Thirty were off-duty crewmembers, including fourteen flight attendants "deadheading"—flying free—to reposition back at headquarters in San Diego. Obituaries and tributes dominated the news in the days to follow.

For years, ads for Pacific Southwest Airline had featured sex-laden innuendos designed to attract traveling businessmen—lines such as *I'm going to fly you like you've never been flown before.* But now, the thought of those attractive flight attendants made me queasy. All of a sudden, they were corpses. Their body parts had been strewn across a smoldering block in the North Park section of San Diego. As a result, a new sense of mortality crept into my brain, etching itself indelibly for all of eternity—at least eternity as I understood it.

* * *

Performing surgery was lucrative. The requirements were years of education, manual dexterity, mental acuity, physical agility, endurance, and confidence in functioning under pressure. Mom scheduled my office appointments tightly to ensure maximum productivity. Margaret managed the finances, watched the overhead like a hawk, and attacked over-expenditures with an immediate inquiry. On the side, I moonlighted in several academic slots, and the income flowed.

Tired of driving Chevrolets, in early 1978, I bought a two-toned, blue-and-gray Datsun 280 ZX with a T-Bar hardtop roof that allowed an easy conversion to a convertible. I'd been thinking about a car like that since riding to LA with Arnold. In retrospect, my new vehicle was tangible evidence that my pride had been taking hold. My Datsun was not a Maserati, although the overall styling was similar. But it had been affordable. And with its AGUMDR vanity plate, striking colors, and design, many patients saw it in the parking lot and guessed it was mine. Many times I'd heard the same thing. "Hey, Doc. I see I bought you a new car!"

Invitations continued to arrive, requesting me to speak at future regional and national meetings, including a featured spot at the 1979 Annual Meeting of the American Dental Association in Dallas. Such demand boosted my self-esteem and encouraged me to attempt other endeavors beyond the confines of my office.

RCA had recently developed a videocassette recorder. This two-piece combo was far superior to the Super-8 camera that produced silent films projected on a screen, often accompanied by noise, heat, and a vibrating image due to the projector itself. The growing popularity of the camcorder intrigued me. Its movies were clear, and they captured sound as well. With its 6:1 zoom and compatible video, the RCA product weighed but fourteen pounds, and its handle made it easily portable. I was excited by the promise of bringing this equipment to the soccer field and watching Wayne and Mark grow up on our TV.

I envisioned a business use as well. I could record lectures of medical and dental professionals, edit the tapes, and market them, along with the equipment itself, to physicians and dentists. When I approached Dr. David Tagge, my new associate, as a possible partner in a video business, he said his wife Lynn had talents that would make her a better fit. So I presented the idea to Lynn, she agreed, and we formed Videodontics, a company to make continuing-education videocassettes for dentists. We believed it was the first such venture in the nation.

In October 1978, we began video-recording faculty members at the UCLA medical and dental schools. Soon, an international opportunity to plug the equipment and courses of Videodontics materialized with an invitation to lecture in Mexico with Dr. Alex Koper.

Since its debut four years earlier, the USC Annual Periodontal Symposium had been the largest moneymaker for the Department of Continuing Education. Dr. Koper, thrilled with me for managing the annual program, suggested we lecture together, along with his protégée, Dr. Howard Landesman, a talented prosthodontist, for the dental society of Mexico City. He'd been contacted by Dr. Luis Rodríguez, head of *La Asociacion Dental Del Distrito Federal*, to arrange a program for their November meeting.

"Bring your wives," Alex said. "The Mexican dental society will pay airfare and expenses in Mexico City. Then we'll fly to Zihuatanejo on the Pacific coast for some sun and sand."

Zihuatanejo was one hundred fifty miles northwest of Acapulco. A new international airport had been built there two years earlier. We were to spend three nights at the charming *Sotavento* hotel, paying for it ourselves, but Alex assured us it wasn't expensive. He was a renaissance man who took pride in finding good deals, including delicious yet inexpensive wines at Trader Joe's. This talent impressed Margaret, who constantly researched better prices for our office purchases. In that respect, they were two of a kind.

"The *Sotavento*'s a real find," Alex assured us. "We *could* stay in the new government resort at Ixtapa, but why spend the money? The *Sotavento*'s charming and romantic—no TVs, just king-size beds and spacious ocean-view balconies."

And so, on October 31—the onset of *Día de los Muertos*—Margaret and I flew to Mexico City with Alex, Corinne Koper, Howard, and Lynn Landesman and checked into the 60-room *Gran Hotel Ciudad de Mexico*. Built in the heart of the city in 1885, it is located just off the huge *Zocalo* plaza. Inside, a massive stained-glass ceiling tops a four-story Art Nouveau lobby. In honor of the holiday, porters were wearing black top hats, black pants, and long-sleeved black shirts, painted front and back with white skeletons—somewhat anatomically correct, as I duly noted. They'd also painted their faces white, contrasting their dark noses and blue-circled eyes. Vertical black lines, inked on their lips, gave the macabre impression of age and desiccation.

During the next three days, Alex, Howard, and I lectured in tandem in two-hour time slots. Evenings were for social events with our spouses, the most memorable being a formal dinner hosted by the dignitaries of the Mexico City dental society at the *Hacienda de Los Morales*, Mexico City's iconic restaurant. Constructed in 1526 as a silkworm factory, the two-story structure was enhanced with arched windows, columns, fountains, and numerous flowers in clay pots.

Dinner was in the main dining room, at a long table set for sixteen with crystal and silver flatware. The black, straight-back chairs bore ornate designs. Margaret sat to my right, directly across from Linda Rodríguez, the lovely wife of Dr. Rodríguez, who sat across from me. Beautiful and composed as always, Margaret wore a simple black evening dress. Linda Rodríguez, an attractive, charming, bilingual woman with a contagious laugh, wore a lavish red number with puffed short sleeves. One of her parents had been born in the United States, so she spoke perfect English. She and Luis had four sons, the two older ones similar in age to Wayne and Mark. Luis and I talked dentistry, and I plugged my business adventure with Videodontics. Linda and Margaret discussed faith and children.

The mariachis were singing at our table when I heard Linda say, "Margarita, maybe you and John could bring your boys and stay at our home. Francisco and Jose are the same ages as Wayne and Mark. Manuel and little Alejandro would enjoy playing with the big boys."

"*Si, Juan.*" Luis had heard, too. "*Mi casa es su casa.*"

"*Gracias, Luis,*" I said, adding, after a pause, "*mi amigo.*"

Novedades, the local newspaper, reported on our prestigious conference during the week. I saved those clippings for years—an indication of the pride I felt in my first experience as an international notable. Meanwhile, down the table from us, Alex and Corinne and Howard and Lynn were similarly engaged in conversation. But Alex seemed to be thinking, *This is cool, but wait 'til they see the Sotavento!*

Chapter 18   Paradise Lost and Found

THE BAY OF ZIHUATANEJO could be seen through a framework of palm branches beneath our hillside patio—all sandy beach to turquoise water. Farther out, the sea turned Tiffany blue, then teal, ending in an expanse of azure beneath a light blue sky. High white clouds enhanced the sultry afternoon, floating lazily above a smattering of fishing boats. To our left lay the jungle foliage of the *Punta Garrobo* peninsula. The only negative factor I'd discovered when we dropped our suitcases in our rooms and headed for the beach was that the *Sotavento* lacked air conditioning.

Then it was off to dinner at the *Garrobos* restaurant to feast on garlic-laden red snapper. The Chilean white wine, selected by Alex, was perfect. Then the six of us strolled back to the *Sotavento*, ignoring the mosquitos and humidity.

At 3:00 a.m., I woke to the whirring of the wooden ceiling fan and the roar of the ocean. The temperature had dropped into the eighties, but the Pacific breeze—which had cooled us during the day—was non-existent, and the humidity hadn't dropped at all. Although the fan's hum was soothing, its rocking motor, silhouetted against the white plaster ceiling, was disconcerting. Lying there naked, I imagined my father studying the ceiling at St. James Church in Stratford; then, I wondered about Mexican building codes and the stability of the whirring fan overhead. My naked-ness, a comfort in the heat, was an invitation to the mosquitos. Margaret was sleeping, however, fitfully.

Two hours later, still sleepless, I turned on the bathroom light, scattering large dark roaches into hiding.

"Margaret," I called. "I can't sleep in this place. Let's walk on the beach."

I hated to wake her. She groaned, rolled over, and slipped out of bed. Minutes later, we descended an illuminated dirt path toward the water. To our surprise, another couple was on the beach—Howard and Lynn.

"What are you guys doing here?" I said.

Howard was agitated. "Damn heat and bugs—we had to get out of that room!"

"Can you imagine two more nights here? Let's try the *El Presidente* hotel in Ixtapa," I said. "My guidebook says it's air-conditioned and only a 20-minute drive." I hesitated. "But I don't have the heart to tell Alex." Alex had been hinting at sending me on future trips out of the country—he'd even mentioned Tahiti—and it was something I didn't want to jeopardize.

"I'll tell him," Howard said. "He and I have endured a lot together over the years."

The following day, at the *El Presidente*—while we were all drinking margaritas in the swimming pool beneath an expansive *palapa* of dry palm branches—Howard confided that Alex had seemed relieved. He and Corinne couldn't have spent another night at the sweltering *Sotavento*, either. I was glad to hear it. I could now savor the salt of my margarita on the rim of my wide-mouthed glass as ice chips floated on the surface.

"That hotel's deteriorated since I was last here," Alex admitted, unable to conceal his embarrassment. "I'm so sorry."

"Let me tell you what happened last week," Corinne said, abruptly changing the subject.

I cringed. Corinne was always frank with her opinions. She and Alex lived in Brentwood, near UCLA and the VA hospital, one of the wealthiest neighborhoods in West Los Angeles—home to celebrities, corporate executives, and professional athletes. At all times, the residents were well aware of who should be on their streets. During normal daytime hours, construction workers and landscape laborers were expected. But at 6:30 in the morning, as Corinne explained, you had to keep an eye out.

"I was up early, pulling weeds in the yard, when a Black man came jogging by. He was looking at our house, probably casing the joint, so I yelled, 'Excuse me, do you live around here?' Well, to my surprise, he said, 'Ma'am, don't you know me? I'm O.J. Simpson.'"

Suddenly, Corinne's story interested me. In Stratford, the most recognizable name on a list of notable residents was Stephen King, who'd lived in town briefly as a child. It would take many years for me not to be fascinated by famous people, and LA certainly had its share.

"Well," Corinne continued, "I smiled and said, 'Have a nice day!'"

Then, like Alex, she admitted her embarrassment. She had no idea—how could any of us—that sixteen years later, O.J. Simpson would be implicated in the murder of Nicole Brown Simpson, only blocks from where she'd been weeding the yard.

Alex changed the subject. "I'm thinking of adding your husband to the faculty of our new travel-and-learn program," he said to Margaret. "I hope you'll come along. We'll have courses in some very exotic places."

Margaret had charmed Alex with her account of our office economies, so I wasn't surprised that he announced this choice to her. Nor did I think much would come of it. Nonetheless, in early January 1979, a pink envelope arrived for Margaret. Expecting something from Alex and Corinne, she found, instead—on quality stationery, bordered with roses—a beautifully hand-written note from Linda Rodríguez.

Dear Margaret, it began, *Luis and I so enjoyed our visit with you and John at the Hacienda de los Morales and the opportunity to learn about your family. We would like to invite you and your sons to visit us for Holy Week. We call it Semana Santa, and it is a week of feasts and festivities. We have a large home, and you will be very comfortable. Mexico City is so exciting during the Easter holiday.*

Specific details for the visit followed, and three months later, we were back in Mexico, on the day before Palm Sunday, for a one-week stay. We planned to leave the day before Easter to celebrate what Margaret considered the holiest day in Christianity—with Mom, Dad, and my sister Janet's family.

Janet and her husband Glenn had recently moved with their four children from New Jersey to Rancho Bernardo, induced by our family Christmas photo at San Diego's Sea World—in shorts, with wading pink flamingos, and a row of palms. Soon after their move, they opened *Tots 'n Teens*, an exclusive children's store, featuring quality furniture and expensive baby carriages imported from Italy. Margaret and I were looking forward to spending time with them.

Meanwhile, the Rodríguez family home was as large and comfortable as Linda had promised. It was exquisite—a two-story, white stucco contemporary tucked behind a tall black wrought-iron fence. Arrowhead-like finials, topping the barrier from front to back, pointed toward the sky. As we removed our suitcases from Luis' car in the circular driveway, I peered through the fence to the far side of the street, where another prominent residence had a similar fence, plus a uniformed armed guard pacing the sidewalk, back and forth, to the property line.

Observing my stare, Luis said, with a broad grin and strong accent, "Juan, eets zee *casa* of zee Mayor . . . we spleet protection." I'd heard of Mexico City's high homicide rate—kidnappings for ransom were becoming more common—but Luis said we'd be safe. He intended to confine our visit to protected roads and places with large crowds. Reassured, I settled in for a week of sightseeing—from the pyramids of the Gods at the Aztec city of *Teotihuacan* to the gondola-like boats on the waterways of *Xochimilco*.

On Holy Thursday, our last day for touring, we visited Puebla, 80 miles to the southeast, a city founded by the Spanish in 1521 to protect the trade route between Mexico City and Veracruz. Margaret was disappointed to miss the Basilica of Our Lady of Guadalupe in Mexico City, with its famous image of the Virgin Mary on a *tilma*, which miraculously appeared on an indigenous man's shawl of cactus fibers. It belonged to Juan Diego Cuauhtlatoatzin, whose conversion was thought to be responsible for bringing the indigenous people of Mexico and, ultimately, all of South America to Catholicism. I, however, considered this to be another fairy tale, a "miracle" story like that of Andy Brose, my father's friend who'd supposedly been cured of severe asthma at the shrine of St. Anne de Beaupré.

As we prepared to depart, seven-year-old Mark asked why we hadn't seen the Easter Bunny or any Easter eggs. "The Mexican people," Margaret explained, "understand better than Americans the true meaning of Easter."

She didn't tell Mark, as Linda Rodríguez had explained, about the reenactment of the Passion of Christ in nearby Temoaya. During Easter Week, a man is scourged and then, accompanied by "Roman" soldiers on horseback, walks uphill with a wooden cross on his back. Atop the hill, he joins two other men, each bound to a cross, then the crosses are hoisted and kept upright for thirty minutes. But all I could think of was the Russell Stover, solid-chocolate Easter Bunny that Aunt Josephine used to give Janet and me at Easter. It certainly was less stressful for kids than watching three guys hanging from a cross.

Was the Easter Bunny a sham substitute for the true meaning of the Easter holiday? Thinking of the addictive behavior I'd witnessed in Las Vegas—my own included—I wondered if religious faith might be a way to overcome such addictions, the Seven Deadly Sins included. *If so, were kids in the United States—my own included—being shortchanged?*

* * *

Not two weeks later, speaking in broken English, Luis Rodríguez called my office. I thought this was unusual. Usually, his wife Linda wrote to Margaret as his preferred method of communication. Luis tended to lapse into "Spanglish" when excited.

"Juan," he said in a rapid staccato, "ever seence you show me . . . deese peek-tures . . . I want dee veedeo cam-eera."

I'd left him a Videodontics brochure, which included an ad for the portable RCA system. As best I could understand, he wanted to purchase the entire works. He was willing to pay for me to bring the equipment to his home and suggested the first weekend in June. Given the import taxes, the same equipment in Mexico City would be double the cost.

"What about Customs?" I said.

"*No problema.*" American tourists, Luis assured me, passed through Customs without having their luggage inspected.

I was being cautious. I didn't want to wind up in a Mexican "hoosegow." As I'd learned, that familiar term was a corruption of the Spanish *jusgado*, meaning "court of law." Such courts were usually in the same building as Mexican prisons. English-speaking Southwesterners, unfortunate enough to experience them, had coined the term, spelling it as they heard it.

Since we'd just visited Mexico City and passed through Customs without inspection, I acquiesced. Grandma Sottosanti had resorted to occasional shoplifting to feed her family in difficult times, and Dad had obtained an education without following all the rules. For them, it was like driving sixty miles per hour in a zone posted at fifty. Some dictates, my heritage seemed to say, begged to be ignored. In Sicily, many statutes were often not rigidly enforced; evidently, it was the same in Mexico. Maybe that was why Luis and I, in a very short period of time, had become like brothers. How could I refuse? He'd just hosted my family for a weeklong vacation.

Packing the new video equipment in two large suitcases, I protected it from damage with my underwear, towels, clean slacks, and a polo shirt. Still, I watched nervously as those suitcases circled the baggage conveyor belt at the Mexico City International Airport. Other passengers—many appearing to be Americans—had already picked up their luggage and were in line for inspection. Everyone else was queuing up.

The lines were long. But something was amiss. Leaving my luggage on the conveyor, I walked to the front, where an elderly U.S. woman, who looked in her eighties, watched a Customs inspector scrutinize her underwear. Did he think she'd sewn drugs into the lining? My heart rate and perspiration increased.

As I returned to the carousel, my suitcases reappeared, having circled back through the loading area. Then a porter materialized out of nowhere. "Meester, *keen* I help you?"

"*Si, gracias.* I'm late." I pointed to my wristwatch. "Can you help me . . . *rapido?*" I pointed to the tall glass barrier. Limousine drivers, just beyond it, were holding up signs, and relatives and friends of arriving passengers were eagerly waiting. I removed a ten-dollar bill from my wallet, and the porter's eyes widened.

"*Si, meester.*" Picking up my suitcases, he seemed undisturbed by their considerable weight. Then he motioned for me to follow, pausing briefly to move a stanchion to bypass security. When the armed guard at the baggage check table looked at us, the porter simply waved him off. The guard understood that money had been exchanged and would be divided between them later.

We walked under the *Salida* sign, passed through the glass doors, and there was Luis with a worried look on his face. I couldn't conceal my annoyance.

"You said there'd be no inspection."

In his fractured English, Luis explained that—just the day before, without notice—his friend and neighbor, the former mayor, had been replaced. And the new mayor immediately changed the rules. Months earlier, there'd been a sign instructing U.S. citizens with nothing to declare to pass directly through Customs. But that sign had been removed.

I had no remorse about breaking the law to help my friend—I was both proud and relieved to escape confinement in a Mexican jail. Hadn't I avoided a court-martial and imprisonment at the Nellis dental clinic? But my behavior, in this case, felt different.

* * *

"Dad," I said, early in the summer of 1979, "can you build me a redwood deck for the hot tub I'm gonna buy?"

I considered redwood tubs, with their vertical wooden slats and stabilizing metal band, more aesthetic and romantic than the new acrylic ones, despite the hygienic benefits of the latter.

"Certainly," Dad said—"if you promise me that third grandchild I've been waiting for." I didn't promise, but by early September, Margaret was pregnant. Mom and Dad were delighted, and Margaret and I began considering a larger home. My practice was thriving, so money was not an issue. Mom kept my schedule full, and Margaret rode herd on the books.

Meanwhile, true to his word, Alex Koper assigned me as the USC professor for a nine-day travel course the following February in Papeete, Tahiti, and the nearby island of Moorea. Traveling to French Polynesia was beyond my imagination. Growing up in Stratford, I'd seen palm trees only in pictures, until first going to Mexico. Now I had an all-expense paid trip with Margaret to the South Pacific. I was flying high. *Who needs Heaven when there's heaven on earth?*

"What shall we call the course?" Alex said. "Make it catchy, so it'll sell out."

"*Periodontics in Paradise,*" I said.

And it *did* sell out, so in February, while Margaret—five months pregnant—lounged on the beach, I relaxed in a hammock between two palm trees on the island of Moorea, eleven miles northwest of Tahiti, considering myself the most fortunate surgeon in the world. Instead of incising human tissue and facing the daily pressures of a surgical practice, I was eating *poisson cru*—the Tahitian version of raw fish cured in citrus juices—washing it down with icy cold local beer.

I lectured for four days of the ten-day trip—travel days excluded—to satisfy the IRS regulations for tax deductions. Using a Kodak Carousel projector, I spoke for two hours in the morning while Margaret enjoyed the breakfast buffet. I lectured again between four and six when appetizers were offered, and a bartender prepared Mai Tais, banana coladas, and martinis. The "classroom" tone was casual and joyful. While speaking, I didn't mind competing with the noise of ice being crushed or shaken.

The flight back to Los Angeles stopped in Honolulu, and as we re-boarded the plane, we were surprised to see Lawrence Welk, the TV accordionist and orchestra leader, sitting in first class. Born into the German-speaking Catholic community of Strasburg, North Dakota, Welk had remained a Catholic throughout his life, receiving Holy Communion daily, whenever possible. In interviews, he readily acknowledged that the Christian principles of honesty, charity, and trust had been important to him in his rise to success in the entertainment and business worlds. He owned multiple buildings in Santa Monica and a 900-acre resort in Escondido, a small city in north San Diego County.

After landing, I found him standing beside me as we waited for our suitcases in baggage claim. Feeling confident and heady due to my professional success, I didn't hesitate to speak.

"Headed to Escondido, Mr. Welk?"

Looking past me, he smiled at Margaret. "Excuse me, ma'am. Are you a singer?"

Without missing a beat, Margaret said, "No. Not at all."

"Well, if you *were* a singer, I'd personally audition you. You have the look of the ladies I like to have on my show."

Among the attractive and wholesome female singers on the Welk show were the Lennon sisters, who, like their boss, were devout Catholics. Their album—*Lawrence Welk Presents the Lennon Sisters: Best-Loved Catholic Hymns*—was one of their most successful.

What is it with this Catholic thing? I remember thinking. *I can't escape it!*

I was beginning to see that the adjective *devout* didn't apply to me. Though born a Catholic, I was Catholic in name only and had never considered myself dedicated to, or knowledgeable in, the Catholic Faith. I didn't take the Sacraments seriously, while Margaret was pious in all these ways when I met her. Nor—as when she wound up on national TV—did the attention of Lawrence Welk pique her pride, whereas mine had been slighted when he overlooked me.

Back in San Diego, I began to reflect on the Catholic celebrities I'd known or knew about. William Lundigan and I had never discussed religion, but he'd enjoyed a long marriage and was buried at the Holy Cross Catholic Cemetery in Culver City, a few miles from the V.A. hospital. Jimmy Durante would eventually be interred there, Lawrence Welk as well, while Danny Thomas was interred on the grounds of St. Jude Hospital in Memphis. Both Rosemary Clooney and Angie Dickinson had strayed from their childhood faith, leading to lives quite different than Lundigan, Durante, and Welk.

Was Catholicism too strict for the times, or was I missing something?

Such thoughts didn't remain with me for very long. Home from Tahiti, I had surgeries to perform, fees to collect, lectures to give, and new things to purchase. Meanwhile, on June 7, 1980, Margaret gave birth to our third son, Paul Brian Sottosanti, an unplanned blessing in our lives. His grandparents were thrilled.

Chapter 19   Sun City Surprise

In November of 1980, I invited Dad to fly with me to Italy to find his ancestral home in the town of his birth. Renting a car in Rome, we headed south through Reggio Calabria, where Grandpa and Grandma Russo had been born, and as we left the ferry for Sicilian soil, Dad became emotional. His excitement increased as we drove along the island's northern coast, headed for Mistretta. Ninety-three miles west of Messina, we came to the town of Santo Stefano di Camastra. There, we exited the main highway and proceeded south to a curvy, twelve-mile road, gaining altitude, all the while, into the foothills of the Nebrodi Mountains.

I can remember a conversation Dad had with Aunt Liboria many times when he would tell her he remembered the street address in Italy. "Johnutz," Aunt Liboria would say, "when you go a-back to Italy someday, how you gonna say-a 'We-a lived in Numero Quatro, Via Petronilla.' You were a little boy, I-a only twenty. I no remember, how could-a you?" Then they'd both laugh, playing their little game for all to enjoy. Now, in Italy, came the moment of truth. Would Dad's memory prove true?

We entered the town square of Mistretta, an ancient city of eight thousand, with roots dating to the Phoenicians and Carthaginians. Parking the car, we walked to an old stone building with a large white sign in black letters: POLIZIA. Inside, the officer at the desk wore a blue, short-sleeved uniform. Another, similarly dressed, stood towards the back of the room.

"*Ciao,*" Dad said. He looked dapper in his tan, flat, small-brim cap, yellow dress shirt, brown sports jacket, and matching striped tie—fitting apparel for one about to enter the "old country" where he'd been born, in the company of his son, the doctor. All we had to do was locate the house. "*Dov'e via Petronilla?*"

The officer turned his palms up. "*Non lo so.*"

Looking deflated, Dad turned to the older officer across the room and shouted the same question. *"Si, si!"* the officer replied. Moving toward a large map on the wall, he motioned for us to follow. Then he pointed to a short street. *"Via Petronilla."*

Speaking in a Sicilian dialect, Dad asked for a pen and paper to take notes. He was much happier now. *"Grazie, mille grazie!"* he said as we left.

We drove from Mistretta's Town Hall along Via Liberta to the square near the *Chiesa della Santissima Trinita*, the Church of the Holy Trinity. From there, we walked two blocks down Conte Ruggero until we came to a street that sloped into a long underground passageway beneath a two-story stone residence. At the front of this tunnel was a Roman arch, its design and capstone similar to the one Dad had included in the shrine to the Virgin Mary he'd built in Connecticut.

Stopping at the entrance, Dad pointed to a square white stone set into the wall of the archway. Its black letters said: "Via Petronilla." I snapped a photo. Now for *Numero Quatro*.

The long passage—Dad led the way—exited onto a one-block continuation of Via Petronilla. Stone houses lined the street on our left, a stone wall on our right, and as we passed each house, we began counting: *numero uno, numero due, numero tre, numero . . . cinque?* A small white plaque marked each home by the doorway, the numbers deftly carved into the stone. But where was *quatro?* Dad looked more disappointed than at the police station. Tears welled up in his eyes. He seemed to doubt his memory.

"Hey!" I said from a distance—I'd retraced my steps. "This house has two doors! Come back here!" And there it was—*Numero Quatro, Via Petronilla*, Mistretta, Sicily. The number was barely visible, worn thin from a hundred years of Sicilian wind and rain. Dad's memory was, indeed, as sharp as ever. Catching up, he caught his breath and proudly knocked on the door. He was home.

A man in his seventies greeted us. *"Buongiorno."*

"Ciao," Dad said. He then hastily explained that we'd traveled nearly seven thousand miles to see this very house—the house of his birth.

The old man readily invited us in. He was spiffily dressed in a white shirt with blue pinstripes, dark slacks, and a heavy, black, V-neck sweater. His flat hat was identical to Dad's, except that it was gray. Even his thick, black-framed glasses were similar, though Dad's were tan. It was a cold, late November day, and the house lacked central heating. The only heat source was a bronze brazier—a two-handled shallow pot—on the living room floor.

After nearly an hour of conversation around the hot coals, the old man introduced us to his wife and daughter and invited us into the dining room for coffee and pastries. Speaking in Sicilian, Dad said he'd like to take some pictures. The old couple smiled, ready to pose, but the daughter—a dark-haired, attractive woman about my age—was adamant. "No!" she said.

Dad was tenacious. *Why couldn't he take photos?* The woman responded in Sicilian. *"My husband is working hard in the fields all day long. I would never want him to see a picture of me having a party with two strange men while he was gone."*

I was struck by this deep-seated loyalty to her husband and wondered about its source. Did this young woman attend Mass daily like Dad's old friend Andy Brose? The *Chiesa della Santissima Trinita* was only a few blocks away—easy access for habitual church-going, thus enhancing and sustaining one's faith.

Dad was proud to have located his birth home in Sicily. But my pride was different. I was pleased I had the money to treat him to such a trip. My flourishing surgical practice, jet-setter mentality, and thirst for success were propelling me in many directions at once. And so the 1980s would become my personal *Tower of Babel*, which I built like the Babylonians, who, having fashioned a great nation, wanted to construct a tower to the heavens, to be like the gods. *But who needed God when all was well?*

Pride infects the soul—which, as some believe, is the essence of a person once the body's stripped away. But I wasn't among those believers. My tower was a self-aggrandizing attempt to credit myself with the talents that had wrought my success. These hadn't come from a higher power—I felt I'd fashioned them myself. My addiction to pride was an attempt to answer a nagging question: *Are you good enough?* Mr. Hathaway, my math teacher at Stratford High, had become my early personal symbol of the need to prove myself. He'd predicted I would flunk out of Penn my first semester. Does everyone possess such a person who periodically resurfaces to guide or goad? In Genesis, God punished the pride and arrogance of the Babylonians. *Was I setting myself up for a fall?*

Nonsense.

* * *

In November of 1981, pleased with the successes of the annual periodontal symposia, programs I continued to orchestrate, Alex Koper invited me to lecture for a two-week travel program to Australia, New Zealand, and Fiji. This time I called the course "Periodontics Down Under," an appropriate pun, since periodontal disease progresses beneath the gums, destroying bone before surgery can arrest the process and rebuild the bone. Again, the course was a sellout.

In addition to my private practice, my life was busy with traveling, lecturing, and trying to manage Videodontics. In the process, I abandoned my family. Lynn Tagge was no longer my business partner. She'd found Videodontics too taxing or perhaps sensed it was doomed to fail. Meanwhile, I'd purchased equity in a new professional building and moved my practice there. Seeking to expand operations in various ways—rather than focusing on Videodontics, as I should have—I started a second company called American Family Health, which produced *Save-A-Smile*, a bubble-pack kit developed to motivate children to reduce cavities and achieve oral health. With professional design and appeal, the kit included a four-color storybook and a cassette tape that featured Wayne and Mark talking and singing. A professional actor played the role of a wise wizard, counseling the kids. I produced thousands to reduce my cost per kit. It was a substantial financial investment that Margaret did not support, but I proceeded, regardless.

Though I had the creativity, I lacked the requisite marketing skills for such a venture, and my pride prevented me from seeking assistance. Ultimately, neither Videodontics nor Save-A-Smile proved successful. Fortunately, I managed to sell the former for the original price of the equipment. But I wound up giving hundreds of Save-A-Smile kits to every general dentist in the area—for them to give to their patients at no cost— to induce them to send patients needing periodontal treatment my way. It worked—my referrals increased—so Save-A-Smile, like Videodontics, wasn't a total bust. "When life gives you lemons, make lemonade." I learned that cliché concept the hard way.

Meanwhile, Paul's birth had resulted in cramped living quarters in our Rancho Bernardo home, so Margaret and I decided to buy a larger house. The location was the big question. I'd received an offer to practice, one day a week, in the office of a periodontist in La Jolla, a toney coastal suburb of San Diego. I didn't need the extra work or money, but I'd always loved being close to the beach. Wayne and Mark, excelling in public schools, had just been accepted into The Bishop's School, an elite private Episcopalian school in La Jolla. So I took the offer and fulfilled another of my dreams, purchasing a home with an expansive ocean view—and countless palm trees—on a half-acre lot.

By 1984, having built a national reputation with the Annual USC Periodontal Symposium and my lectures at major dental meetings throughout the United States, I received referrals from periodontists nationwide. These were for patients moving to San Diego and needing to continue their periodontal care. Then, one day, there was a recognizable voice on the phone with a distinct New York City accent.

"Hello, John," said Dr. Alan Bloom, a prominent New York City periodontist who knew me from my reputation at the USC Periodontal Symposium. "I've got a patient moving to your neck of the woods. She's an actress, and I told her to see you. Be on the lookout for her, and do me a favor—take good care of her."

For privacy reasons, I will use a fictitious name for the actress and change the movie's title. All conversations and interactions are as I remember them.

"Good to hear from you, Alan. What's her name?"

"Candace Farrell. Most of her work's been on television, but she's starred in one recent movie and needs to be in L.A."

Having no spare time since I entered professional school, began to practice, and lectured extensively, I knew very few television stars. So the name meant nothing to me.

Since my new office had tripled the square footage and doubled the staff, Mom had retired, but our new receptionist, Nancy, recognized the name immediately. Candace Farrell had played many roles on television and had a particularly long run in a popular soap opera.

Remembering meeting Angie Dickinson, I told Nancy to give Candace Farrell preferential treatment if she called, as I wanted to be of assistance to Dr. Bloom. If this aspiring movie star was willing to make the two-hour drive from West Los Angeles to San Diego, we should accommodate her. And she *did* call, asking for an appointment when the office wouldn't be too busy. She liked to avoid the annoyance that her celebrity status entailed. Nancy scheduled her for an early Friday afternoon.

For her initial visit, Candace arrived in oversized sunglasses and casual clothing. She was lovely, with a keen sense of humor; however, she was visibly uncomfortable in a dental office, so I did my best to be gentle and reassuring. "She's adorable," Nancy said after Candace had left. "Even more beautiful than on television. And she's so warm and kind."

I found Candace Farrell very attractive, with penetrating blue eyes and a vivacious personality. Almost as tall as Margaret, she wore her blond hair cropped in a pixie, highlighting delicate facial features and a slender, turned-up nose.

"Candace," I'd said during her visit, "I realize you need special appointment times, so next time you call, ask for me personally. I know my schedule better than anyone."

"I'll do that," she said, looking me straight in the eyes, a look that caused a flitting in my chest. It was an innocent moment, but that's how such things begin.

* * *

As my relationship with USC continued to thrive, Alex Koper sent me, in March of 1984, on a two-week teaching trip to South Africa—the land of diamonds, gold, scenic beauty, and wild animals. Margaret accompanied me on this whirlwind tour to six major destinations. Intermittently, I lectured to a group of ten dentists who'd accompanied us from the States with their wives for a tax-deductible, travel-and-learn program. Although exhausted from the long flight from Los Angeles, I began lecturing shortly after our arrival.

During a stop at the Department of Periodontology at the University of Witwatersrand in Johannesburg, while conversing with the dental staff, I noticed on the counter a copy of the latest edition of *Glickman's Clinical Periodontology*, the most circulated periodontal textbook in the world. Its editor, Dr. Fermin Carranza, was my UCLA teaching mentor. I immediately opened the text to the chapter that contained many of my research photos—of subgingival pathogenic bacteria, taken through a scanning electron microscope. Beneath each picture was the citation: "Courtesy of Dr. John Sottosanti, La Jolla, California."

Halfway around the world, I found it impossible not to bask in the limelight. My pride was full-blown.

We'd gone to South Africa during the Apartheid period, when, due to extreme segregation, interracial marriage was forbidden, and many jobs were for whites only. But our trip was sheltered from the discriminatory policies forced on the non-white majority by the minority Afrikaners, the white descendants of Dutch settlers who'd arrived at the Cape of Good Hope in the seventeenth and eighteenth centuries. Afrikaners dominated politics and the economy as well.

Oblivious to the prevailing injustice, we anticipated our visit to Kruger National Park, one of the largest game parks in South Africa, where our roving contingent stayed at the adjacent Mala Mala Game Reserve for a photographic safari. Day or night, each safari had its own enhancements, including cocktail parties in the middle of the bush. After following animal tracks in the late afternoon, all nine Mala Mala jeeps—rifles mounted for safety—would emerge simultaneously into a clearing from different directions for a "sundowner" of appetizers and drinks.

Dinners at the reserve headquarters were behind iron fences, not unlike that at the Rodríguez home in Mexico City. These were part of a protective *boma*, where elephants might peer in as you looked out, attracted by the smells of barbecued venison. We ate under an ancient jackalberry tree, illuminated by candles and a roaring fire. Wine was being served, when one of the fourteen guests, unknown to me, asked, "Where you guys from?"

My reply set off a small commotion. "La Jolla, in California."

"We are too!" a second couple said. "So are we!" another exclaimed.

Incredibly, eight of Mala Mala's guests, always limited to thirty-six people, were from our new hometown. We were ten thousand miles from California, at one of the most luxurious private game reserves in the world—all expenses paid—and my La Jolla neighbors comprised twenty percent of the guests. I knew I'd earned the right to be there, but my head swelled again as it had in Mexico City.

Afrikaner dominance had led to restrictive rules that imposed Victorian-era mores on the entire country, whites included. And so gambling, or any public display of nudity, was strictly forbidden. But to spice things up for our traveling group, our local hosts had scheduled our final two nights in Sun City—a luxury resort and casino in South Africa's North West Province. Developed four years earlier in Bophuthatswana, Sun City had been declared independent by South Africa's government in response to a UN cultural boycott condemning Apartheid. This freed the developer to entice stars like Frank Sinatra, Liza Minnelli, and Elton John to perform, and to offer gambling, topless showgirl extravaganzas, and R-rated movies. The proximate metropolitan cities of Pretoria, the seat of the government, and Johannesburg, the country's largest city, assured that the resort would never lack for visitors.

I'd come full circle from Sin City in Nevada to Sun City in South Africa, battling the Seven Deadly Sins. One, in particular, would become potentially deadlier, starting right here in Bophuthatswana.

On our last night before departure, walking with Margaret near a fashionable shopping area, I saw a sign for a movie theater and suggested we check it out. I couldn't believe what I saw.

"Honey, that's my patient!" I exclaimed, surprising Margaret even more than me.

A large poster showed Candace Farrell sitting provocatively on a bed, wearing a sheer negligee, barely covering her pink skin, sufficiently transparent to outline a nipple. Across the top of the poster, on a black background, white letters proclaimed: "America's newest and sexiest star— Candace Farrell— in a movie that's elegant and erotic." The title, scrawled at the bottom in lipstick red, was "Sensual Interludes." A famous director's name was prominently displayed on the poster.

Margaret was tired and unimpressed with the image and the movie's description, and it was too late to see the movie—we had to be up and out early in the morning—but that chance "encounter" with one of my patients "blew my mind." I knew it was a coincidence, but, nevertheless, it startled me.

The next morning, we flew to Johannesburg, then to New York, and after a short layover, on to Los Angeles. On Monday, thoroughly exhausted, I was back in the office, checking the correspondence on my desk, when Nancy's voice came over the intercom, "Candace Farrell's on the phone for you, Doctor."

I couldn't believe the timing. It was as if someone had scripted a play, made me the protagonist, and placed a movie poster and a telephone in sequential scenes to develop the plot, to tempt me beyond the limits of my self-control. I decided to play along, believing no harm would come from my minor infatuation.

"Hello, Candace. How—how've you been?" I paused while she spoke, picturing her on that Sun City poster, her blue bedroom eyes staring at me from above her right nipple, camouflaged by a diaphanous nightgown. "Well, if you're having some discomfort, I can fit you in."

"Wonderful—" Her voice was charming. "I'd appreciate it."

"Friday at one? If you arrive early, we could do lunch."

"Perfect."

"See you then." And so, I hung up, looking forward to Friday with anticipation and apprehension.

Chapter 20   A Light From Above

BACK IN 1976, WHEN Margaret and I, at the recommendation of friends, had attended our church's Marriage Encounter Weekend, hoping to grow closer together, the topic of one speaker—Father Chuck Gallagher—was "Avoiding Temptation When Married." Margaret and I certainly had our differences, often revolving around birth control and how we spent our money, so the story Fr. Gallagher told began to resonate all the more. As I had suspected, and later learned for sure, Margaret had never forgiven me for that junket I'd taken to Japan just weeks after Mark was born.

"Joe was married," Fr. Gallagher began, "but didn't wear a wedding band. He worked for a large firm, spending most of the day in his six-by-eight cubicle. One Monday morning, when he took a coffee break, he met Charlotte, a beautiful young addition to the secretarial pool. They chatted for ten minutes and, on the way back to his cubicle, Joe checked his watch. It was 9:55. The next day, he began checking his watch at 9:00, and, with no overt evil intention in mind, he headed for coffee at 9:44. A minute later, Charlotte arrived, and they had a pleasant chat. This continued for the next four days. The following Monday, Joe asked Charlotte to lunch at a local deli—then to a happy hour on Friday afternoon, after which he offered to drive her home because it was growing dark, and she shouldn't walk the six blocks to her apartment.

"You can guess the rest of the story," Fr. Gallagher said. "And that's how things happen. They evolve, and in the blink of an eye, a faithful husband and father commits adultery, potentially ruining his marriage and alienating his family. Joe wasn't evil. He never dreamed something like this would happen to him. But he yielded to temptation."

Fr. Gallagher looked intently at the couples in the audience. "There were four steps involved," he said. "Joe was at the coffee machine when Charlotte coincidentally arrived. He was innocent. Step One involves 'intention.' The next day, Joe consciously increased the chances of meeting Charlotte at the coffee pot. Step Two is 'continuation.' Joe could easily have gone for coffee each day whenever he thought of it, but he chose the time when he'd most likely meet Charlotte."

A stern look appeared on Fr. Gallagher's face. "Step three is 'deception.' He didn't tell Charlotte he was married, and he lied to his wife about why he was late. Arranging for a happy hour with alcohol—which, as everyone knows, can quickly stifle good judgment—and then escorting Charlotte to her apartment to protect her from unknown and improbable dangers, provided the likelihood for Step Four, 'enactment.'"

Pausing dramatically, Fr. Gallagher shook his head and then looked slowly about the room, re-establishing direct eye contact with each couple. "Step Four would never have happened had Joe not taken a coffee break at 9:44 on the second day. He should have never let Step One happen. Satan—prince of darkness, temptation, and damnation—will find the slightest crack in your innocence and insert the tip of his bat-like wing, as Dante so vividly described it, to open you up to condemnation for eternity."

That bat-wing image, as vivid as the poster of Candace Farrell in Sun City, had stuck with me. And now, eight years later, it had me wondering: *Had I already committed Step One?*

* * *

Reaching for my wine glass, the chaise lounge shifted against the redwood deck, emitting a squeak—like chalk on a blackboard. Swirling the mellow yellow liquid, I caught a whiff of flowers, peach, and honey. I'd purchased the wine weeks before—a 1983 DeMorgenzon Reserve Chenin Blanc—in Stellenbosch, thirty miles east of Cape Town.

Life was good. The ocean was an Air Force blue on this sparkling evening. The waves, a steady roar with peaks and valleys, pounded the beach of La Jolla Shores several blocks in the distance. After six hours of surgery, serenity was just what I needed.

Seagulls hovered above the water, intermittently diving to confiscate morsels of food left on unattended blankets. Margaret was inside, preparing one of Mom's recipes—linguini with squid and clams, in garlic, butter, and lemon. Which only intensified my guilt, as I imagined tomorrow's lunch date with Candace Farrell—if all worked out as I hoped. It seemed silly to have lunch with a patient before a dental appointment, but I had plenty of sample toothbrushes and toothpaste in the office. I had it all figured out.

So why hadn't I mentioned this lunch to Margaret? I could excuse it as an innocent gesture, a courtesy lunch, on behalf of a patient who was driving two hours for an appointment. She was, after all, a friend of Alan Bloom. Lunch might not even happen if she were late . . . Why stir up trouble?

During my childhood in Stratford, as the son of an Italian immigrant, I'd only wanted to blend in. La Jolla and Stratford were similar in only one respect—they were coastal communities with thirty thousand residents. Other than that, Stratford was flat, covered with snow and ice in the winter, and suffering relentless heat and humidity in summer. Here in La Jolla, the weather was ideal, with low humidity and an annual average temperature of seventy-one degrees. Beauty surrounded us. To the southeast, a thirty-foot cross rose from the summit of Mt. Soledad. In a few weeks, a multitude of Christians would go there for the annual Easter sunrise service. Beyond the cross, green trees and red-tiled rooftops dotted the slopes, descending to La Jolla Cove, a secluded area protected by tall sandstone bluffs at the tip of a peninsula jutting into the Pacific. To the north, the coastline curved past the famed Torrey Pines Golf Course, a municipal layout along five hundred-foot cliffs, home to major PGA tournaments. After sunset, the lights of Del Mar, Carlsbad, and Oceanside would begin to twinkle.

The locals call La Jolla "The Jewel." Visitors call it the "Beverly Hills of San Diego," with its pricey Girard Avenue shops and ocean-view, four-star restaurants on Prospect Street. We were so fortunate to be living here.

A few miles north, the Salk Institute, named for its famous founder, Jonas Salk, sits on the Torrey Pines plateau high above the Pacific. Designed in 1960 by the renowned architect Louis Kahn, the Institute consists of twin futuristic structures, each six stories tall, bordering a courtyard with its ocean view. It is the perfect place for contemplation, reflection, and scientific innovation. The beautiful campus has received numerous awards, and many consider it the finest architectural site in San Diego.

But Salk, who perfected the anti-polio vaccine, was not necessarily the most famous La Jolla scientist. In 1953, while at Cambridge, the Englishman Frances Crick and the American James Watson discovered the structure of the DNA molecule, the "secret to life," as Crick was fond of saying. Nine years later, along with Maurice Wilkins from nearby Kings College, Crick and Watson received the Nobel Prize. Then, on a 1976 sabbatical from Cambridge for research at the Salk Institute, Crick fell in love with La Jolla and moved to California permanently with his wife, Odile. He was but one of the many world-famous residents of La Jolla—among whom I now counted myself.

Margaret brought a premature end to these thoughts. Since our wedding day, she'd addressed me as "honey" when all was well. And so it was now, which only increased my guilt, given what I was thinking.

"How was your day, honey? I've got a few minutes before putting Paul to bed."

"Tough. Six hours of surgery. I had some difficult cases. My back's killing me."

"I'll give you a backrub later. What's your day like tomorrow?"

"A difficult surgery in the morning." I didn't tell her that the surgery, difficult or not, would end on time because I had a lunch date with a gorgeous movie star. I was accustomed to lunching in local restaurants with female staff members to do their quarterly reviews. But I called them "meetings," not "dates." Was this Fr. Gallagher's First Step—*intention?* I hastily dismissed the thought. I hadn't lied to Margaret. I just didn't provide all the information.

* * *

"Candace," I said, "what's it like being on TV?" Nancy, an avid fan of the soaps, had told me about her role in a soap opera that ran daily for years. "How can you memorize all those lines?"

"It's humbling." Candace furrowed her brow. "Up to thirty pages a day." Then she laughed. "But you don't have to be line-perfect, like in the movies." Her smile widened. "That would be impossible. In the soaps, you get to ad-lib a bit. It was fun. I was always amazed when one of the characters would stray from the script, yet it still worked."

We were in a back booth at Trattoria Napoli, a few blocks from my office, and I felt so comfortable talking to this charming, tall, beautiful, blond woman. In many ways, it was like talking to Margaret. *So why was I obsessed with Candace Farrell?* Our lunch conversation was interesting and innocent— I told her about the elephants and giraffes at the San Diego Wild Animal Park, and she told me about all the scrambling on a soap opera set.

When I mentioned that I'd seen the poster for "Sensual Interludes" in South Africa, she seemed briefly embarrassed, lowered her eyes, and then looked deeply into mine. "I was really uncomfortable in that role," she confessed, "but who'd miss an opportunity to work with a famous director? The material wasn't great, but it gave me the opportunity to travel."

She paused, grew quiet, then looked right through my eyes to the back of my skull.

"I'm really a small-town girl. I was born in Kansas and went to college in Nebraska, where I studied drama. I acted in regional theater until I was invited to New York City to do bit parts. Soon I was discovered and given a featured role in a soap with good daily viewership. That lasted a few years until I was offered a role by a well-known director who promised if I played this role, I could travel internationally and follow in the footsteps of Marilyn Monroe, Raquel Welch, and Sophia Loren. Who wouldn't want that?"

I didn't have an answer. But, I certainly understood the lure of travel. I'd done everything I could to leave Stratford behind and see the world.

"I've no regrets, John," Candace continued. "That role wasn't me, but we filmed in Thailand with an international crew. Then the movie was released in Europe. It was so exciting!"

Still smiling, she picked up the menu. "What's good here?"

Reaching for my own menu, I realized I wasn't wearing my wedding ring, a simple gold band, inscribed on the inside: *MAK to JSS 8-10-1968*. The memory of my mentor, nine-fingered Major Jim Hardeman, who'd lost a battle with the engine fan of his car—along with the unhygienic nature of a ring during daily surgery—justified keeping it safe in the drawer of my nightstand. *How convenient!*

I could relate to Candace Farrell taking the role in *Sensual Interludes*. Once back in San Diego, I went alone to see the movie. Wanting to go unnoticed, Candace arrived at my office wearing loose clothing, a hat, no makeup, and large sunglasses. In the film, she played a sexually frustrated wife who experiences erotic fantasies. I'd done almost anything to please Alex Koper, so he'd send me on USC-financed junkets around the world because, at times, the rhythm method left me sexually frustrated.

"The pasta's fresh," I said after a considerable delay. "It'd be my first choice."

"Carbs are out," Candace said. "I have to watch my diet. I work out a lot and do yoga every day."

According to Margaret, yoga was controversial for many Christians. Originating in India as a pathway to spiritual growth and enlightenment, it had overtones of pantheism, wherein everything—God included—is one and the same. Some adherents even believe in multiple gods. Unsure of my own beliefs, I certainly wasn't going to ask Candace Farrell about hers.

Later, after her appointment, Candace smiled warmly. "I can't believe I went to the dentist and had fun." She squeezed my hand and gave me that penetrating look. "Thank you."

"My pleasure. I should check that area of your gums in a month." Then I heard myself saying, "Can we have lunch again?"

And there it was, Step Two—continuation—on the pathway to infidelity and destruction. And I realized that I simply didn't care.

* * *

In early May, Candace Farrell and I had lunch again—in the same restaurant and in the same booth—avoiding all talk of our personal lives. The subject seemed taboo, and we danced around it. Following my instructions, Nancy scheduled Candace's next appointment for three months later.

But on the first of June, a Friday morning, I was doing surgery when Nancy stuck her head in the room. "Doctor, Candace Farrell's on the phone. She says it's urgent."

How unusual, I thought, surprised—yet excited—for the intrusion. "Tell her it'll be a few minutes." I would have to break away from surgery to return her call. Fortunately, it was a good time—the patient needed a second injection of lidocaine, which would take a while to kick in.

"John," Candace said, "I had a sudden terrible pain in my upper jaw last night." She sounded anguished. "I need to see you as soon as I can get down there."

"OK. It might be a root canal problem unrelated to your gums. We'll take an x-ray when you get here. I may have to refer you to a specialist, but he's right here in the building."

Three hours later, about mid-afternoon, Candace came in, severely distressed, and her x-ray revealed what I'd expected. So I called Dr. David Monson, an excellent endodontist, in an adjacent office, and asked for a favor.

"If it can wait until four," Dave said, "I'll see her when my schedule ends."

When I introduced Dave to Candace, she motioned for me to follow her to the treatment room, then slipped into the dental chair. I retreated to a corner seat usually reserved for friends, relatives, and spouses. For most people, "root canal" brings instant trepidation. Candace looked at me with pleading eyes. "Please move your chair by my side."

Well, there's not much room next to a dental chair. The doctor's positioned at the patient's right shoulder, the assistant on the left. Candace's request put me as close as possible to the assistant without hindering the transfer of instruments and other movements.

"Give me your hand," Candace said. "I'm scared."

"Of course." My voice reflected concern while I relished the warmth and softness of her hand.

For the next hour, I held the hand of an alluring and seductive movie actress. I was gloating. *If those guys from Stratford could only see me now!*

Whenever Candace felt increased stress, she squeezed my hand, occasionally stroking my palm in what I considered a sensual manner. I reciprocated, not wanting to seem apathetic. But I couldn't shake thoughts of Fr. Gallagher, even though that Marriage Encounter had been eight years ago. I was plainly guilty of Step Three, *deception*. Two counts of it, in fact—Candace didn't know I was married, and I hadn't told Margaret of my interest in another woman.

David Monson ended these thoughts by holding up the post-op x-ray, using the ceiling light to illuminate the film. "Looks good," he said. "You should do well. My assistant will give you two ibuprofen, but I doubt you'll have any pain."

I thanked Dave for stepping in, and he left the room. Candace still had a firm grip on my hand. "Traffic might be bad going back to LA," I said. "Drive carefully." I squeezed her hand and then released it, unprepared for what came next.

"After what I've been through," she said, "there's no way I'm going to drive home. Do you know a good motel?"

Fortunately, since I was unprepared to respond to Candace, the dental assistant entered briskly with a water-filled paper cup and two pills. Then turned and left.

"Let me think. Take your pills while I use the restroom."

Wrapped in confusion and indecision, I headed down the hallway. It was as if two voices were whispering to me simultaneously: *This is a once-in-a-lifetime opportunity. This could lead to adultery. We could have dinner, split a bottle of wine. This is deceitful and unacceptable. She's beautiful, such a lovely body. I saw that movie poster. How could you do this to Margaret and the kids? You've put up with the rhythm method for too long. Today's a "no" day. Your reputation will be ruined. You can brag about this night for the rest of your life. But you'll be sorry for all of eternity.*

Maybe it was that word—*eternity*—that brought me to my senses. Until that moment, I'd felt like the young Tom Hulce in the 1978 film *Animal House,* when his half-undressed teenage date passes out on a bed during a fraternity party. On one shoulder, a miniature version of himself, dressed as a red devil, urges him to take advantage of her. On the other, another, clothed as a white angel, warns him not to because he'll be sorry his entire life.

But that was a comic scene in a funny movie. This wasn't a movie, and it wasn't comic, although a movie star was involved. Fr. Gallagher would say I had Satan in one ear, but who was in the other? *My conscience?*

Margaret would call it the Holy Spirit or my guardian angel. Regardless, the decision, once made, was clear, precise, and resolute, as if a light from above had given clarity to my thoughts, guiding me at a critical moment. I asked Dr. Monson's receptionist, loud enough for Candace to hear, "Is there a phone I can use? I need to call my wife."

She directed me into Dr. Monson's private office and closed the door behind me.

"Honey," I said to Margaret. "I've got a patient from Los Angeles who's just had a stressful procedure and can't drive home. Remember that poster in South Africa?"

"No way!"

"She needs a place to stay, with a meal of soft food. Can we host her?"

"Sure, why not? There's plenty of pasta from last night."

"She doesn't do pasta," I said.

"We'll figure something out."

Margaret was amazed when I walked in with Candace—the woman we'd seen on the poster in South Africa, but now with much more clothing. Candace was just as amazed to meet Margaret. Less than an hour ago, she believed I was single. It didn't surprise me that they got on well together. Whatever their different thoughts and roles in life, they were both genuinely warm and kind individuals.

We had a late dinner—soup for Candace—and the boys obliged by keeping quiet in their rooms. Later, when I showed Candace our second-story guest room, I opened the doors to the balcony overlooking the ocean. Staring at the view, she said sincerely, "Thank you for everything, John."

At breakfast, Candace invited Margaret and me to the upcoming private premier of the first episode of her new weekly television series, scheduled for an evening primetime spot. Naturally, we accepted her invitation, and that evening we mingled with Hollywood stars, sipping wine and munching hors d'oeuvres before the show.

Candace played the role of a devoted wife and mother of three kids in a family challenged by the turbulent sixties when her husband had to travel to defend his country during the Cold War. The show aired for twenty-two weeks, in hour-long episodes, but then the show ended abruptly as audience appeal for the thematic plot suffered. But Candace did the same to our relationship much sooner, canceling her very next appointment after the series debut. I understood her rationale and have continued to experience guilt over my deception.

The next time I saw her was several years later when she was on the silver screen, again playing a loving and compassionate mother in a popular high-grossing movie. One movie reviewer applauded her role, characterizing her as "the mother of all movie mothers," while Margaret, Andy Brose, and maybe even Dad, would say that the true mother of *all* mothers is the Virgin Mary.

Chapter 21   Oh Lord, Won't You Buy Me a Mercedes-Benz?

LIKE AN APPROACHING TORNADO, a distant roar grew louder by the minute. I pressed my thighs around the rubberized J-rig pontoon and grabbed a nylon rope. As the rumble increased, so did my stomach acids, triggered first by the morning's strong coffee and now by distress. My gut was burning, anticipating the upcoming rapids.

Sons Wayne, Mark, and I were on a weeklong Grand Canyon river rafting trip. Having negotiated the rapids successfully, guide Tom Oliver shouted, "We'll be pulling over to the shore on our left." Securing the raft on the Marble Canyon sandbar, Tom and his assistant, Susie Wendover, helped us remove and store our life jackets.

"You're in for a real treat," Tom said. "There's some important history here. In the '40s, this spot was designated as the site for a proposed dam. It was to be three hundred feet high, to harness cheap hydroelectric power, but with total disregard for reducing the Colorado to a trickle in much of the canyon."

In 1951, exploratory drilling began on the rim, cutting through porous sand and limestone to the canyon floor. The base of the first pilot hole was only a hundred feet from the river and reachable from a tunnel at the base of a sheer rock wall.

"It'll be dark for the first ten minutes," Tom explained, "but I'll lead you to a natural room deep in the cliffs. Light from the rim above shines down, over a thousand feet, through the drill hole. It illuminates a bronze plaque, commemorating the start of construction."

Clutching his flashlight, Tom led our group of twenty into the tunnel. Susie brought up the rear with a light of her own. Plodding across the soft wet sand, we turned left and right several times before entering an irregular, ten by fifteen-foot chamber. And that room, contrary to what Tom had promised, was dark! Something had blocked the light from the drill hole.

Tom waved his flashlight across the far wall until it stopped on the impressive plaque. "Martin Litton of the Sierra Club had pressured the government to halt work on the dam," he explained. "His efforts catapulted the club into one of the most powerful conservation organizations in the country." His informative talk continued for ten minutes.

I'd been noticing that the flashlights of our guides were decreasing in intensity. When we entered the tunnel to return to the river, Tom's went out completely. Susie's was just bright enough to show Tom up ahead. He was feeling his way along the walls with his free hand, searching for the next turn. Then Susie's light went dead.

Twenty steps from the turn, we were in ankle-deep water, in total darkness, holding hands as Tom instructed so as not to leave anyone behind. "We're turning left now," he called out, and the water felt deeper as we did. Soon it reached the bottom of my calf. The silence—except for the splashing of legs—was surreal. Wayne was in front of me, Mark behind, and I clutched their hands tightly. In my head, I could hear the strange voice of Long John Nebel, broadcasting late at night in the fifties to listeners in the New York region, reading from Edgar Allan Poe's *The Cask of Amontillado*: "*We walked on for some time. We were now under the river's bed, and water fell in drops upon us from above. Deeper into the ground we went . . .*" But I'd been in bed then, the radio under my pillow, not in a cave at the bottom of the Grand Canyon.

"Stay put," Tom shouted, obviously trying to disguise the fear in his voice. "I'll find the way out and come back for you!"

The water was now to my knees. I imagined a rainstorm on the rim.

Women began crying while the men held their breath and fought back tears. Wayne and Mark, perhaps unaware of the seriousness of the situation, remained calm—if, in fact, that was the meaning of their silence. *Is this it?* I wondered silently. *There has to be more to life! How could I have exposed my sons to this danger? What could I do? What awaits us on the other side of life? This darkness—or is there something more?*"

I passed the next fifteen minutes in silent anguish, punctuated by fleeting moments of tranquility as I repeated the three short prayers I knew. Then, barely above the surrounding sobs, I heard a distant voice screaming. "I found it! I found it!"

Tom grasped the hand of the leader of our human chain and led us out of the water, making three turns—two right, one left—until, far ahead, I saw the most beautiful light I'll ever see. I knew then that there's truth to the stories told by survivors of near-death experiences. They always mention "seeing the light," and we had seen ours.

Besides that frightful scare, our week was filled with breathtaking scenery, spectacular hikes, and thrilling rapids. The trip was one of the best I'd ever taken, though that cave brought me face to face with my own mortality even more than the PSA crash. Now I had to live with the sobering realization that the pursuit of excitement and adventure—instead of peace and tranquility—could have cost me my own life and the lives of my sons. And there were still more lessons to be learned.

* * *

In June of 1984, several months before the Grand Canyon river trip, the movie *Ghostbusters* had been released, starring Dan Aykroyd and Bill Murray, both known for their stellar performances on *Saturday Night Live*. But Margaret and I had no interest in seeing it as it was not a movie for the whole family. The *Catholic News Service* had criticized its frivolous occult elements, implied premarital sexual activity, and sexual humor. Then, in early January of 1985, came the first of a series of events that made me think not only of *Ghostbusters* but the occult peculiarities I'd encountered years earlier on the Long John Nebel radio show.

Margaret and I had just slipped into our Jacuzzi to watch the sunset. Bright rays gilded the underside of a flat bank of distant clouds as the colors around the sun changed from amber to apricot. Then there was a sudden green flash just before the sun dropped beneath the ocean.

Along the boardwalk in nearby Pacific Beach was a restaurant called the Green Flash, but I'd never given it much attention. Then there was Delphine, a character in Jules Verne's novel *The Green Ray*, who believed anyone seeing such a flash is blessed with "heightened perception." Margaret said she'd just been thinking about Nature as a palette of celestial colors in a universe created by God, and then the flash happened, as if confirming her idea. But my mind had been elsewhere—on automobiles. Not Arnold's Maserati or my gaudy Datsun, but a black, spacious Mercedes-Benz S-Class.

"Margaret," I said after a pause. "I want to buy a new car." Then, in a throaty voice cracking on the high notes, I imitated Janis Joplin singing, *"Oh Lord, won't you buy me a Mercedes-Benz?"*—a blues song about happiness promised by the possession of worldly goods.

Margaret didn't find it funny—maybe because, fifteen years earlier, Joplin had died from an overdose of heroin at the age of twenty-seven. "Your car isn't that old," she said.

"It's not right for La Jolla."

I then told Margaret about an afternoon I'd spent with Paddy Rain-water, the real estate agent who'd taken me house hunting in La Jolla. We were heading into the exclusive La Jolla Shores area, stopped in a double left-turn lane at one of San Diego's busiest intersections—Torrey Pines Road and La Jolla Shores Drive—when I realized that we were surrounded by just one make of automobile.

"I've never seen so many Mercedes!"

Paddy had laughed. "It's the Ford of La Jolla." Her own Mercedes, with its all-leather interior, was roomy and exuded an aroma of newness and luxury. "S-Class stands for *sonderklasse*," she said. "*Special class,* in English."

I'd told Paddy I wanted a four-bedroom house with a view, but when I mentioned my price range, which I thought sufficient, she showed me small homes, at least thirty years old, with "peek" views. That is, if you leaned out a window and peeked through the neighbor's trees, you might catch a glimpse of the ocean over rooftops and chimneys. Frustrated, I asked her for a copy of a recently-expired Multiple Listing Services book, a phonebook-sized guide to local homes on the market.

A week later, back out house-hunting with Paddy in her black Mer-cedes, I asked why she hadn't shown me a particular house on Calle Chiq-uita. Of course, I didn't mention that I'd climbed the long asphalt driveway to see its unobstructed ocean view. She explained that the house was pricey and that Dan Broderick, the famous malpractice attorney, had bought it, although the escrow hadn't yet closed. Moreover, a rumor was circulating that the home's owner, retired Major General Doug Peacher, was upset with Broderick's shenanigans and non-compliance with various deadlines. "You could make an offer," she said.

Following her suggestion, although it was a stretch, I did present an offer I thought we could afford, and the General accepted, which infuriated Broderick. And so, we had our house with an ocean view.

Years later, the world would learn that when Broderick was planning to buy that house, he was having an affair with his young receptionist, a former flight attendant he later married. Subsequently, his first wife, Betty Broderick, murdered the couple in their bed. The film—*A Woman Scorned: The Betty Broderick Story*—premiered on CBS. The murder resulted in nu-merous books and TV shows on the theme of marital infidelity, the shat-tering of an American suburban dream, and the mental torment of a wife who'd supported her husband, paid for his medical school, and then was abandoned for a pretty young woman.

All that lay in the future, while—oblivious to any such themes—I was lost in my pursuit of money, prestige, and power. "Besides," I explained to

Margaret, trying to justify a new Mercedes, "ever since that experience in the cave, I've got claustrophobia. So I need a big car."

"An Impala's a third the cost. And just as roomy."

"Anyone who's anybody in La Jolla wouldn't be caught dead in a Chevy."

"So, it's not the car, John—it's your ego."

Margaret was annoyed at the thought of another large expenditure when our new house needed remodeling. But, even with the communication lessons I'd learned in Marriage Encounter, my self-will prevented me from giving in. I wanted that car!

Two days later, I stood in the Mercedes-Benz of San Diego showroom, dressed in a coat and tie. I needed to look like I belonged in a Mercedes. So I selected a new black S-Class, with leather seats and natural-grain wood trim. Steve Robinson, the salesman, suggested we see how the car performs.

A few minutes after my test drive, sitting at Steve's desk while he calculated the total—with options and sales tax—I was astonished by the price. "Would you have something slightly used," I said meekly. "Same model and color?"

Fortunately, a car similar to the one I'd just driven, with less than five thousand miles on it, had recently been traded in. The discount was substantial, and so I bought it on the spot—just in time to chauffeur several prestigious speakers to the Friday-night dinner of the USC Annual Periodontal Symposium, which I was chairing. The speakers included Dr. Robert Genco, a world-renowned researcher in oral biology from the State University of New York at Buffalo, a pioneer on the impact of oral health on systemic health, and Dr. Sigmund Socransky, Director of the Forsyth Institute at the Harvard School of Dental Medicine, the world's foremost periodontal microbiologist.

I chose Lawry's on La Cienega Boulevard, on Restaurant Row in Beverly Hills, which had been in business since 1938. The restaurant had the feel of a traditional English gentlemen's club, from its gilded chandeliers and high-backed chairs to original eighteenth-century portraits. Our table for twenty-two was in the private, pine-paneled Vintage Room, surrounded by murals of countryside vineyards. For another sold-out symposium, Alex Koper had ordered multiple bottles of 1980 Joseph Phelps Cabernet Sauvignon, far better than what Trader Joe's had to offer and all paid for by USC.

Leaving the restaurant with Margaret, Professor Genco, his wife, and Dr. Socransky, I handed the valet my ticket. "It'll be a few minutes," he said. On a Friday night in Beverly Hills, even a new Mercedes didn't qualify for a premier parking spot in front of the restaurant. A silver Rolls Royce, a powder blue Bentley, and a red Lamborghini, among other prestigious cars, were parked there for all to see. Margaret and our guests entered my car while I waited on the sidewalk.

I looked up as another valet pulled a car in behind mine, a late-model Volvo sedan belonging to Dr. George Bailey, Chair of the USC Periodontal Department. He was with his wife, Mary, and they waved goodbye before entering their vehicle. It had begun to rain as we waited under the porte-cochère. Suddenly, the noise of heavy traffic along La Cienega Boulevard was topped by the sound of a car being floored in neutral, then ground into first—followed by squealing tires and a resounding crash. We watched in horror as the Bailey's Volvo catapulted my driverless car forward, scraping the sides of the three luxury cars. The Mercedes came to rest several feet into the street. Cars slammed their brakes to avoid broadsiding it.

I ran to my car, and everyone was fine, though shaken. The front bumper of the Volvo had smashed the trunk of the Mercedes. Mary jumped out and ran around the car to strike George on the head with an unopened umbrella. "How could you?" she screamed. "This is the most embarrassing thing that's ever happened to me!"

Unlike his wife, George was calm and, in the manner I'd come to expect from this compassionate and amiable colleague, said, "I don't know what happened, John. All I did was turn on the ignition and the car took off."

"Fortunately, no one's hurt."

"Take your car to the dealer and get it fixed. My insurance will pay."

The Mercedes' rear bumper was smashed in, the right side dented and scratched along its entire length, but George's insurance did pay for it —an exorbitant amount—leaving me wondering what it must have cost to repair the Rolls Royce, Bentley, and Lamborghini.

* * *

Ten days later, the Mercedes was restored to its pre-accident condition.

Meanwhile, David Tagge, who had left our office to establish his own practice in Escondido, was replaced by Bruce Johnson, a periodontist who'd also trained at the VA Hospital in West Los Angeles

On Wednesday, February 13, I headed for a dinner meeting with Bruce at a University Town Center restaurant, in a shopping center on the northern fringe of La Jolla known as UTC. Bruce wanted to discuss a La Jolla partnership, as Dr. Stewart now wanted to sell the practice.

Arriving early, I parked the car and walked to Ben Bridge's, an upscale jeweler, to purchase a Valentine's gift for Margaret. Although she eschewed fine jewelry as too costly and excessive, I loved the way it enhanced her natural beauty. Taking an elegant wife to professional events, especially the national meetings of the American Academy of Periodontology, assured me of the admiration of my male colleagues. The gift I selected—a fourteen-karat yellow gold necklace with the blues and greens of a large opal—would complement her eyes.

I parked the Mercedes within sight of the restaurant but left the little bag with the necklace in full view on the front seat. Bruce and I had just finished dessert when a police officer entered the restaurant to announce in a loud voice: "Does anyone here drive a black Mercedes? License plate UVH189?"

The Mercedes dealer had discreetly advised me to abandon my vanity plates, so it was the "black Mercedes" that captured my attention. Jumping up, I followed the officer outside, fearing the worst.

"I can't figure out why anyone would do this," the officer said. The rear window had been smashed by a large rock, which lay on the back seat. The officer pointed through the hole, saying, "Is anything missing?"

"No, sir."

Incredibly, my Valentine's gift was untouched on the front seat. But my Mercedes had been damaged once again.

Chapter 22   Mercedes-Bent

THE FOLLOWING DAY I took my car to Mercedes-Benz of San Diego, and a few days later, with the window replaced, Margaret and I lounged on the deck, awaiting another spectacular sunset over the Pacific.

"You've had bad luck with your car," Margaret said.

"I can't believe they didn't steal the jewelry. That necklace wasn't cheap."

"We need to talk about that. I appreciate these gifts, John, but you spend a lot of money foolishly."

Once again, she mentioned my vanity. "I want to be appreciated for who I am and for what I believe, not for what I wear or the car I drive."

The very next day, while running errands, I found a vertical ding in the door of the Mercedes, marring its restored brilliance. The white paint matched that of the adjacent Volkswagen. Enraged, I reached into my pocket for my keys, tempted to inscribe an identical mark on the VW. Then I cussed and settled down. I was proud of my car. I wanted people to see me driving a luxury Mercedes, not a dinged-up one. Disgusted, I got behind the wheel and just sat there.

I felt anger towards the owner of the Volkswagen. But there I was again, guilty of three of the Seven Deadly Sins—pride, greed, and wrath. I thought of the red Lamborghini at Lawry's—a low, two-door fastback, sharply angled with "Italian Wedge" styling, alloy wheels, white leather seats, and a rear engine. *What I wouldn't give to have that car!*

"God!" I told myself. *"I've added envy to the list!"*

Margaret hated it when I took the Lord's name in vain, words prohibited by the second of the Ten Commandments. I was chalking up sins left and right.

But I still didn't care.

* * *

One evening two weeks later, Margaret and I headed out in the Mercedes for Symphony Hall in downtown San Diego, for an evening of Bach and Beethoven. Leaving Calle Chiquita, before long we were stopped at the busy T-intersection with Torrey Pines Road, where I'd been with Paddy Rainwater, and noticed all those Mercedes.

As usual, traffic was heavy. Cars were lined up in front and in back of us as we waited to turn left toward I-5, the quickest route into downtown San Diego. Meanwhile, without its front bumper, a gray Ford Fiesta was readying to turn right from a corner Shell station. Somehow, for such a jalopy, its headlights, sticking out from its rusty hood, were working. When the light changed, just as the Fiesta turned, its driver-side wheel—not just the tire, but the entire wheel—broke from the vehicle and rolled toward us, bouncing across the yellow stripe on the pavement. I leaned towards Margaret as it creased my door, shattered the window, and rolled over the roof.

Our light turned green, but how far could a three-wheeled car go? So I turned left, but it was three miles before I could make a U-turn to return to the intersection.

"Slow down!" Margaret yelled.

But I was angry, and several long minutes later I became angrier as we approached the Shell station. The Ford Fiesta was nowhere in sight. Then, on a hunch, I swung around behind the building, and there it was, collapsed at a lopsided angle. Standing alongside was a man in his sixties, in ragged clothing. I was wearing an Armani herringbone sport coat, Givenchy trousers, Mantellassi shoes, and white shirt with matching tie. Leaping out, I glared at him.

"Be kind, John," Margaret called after me.

"Oh, it's your car my wheel hit," he said. "I'm so sorry. I'll cover the damage." He had a warm smile and a fleshy nose. Unkempt hair stuck out from his tattered Padres baseball cap. His white mustache had a reddish tinge that extended to the corners of his mouth, where it faded into a full white curly beard. He was missing his right central incisor, and his beard needed a trim. Nonetheless, he was a handsome, kindly man, and I suddenly felt sorry for him.

"It's OK," I said. "My insurance will cover it."

He smiled and thanked me, and I slipped back behind the wheel, silently bemoaning this third trauma to my new Mercedes.

Margaret put her hand on mine. "That was a wonderful thing you did."

"How could I not?" I heard myself say. "I've been given so much."

Then that strange thought hit me. *I've been given so much.* That's what I said. But who had given it? *Hadn't I earned it?*

* * *

The very next evening, as if chastened by recent events, Margaret and I lingered over dinner. She cherished the moment because I would later busy myself with patient charts, preparing a lecture, or watching a ballgame. Casual conversation was important to her but not to me, except this evening, when strange thoughts plagued my mind.

"I feel odd about this car," I began. "It's been to the Collision Center three times in two months." Then I laughed. "I know all the guys there by name. Before that—" I paused, as if to let the significance of what I was trying to say sink in—"it's been ten years since I've had to fix any of my previous cars."

"Coincidences happen," Margaret said. "I'm sure they'll stop. Let's concentrate on Easter. There'll be your parents again, and your sister's family, and the five of us." She looked preoccupied. There was a lot of work to be done.

But I was unwilling to end the discussion. "My father, his parents, and Wayne were all born within the same three days in October. That's a coincidence. I'm not sure about the car." I didn't mention my father's experience, Andy Brose, and the number 653—the Rosary's six "Our Fathers" and fifty-three "Hail Marys"—which defied mathematical odds. *And if that were the case, what was the cause?*

I didn't know. I was a scientist and a surgeon, skeptical of anything not observable, evidence-based, or data-driven. I'd been trained to support any statement in a scientific paper with a citation from peer-reviewed literature—whatever it took to avoid looking like a fool.

"I guess you're right," I finally conceded. "These problems with the Mercedes are random. Hopefully, they're over now."

But they weren't.

At 7:05 a.m. on the Thursday after Easter, I was driving to the Rancho Bernardo office when the unbelievable occurred. Stopped at a red light in the middle of three eastbound lanes on La Jolla Village Drive—at the busy intersection with Genesee Avenue—I had no time to spare. My first patient was due at 7:30. When the light turned, I took full advantage of the power of the Mercedes, though keeping within the fifty-mile-per-hour speed limit. Checking my side-view mirrors as I approached the next intersection, I saw two cars close behind. The light was green, and I planned to cruise on through.

But an approaching car, making a quick left, hit me head-on, flinging my body into the seatbelt and shoulder harness while snapping my head backward. The crunch of metal and glass reverberated through the intersection. The front end of the Mercedes, designed to protect the passenger chamber in a high-speed collision, had become an accordion, absorbing much of the force and protecting me from major injury or death. The young woman, disregarding her red light, had tried to dart into the parking lot of her health club, which—ironically—sat adjacent to the UTC restaurant where someone had thrown a rock through my rear window.

"I hadn't had my morning coffee," she explained lamely.

Since our front ends had collided at a slight angle, we both survived. An ambulance took me to nearby Scripps Memorial Hospital, where I was treated for severe whiplash. Subsequently, I had to wear a neck brace for a month and endure a year of intermittent headaches. I didn't know where the other driver was taken. I only knew that her insurance would cover the bills.

A week later, as Margaret and I were talking after dinner, I told her that this woman's insurance company had called. "They want to settle. They're not planning on totaling the car. There's a five-thousand-dollar differential between its value and the cost of the repairs."

"You're *not* getting back in that car, John!" Trained as a nurse, knowledgeable in the sciences, Margaret was thinking rationally, whereas my head was with my beloved Mercedes.

Margaret believed in God, Jesus, angels, saints, and Heaven. And now, she was plainly acknowledging what the Catholic Church had taught all along—that the demonic is real. She cited Thomas Aquinas, the thirteenth-century Dominican friar, Catholic theologian, and author of *Summa Theologica*—fallen angels not only exist, but they also battle against man's salvation.

"What about demonic possession?" I asked.

Margaret shook her head, indicating she had no answer. *The Exorcist* had been released in 1973 when Wayne and Mark were toddlers. Even though the movie was set in Georgetown, not far from my dental school and where we'd dated before our marriage, we hadn't bothered to see it. Friends said it was preposterous. The demonic possession of a twelve-year-old girl had caused her head to spin three hundred sixty degrees on her shoulders.

But the movie had become immensely popular, attesting to a profound interest in the unconventional and mysterious subject of exorcism. I'd since read that, with the onset of filming, casting problems and a fire on the set had resulted in a delay of six weeks. And two actors, Vasiliki Maliaros and Jack MacGowran, whose characters died in the movie, actually did die during post-production before the movie's release. Maliaros, at age ninety, played the role of an elderly frail woman, so her death wasn't a major surprise. But MacGowran, only fifty-four, had been healthy until contracting the flu. I regarded these as strange occurrences but certainly not the work of a demonic force. Still, they intrigued me. If such forces existed, I should be spending more time on my spiritual life, like Margaret, instead of chalking up the Seven Deadly Sins.

Urged by Margaret—and due to my own concerns as I grappled with such thoughts, however bizarre and unscientific—I decided to inform the insurance company that I wouldn't ask for "pain and suffering" damages if they'd award me the high blue-book value for my car. Then I could purchase a new one. I was still singing that Janis Joplin classic: *"Oh Lord, won't you buy me a Mercedes-Benz?"* Thrilled to avoid a major lawsuit, the insurance company agreed, and I became the proud owner of a new black Mercedes S-Class with only twenty-four miles on the odometer. It was nearly identical to the first vehicle, and I hoped to begin with a clean slate. And I loved the intense new car smell.

But once again, I was wrong. I hadn't heard the last from that first Mercedes.

* * *

The last time I saw that car was when I went to retrieve my slides, carousel projector, and screen from the trunk. The screen's straight tripod, now bent into a *V*, attested to the magnitude of the front-end crash. Unfortunately, I never thought to remove the license plates because the one on the front was so crumpled.

A month later, at the Rancho Bernardo office, Donna, our new receptionist, indicated that a lawyer was on the phone from Los Angeles. What now? I wondered.

"This is Dr. Sottosanti," I said somewhat nervously. Was I being sued for malpractice?

"Matthew Sorenson, here." The voice was stern. "Your black Mercedes was in a major hit-and-run accident yesterday in Los Angeles."

"Not my car," I said, relieved but curious. "I sold it to the insurance company a month ago."

"Isn't your license plate UVH189?"

I couldn't believe it. "Yes—but there's gotta be a mistake."

"Dr. Sottosanti, your car ran a red light and hit a pickup truck in the middle of a busy intersection. Then it bounced into a gas station, struck a pump, and disappeared. But somebody got your license number."

"I sold that car," I repeated. "You need to contact the insurance company."

Fortunately, I never heard another thing about my first Mercedes, but my speculations ran wild: *Had it been involved in someone's death before I purchased it? Maybe a murder? Is there such a thing as demonic possession? Can a restless soul stay attached to the scene of its demise? Why does California real estate law require sellers to disclose if there's been a death in a house on the market within the past three years? Haunted houses are popular attractions throughout the United and around the world. If a home can be "possessed" according to real estate laws, why not an automobile? Catholic priests occasionally bless a home before new owners move in. Known as "house healings," such rites are to protect the inhabitants from misfortune—or heal it after an evil occurrence.*

These thoughts spurred me to research haunted cars. Two years earlier, Stephen King had published *Christine,* a novel about a 1958 Plymouth Fury that apparently was possessed by supernatural forces. I watched the movie and found the final scene eerily familiar. A car in Los Angeles, one that earlier had been purposely destroyed, burst through the cinderblock wall of a movie theater, killing the last surviving gang member that had vandalized it.

King's novel was recent. Had there been earlier instances of "haunted" cars? Here's what I discovered.

On June 28, 1914, Archduke Franz Ferdinand, heir to the throne of Austria-Hungary, was assassinated along with his wife by a young Serbian when their open limousine stalled in a parade. The assassination resulted in a declaration of war on Serbia, which escalated into World War I. From the date of the murder, until 1926, when the automobile was installed in a museum in Vienna, it had been owned by fifteen different people, involved in six accidents, and resulted in thirteen deaths.

In 1955, American actor James Dean, age twenty-four, famous for *Rebel Without a Cause* and *East of Eden,* had a chance meeting outside an LA restaurant with the Academy Award-winning actor Alec Guinness. Dean showed the British actor his new car, a silver Porsche 550 Spyder, parked in the restaurant's courtyard. It was a recent present, still wrapped in cellophane and with roses tied to its hood. Dean invited Guinness to join him for dinner, and Guinness later stated—in a 1977 interview on the BBC's *Parkinson Talk Show*—that, after meeting Dean, "a strange thing came over me, some almost different voice, so I said, 'Look, I won't join your table unless you want me to, but I must say something. Please don't get into that car. If you do, you'll be dead by next Thursday.'"

"We had a charming dinner," Guinness said, "and Dean was dead the following Thursday. Days before, he'd nicknamed that car 'the Little Bastard.'" Guinness stressed that nothing like that had ever happened to him before—it was just "one of those odd spooky experiences," for which he had no explanation.

In 1985, my research revealed that a car designer bought "the Little Bastard" for its parts, and when it was delivered to his yard, it rolled off the truck and broke a mechanic's legs. Next, a doctor bought the engine to replace the one in his Porsche and was in a crash the first time he drove it. Another doctor purchased the ill-fated car's transmission and soon was seriously injured in a collision. Two of the car tires made it to the East Coast, where a New York doctor bought them. Both blew out simultaneously, causing a serious accident, but the doctor survived.

When I returned from the library that day, Margaret could sense that I was disturbed by what I'd read. Pouring myself a scotch-on-the-rocks, I sat out on the deck, hoping the waves rolling onto the La Jolla Shores beach would calm me.

Margaret joined me, rubbing my shoulders. "Well, the bad luck's behind you now."

And although she'd said that before, she was wrong.

Chapter 23 *La Famiglia E Tutto*

"LA FAMIGLIA E TUTTO"—the family is everything—had been understood by my sister Janet and me even as toddlers.

More than twenty relatives would be present when the family from Greenwich made the long drive to Stratford. Here, in the home Dad had built on Park Street, we sat at an extended table—a series of aligned card tables—covered with red-and-white checked tablecloths to match the red wallpaper and white line drawings of wine and cocktail glasses, in the basement rec room I'd almost burned down. Mom and Dad joyfully hosted these family gatherings, and Mom was careful not to insult Dad in front of her relatives, even if she disapproved of his behavior. Over the decades, we'd grown to cherish these hours of shared stories, laughter, and food, believing that life was wonderful. We felt safe, surrounded by *la famiglia*.

Grandpa Russo would write in Italian several times a year to his nephew Franco in Calabria, the son of his deceased older brother, and get a return letter informing him of events in the old country. When Grandpa died, Aunt Josephine would receive the letters in Connecticut and forward them to Dad in San Diego, who would translate them for her on the telephone and respond in hand-written Italian letters, which he sent her to read and then mail to Italy.

The concept of *la famiglia e tutto* was dramatically underscored for me in 1980 on my Italian excursion with Dad when we had visited his family home in Mistretta, Sicily. Just before departure, he'd received a letter from Franco, but with no time to respond, he'd placed it in his suitcase. If we could ever find cousin Franco in the mountains north of Reggio, the largest city in Calabria, he would hand deliver it before we took the ferry to Sicily. And that is what we did after locating the village where Grandma and Grandpa Russo were born.

The Audi 5000 sedan I'd rented was large and roomy, and with the crazy Italian drivers on the road, it helped me feel safe (as my first Mercedes should have!) on the narrow, tortuous roads of the Serre Calabresi Mountains. We were in the province of Vibo Valentia, at the southern end of the Italian boot, a region of lush forests of oak, chestnut, and beech, interspersed with abundant olive and lemon groves.

As we entered the town of San Nicola da Crissa (population fifteen hundred), the twisting, rutted road brought us to the piazza in front of the town's church—*Chiesa di Maria Santissima del Rosario*—Church of the Most Holy Mary of the Rosary. As I parked the Audi, Dad asked a teenage boy if he knew of an older man named Franco Russo. He didn't but said he'd ask around town. Minutes later, he returned with several men who said that Franco lived in the hills above—a thirty-minute walk—although someone had seen him in town earlier, and they would look for him.

Before long, two men, each clutching an arm, dragged a nervous old man, who slightly resembled Grandpa Russo, to the middle of the circle forming around us. Since we were from the United States and drove a large sedan—not a small Fiat so typical in the village—we'd become a curiosity to the bored men of San Nicola da Crissa, who spent their days ogling the same young women in a town where any change was a welcome novelty.

Franco, as if frightened by the brutality of the American Mafia in the 1972 movie *The Godfather*, pulled against the tug of his captors. Dad moved forward to embrace him, saying, "*Cugino* Franco!" But the old man recoiled, his eyes widening, his thin-lipped mouth locked in an open grimace. When Dad reached into the breast pocket of his suit coat for the letter he'd brought from San Diego, Franco thought it was a gun. He threw his hands into the air and screamed, *"Non sparate!"*—"Don't shoot!"—until Dad held the letter in front of his face, and he recognized his own handwriting.

"We've come all the way from California to see you!" Dad explained in Italian.

Overwhelmed, with tears streaming, Franco bear-hugged Dad, placing a wet kiss on each cheek, then he kissed me as well. Now elated, he spoke rapidly in Italian, and the only word I understood was—*mangia*. This Russo family member wished to take his wealthy American cousins out to eat. He directed us toward *Carlos Ristorante* for what he called *il pranzo*, or lunch, *al fresco*—outside.

We promptly ordered three *panini al prosciutto*, and Franco proudly informed us that the dry-cured uncooked ham and the pecorino cheese were from a local village. The tomatoes had been picked that morning from the plentiful vines of San Nicola da Crissa. Dad tried to restrain Franco from paying the bill, but every Italian host, as Franco considered himself, had to show love for *la famiglia* by feeding them.

Taking out his camera, Dad snapped a photo of Franco and me in front of *Carlos Ristorante*, a sandwich in our right hand, an Italian beer in our left, sitting on cheap plastic and metal chairs before the antique oak doors of the best restaurant in town. Before meeting Franco, I'd imagined him dressed in the loose blouse and dark pants of an Italian peasant, but, surprisingly, he was dressed virtually like me—same blue sports jacket, navy slacks, black shoes (his were laced, mine were loafers)—except for that gray, flat, short-brimmed hat so popular in southern Italy, whereas I was hatless. Had he had a premonition to dress up on this particular day before walking down the dusty road into town? Nonsense. It had happened by chance.

Or had it? Ever since the incidents with my maleficent Mercedes, I was no longer sure I understood reality.

* * *

Mom was a dyed-in-the-wool Russo. She believed you should do anything necessary to keep the family together. *La famiglia e tutto.* But now—five years after my trip to Italy with Dad—I couldn't believe what she was telling me on the phone.

"I'm divorcing your dad," she announced. "I've had enough."

"What?" I was stunned. "You've been married forty-nine years! You can't get a divorce. I won't let you! I've already reserved a banquet room at the Hotel del Coronado for your fiftieth anniversary. It looks down on the beach."

I thought she'd be impressed if I mentioned The Del. Opening in 1888 as the largest resort hotel in the world; it was a castle-like structure with Queen Anne styling, domes, towers, a massive red roof, and a ten-story turret. From its grand debut until the late 1920s, it had hosted U.S. presidents and Hollywood stars—from Clark Gable and Douglas Fairbanks to Betty Davis and Ginger Rogers. In the summer and autumn of 1958, much of *Some Like It Hot*, starring Marilyn Monroe, Tony Curtis, and Jack Lemmon, had been filmed there.

"You don't know what he's really like!" Mom said.

At times Dad had been like an African lion, the fiercest of the Big Five Margaret and I had seen on safari. But minutes later, he was like a lamb—docile, agreeable, and even-tempered. It was Mom, after all, who had slapped Dad at their wedding dinner after his unexpected kiss, mandated by the clanging spoons of his buddies.

"You want to break up the family? How *could* you?" I was astounded. "This is serious. We need to talk. Margaret and I will be there in an hour."

We immediately left for Rancho Bernardo. Dad was busy building a house for a dentist friend of mine and wouldn't return until late in the day. We sat with Mom in the living room, and Margaret left the talking to me.

"Whatever gave you such a ludicrous idea? I've never heard of divorcing after so many years. Is Dad having an affair?"

"No. It's just that he embarrasses me."

She proceeded to explain that she'd been ironing in front of the TV one afternoon while watching an interview with a best-selling author. "Oh, Johnny, this woman's so smart. She wrote a book saying that women no longer have to put up with their husbands. 'Make demands,' she said. 'And if necessary, hire a lawyer.'"

"And you believe this crap?" When I was really upset, my language tended to match the moment.

"My life's been miserable for forty-nine years. I've put up with your father for the sake of you, Janet, and the grandchildren. But now they're mostly grown, and it's time for *me*."

I shook my head in disbelief. "What's the most serious problem? What don't you like?"

"For starters, he's an alcoholic. I want him to stop drinking."

"He has *two beers* a day. Granted, it's every day—but has he ever missed a day of work or had a DUI? No! And he's seventy-two years old."

"Johnny, I have only another ten years or so left to live. I want them to be peaceful."

Margaret had been listening, unwilling to interrupt a mother-son conversation, but I turned to her to ask what she thought.

"I don't think God wants you to divorce," she said.

"God wants me to be happy," Mom replied. "I've got to do this for *me*."

"Mom," Margaret said, with an observation that made me proud, "it's like you're looking for Heaven on Earth. Life's not easy. Sometimes we have to make sacrifices. To you, this woman on TV seemed to know what she was talking about. But Jesus said, 'I am the way, and the truth, and the life.' So you should listen to Him."

Margaret seemed uncomfortable. She rarely quoted the Bible, preferring to let her actions speak for themselves. But she was determined to make her point. "It was Jesus who said, 'Therefore what God has joined together, let no one separate.'"

I could never argue with my mother from a religious perspective and was relieved that Margaret was doing it for me. Now it was my turn again.

"What do you know about this author?" I said. "Maybe she was abused, or an alcoholic, or a divorcée, herself. And suddenly, she's a marriage expert? She thinks she knows it all—better than God Himself. Who knows what she'll be advocating next year. Research shows that children of divorced parents have behavioral problems, poor academics, and early drug use."

"You and Janet aren't children," Mom said. "And as I said, your kids are nearly grown."

I felt tense and unbelieving. I was determined not to let this happen. I sensed there'd only be negative ramifications if Mom and Dad divorced—a strong sense that it seemed a premonition. We were making no progress with Mom. So I fumed in a loud, deep voice: "You are *not* divorcing Dad. I won't allow it. You'd better be at your fiftieth at The Del —July 4th, 1986—or else!" Standing abruptly, I gave her a peck on the cheek, and we left.

As we drove home in my new Mercedes, I thought of the previous one, the haunted one—if such a thing were possible—how it had begun a series of events over which I had no control, inflicting a year of neck spasms and melancholy. Those accidents had ended with the purchase of a new car. But now there was *this*—Mom wanted a divorce! Who could believe it? After forty-nine years! *What could possibly come next?*

* * *

In 1985, Bruce Johnson and I purchased the La Jolla practice from its founder. I maintained sole ownership of the Rancho Bernardo office, which had been growing in size and provided the majority of my income. Rather than asking our receptionist to answer the phone rather clumsily with: "Doctors Sottosanti, Johnson, Nordland, Roberts, and Adamich." I created a name for us—Periodontal Health Associates—with a logo for the office stationery, an unusual move for healthcare practitioners in the conservative eighties.

Even with the car issues and Mom's determination to divorce Dad, I still believed I was in control of my destiny and could use my intelligence, fortitude, and creativity to fashion a bright future. Wealth and power were extremely important to me, and I revered them without realizing they'd become addictions. At All Hallows Church in La Jolla, on the top of Mt. Soledad, I'd heard Monsignor Fox give a sermon about Moses descending Mount Sinai only to find the Jews worshipping a golden calf. Msgr. Fox warned us to be aware of the idols in our own lives, stressing that they did not necessarily have to be *things*. But the message failed to sink in. My reckless behavior continued unabated. Attending church with Margaret and the boys was simply the obligatory behavior expected of a good husband and father.

Then the stress of professional life began to overwhelm me. I was responsible for two offices, five periodontists, eight hygienists, and a support staff of dental assistants, receptionists, and insurance clerks, not to mention a management team—a total of fifty-two individuals. In addition, the surgeries I performed were more complex—intricate oral plastic-surgical cosmetic procedures, as well as the placement of dental implants deep within bone—during which I had to avoid nerves, blood vessels, and sinus cavities. I felt the tension during the day, bringing it home at night, arguing with Margaret, and being short with the kids.

I'd read that spirituality can be an anecdote for stress, but I didn't want to become affiliated with a church because I felt religious rules were too confining. I was addicted to fame and fortune, building my personal Tower of Babel taller, never considering that there might be a limit to what my body and mind could bear. Alcohol at meals and social events—the equivalent of Dad's two daily beers—assuaged the anxiety momentarily but did nothing to promote a good night's sleep.

In January 1987, TV host Jerry G. Bishop invited me to interact with him on *Sun-Up San Diego,* a daily local version of *The Today Show.* The topic was to speak about the recently-introduced dental implants. A few days later, Jerry's secretary invited me for a return visit because the first segment had resulted in numerous phone calls requesting more information. I was delighted and proud that I'd performed well on television.

And this burgeoning pride at my successes negated my concern for a need to believe in, or understand, God. I believed in God, but whether or not it was a Christian, Jewish, or Buddhist God didn't matter to me. Then I remembered my first examination week at Georgetown and how my spirits had been lifted at the medical school bookstore by a simple sign in the window: "Smile—God Loves You." Without comprehending the attraction, I would notice that sign, almost with a sense of reverence, whenever I felt pressure from my rigorous academic program.

After my TV appearances, I continued to receive invitations to lecture at state and national meetings. The prestigious American Academy of Periodontology—the AAP—asked me to organize local arrangements for the 1988 Annual Meeting to be held in San Diego. One of my duties was to assist the incoming president, Dr. Robert Schallhorn, in selecting the perfect keynote speaker. Dr. Schallhorn, a world-renowned expert in bone regeneration, loved science and research.

"Bob, if you're interested," I said, "I might be able to get Francis Crick. He's been my patient for over a year."

The suggestion excited Schallhorn. "*The* Francis Crick—of Watson and Crick fame? Nobel Prize-winner and discoverer of DNA? To have him speak at my installation would be more than I could ever hope for!" He hesitated. "Can we afford him?"

"We've got a good relationship. I think he might accept the usual honorarium."

I checked my schedule. Francis Crick was due for his annual exam in two weeks.

The day arrived. "How are you, Dr. Crick?" I said, trying to be congenial.

"Just fine," Crick replied. "And how are you, Dr. Sottosanti?"

Undaunted, I went ahead with the invitation, and Dr. Crick accepted, leaving only the topic of his speech to be discussed. Crick suggested the "reverse learning of dreams theory," which he and Graeme Mitchison had proposed in a 1983 article in *Nature*—the same journal that forty years earlier had published one of the most famous articles in all of scientific literature— "Molecular Structure of Nucleic Acids: A Structure for Deoxyribose Nucleic Acid," by J.D. Watson & F.H.C. Crick.

Crick explained his dream theory to me. As I understood it, the neocortex—the part of the brain related to higher levels of thought and cognitive function—becomes clogged with unnecessary connections that need to be eliminated during REM (rapid eye movement) sleep to prevent overloading and malfunctioning. Now, new thoughts can enter, and dreaming achieved that goal. I had no idea whether this theory had merit, but I was not about to challenge this famous scientist. That bold move would come ten years later.

It was "mission accomplished," and I awaited the expected praise from Dr. Schallhorn.

Chapter 24   **Dollars and Sense**

WE HAD HIRED AN office manager at the La Jolla office, a young woman with a winsome smile, sparkling eyes, and curly red hair. Jackie had a gregarious personality—except for every third month when she had to tell us that we might have difficulty making payroll. I couldn't understand how, with busy schedules and surgical procedures being performed each day, there could be months when our practice was in financial difficulty.

Margaret and I, along with Bruce and his wife Debbie, were avid runners, and we encouraged our team members to keep physically fit. And so we had a large staff turnout for the 1987 Rancho Bernardo 10K Run. At the six-kilometer mark, Margaret and I were jogging comfortably when I noticed Jackie up ahead, her fiery ball of red hair, highlighted by the intense summer sun, bouncing with each step. I noticed how slender her body was.

"She talks about running so much," I said to Margaret, "she must run a 10K every weekend." I was thinking about increasing my pace to pull up beside her when she turned left and disappeared into an adjoining street. I imagined she had a stitch in her side and would walk a bit, before recovering and returning to the route.

As Margaret and I crossed the finish line, we noticed Jackie's red hair up ahead. She was standing alone, holding a water bottle, as we approached. I first noticed her lack of perspiration, which was highly unusual given that the temperature was in the mid-80s. The only explanation, absurd as it was, would be that she had parked her car on a side street and driven to the finish line. Which I found hard to believe. I decided to play dumb.

"Jackie," I said, "you certainly made good time. I'm impressed."

Her grin extended from one freckled cheek to the other. "It was difficult in the heat but not as tough as the half-marathon I did last month."

In the 1980 Boston Marathon, Rosie Ruiz had brought her car to a strategic spot near the storied course in order to drive to the endpoint of the race. Seeing a group of male runners approaching, she had pushed through the crowd, re-entered the course, and worked her way within the pack, remaining unnoticed. To her surprise, she crossed the finish line in just over two and a half hours—a fabulous time—and was declared the women's winner until her deception had been discovered.

The following Wednesday, I received a phone call from Art Neumann, our CPA. Art was usually joyful, but now he was somber. He said he was certain that there was embezzlement going on in our office because of discrepancies in the recent postings. Reviewing the past year, he'd found more than sixty thousand dollars missing. He was sure that Jackie was responsible.

On Monday, Bruce and I scheduled a meeting with Jackie to discuss our overdue accounts. As soon as we disclosed our evidence and asked her to comment, she began weeping and revealed her heartbreaking story. She'd been molested as a child, was now bulimic, and had many emotional issues. She pleaded with us not to inform the police. Expressing remorse, she told us that her life was so messed up she couldn't help herself. Thinking she might be suicidal, we quietly terminated her and kept the incident confidential. She had no means of paying back what she'd stolen.

I found myself wondering if God was keeping score. What would it mean for Jackie? Would my example of compassion absolve me from one of my Seven Deadly Sins?

With a new office manager, our finances improved, and we prepared for an inevitable move to a larger space since our lease would soon expire. Having added another periodontist as an associate in the La Jolla office, we looked forward to a modern, expanded facility. Bruce had proven to be a worthy partner in La Jolla, so I sold him half of the Rancho Bernardo practice, which allowed us to combine the finances of both offices.

We signed a ten-year lease with a local bank to rent their vacant second-floor space beginning early in 1988. The suite was triple the size of our present office, but we believed that our financial production, plus that of a busy associate and soon-to-be partner, would cover the cost of the lease, payroll, and loan payments to expand the office and purchase new equipment. For months we'd been negotiating the terms of a partnership with the associate, convinced that splitting the expenses three ways made financial sense.

Then we hired Jain Malkin, an experienced medical and dental interior designer, to design our office. With a degree in psychology and a keen interest in developing soothing and healing environments for patients, she'd written books and articles on the subject and had won many awards. If we were to build a new office in La Jolla, we wanted the design to be utilitarian, comforting, avant-garde, and research-based.

But negotiations with our associate stalled at a time when the new lease for the office space had to be signed. The contractor wanted his down payment, and Jain Malkin needed a deposit. It was then that Bruce and I made a major error in judgment. With the project in motion and contracts signed, the associate informed us that he'd decided not to join our practice. We'd failed to obtain a signed "covenant not to compete," which would have prevented him from entering into competition in the area for a specified time. Had we done so, he most likely would have remained with us.

This was a major financial misfortune. Our calculations included income from three practitioners to pay the skyrocketing overhead. But Bruce and I were suddenly faced with possible bankruptcy but refused to entertain the idea, deciding to do whatever it might take to fulfill our obligations. I never considered prayer, even for solace. Bruce and I would accomplish this ourselves.

Before learning that our associate would be leaving, we'd asked the architect to design our office with three doctors in mind. Then we chose Dooley Construction, feeling comfortable with George Dooley, the company's owner. He was such a pleasant man that we neglected to obtain competitive bids and simply signed the contract—another mindless mistake for a project costing a quarter of a million dollars, an enormous sum in the late '80s. The price seemed excessive, but we thought the price was fair because we had eight treatment rooms—three outfitted for simultaneous surgeries—and all rooms had multiple sinks and drains, ceiling mounted dental lights, and x-ray machines.

But it wasn't. Before Bruce and I made the final payment, we'd failed to have George present us with lien releases from the subcontractors, testifying that they'd been paid. We'd agreed to pay one-third up front, a third halfway, and the balance when the construction was completed. And we honored that agreement.

Nonetheless, arriving early on the opening day of our stunning new office, I gazed at the gleaming, curved, thirty-foot-long reception counter. Made of varnished, light-colored wood with an attractive grain, it was crowned with a sand-colored marble slab, designed to complement our seaside theme and provide a relaxing visual for patient comfort and tranquility. Dad—though lost in the whirlwind of Mom's desire for a divorce—loved it, but he was shocked by how much money we'd spent on the office.

By mid-morning, I was lost in a complex surgery—complicated by adhesions that had formed after a previous operation—when Linda, our office manager, entered silently. Keeping her distance to maintain sterility, she held up a sheet of eight by eleven white paper with bold black letters: SEE ME AS SOON AS YOU HAVE FINISHED.

She shouldn't have done that. Front office employees are told never to interfere during surgery, as any interruption could affect the procedure. But Linda had just opened three envelopes that startled her and was acting out of genuine concern for our collective welfare. A few minutes later, she showed me the first of nearly identical notices. The title was "STATE OF CALIFORNIA MECHANIC'S LIEN."

My heart rate increased, my face flushed, and my neck muscles tightened. I was not yet fully recovered from the head-on collision in my Mercedes-Benz. What I read made me dizzy:

"The undersigned, Crawford Plumbing and Heating, referred to in the Claim of Lien as the Claimant, claims a mechanic's lien for the labor, services, equipment, and/or materials described below, furnished for a work of improvement upon that certain real property located in the City of San Diego, County of San Diego, State of California and described as follows: Sottosanti and Johnson Dental Practice, 7877 Ivanhoe Avenue, La Jolla, CA 92037."

The three liens totaled one hundred and five thousand dollars. I immediately telephoned the office of Dooley Construction but got a message: "This number is no longer in service." Filing a lawsuit on our behalf, our attorney learned that George Dooley had declared bankruptcy.

My auto accidents had ended with the sale of the strange black Mercedes, and then Mom announced she was divorcing Dad. Our charming office manager had embezzled sixty thousand dollars, our promising young associate had left us, and now our friendly contractor had deceived us, leaving us with more than one hundred thousand dollars to pay—money we didn't even owe. But if we didn't pay it, we'd have to close our office.

I recalled Margaret's words after I sold the totaled Mercedes to the insurance company. "Well, the bad luck is behind you now."

Obviously, it wasn't.

Financial problems are usually listed as one of the five top reasons that couples divorce. Although monetary setbacks had placed considerable strain on my marriage to Margaret, they were nothing compared to the stress and tension Bruce and I were feeling—because it affected our partnership. Fortunately, through mutual respect, diligence, and unrelenting commitment, we made the payments necessary to keep our offices open and pay the bills. We began working six days a week, continuing for more than a year without receiving a paycheck while we lived off our personal savings. Our attorney was able to obtain relief from 50 percent of the lien amounts, but his fee, an additional expense, diminished the gain.

In an attempt to reduce the stress, I found myself one Saturday morning at the Deepak Chopra Center of La Jolla, where I subsequently sat cross-legged on the floor every Saturday for seven weeks, palms to the ceiling, reciting to my inner self an individualized mantra given to me based on the time, day, year, and place of my birth. This mantra was not to be shared with anyone—or I would break the aura of tranquility the technique promised. But for me, this transcendental meditation resulted in only a few hours of peace, compared to the ten days of sustained tranquility I'd experienced after my repetitive prayers during a single two-hour session at Penn's Newman Center Chapel, which, in the wake of my Dear John letter, had enabled me to pass my undergraduate exams. Regardless, I never once thought of prayer in my current desperate situation. Faith was a gift, and many, especially Margaret, had it. But I didn't. And it never occurred to me to ask for it or to be prepared to do the work.

Shortly after that, Bruce told me about Wayne Dyer, a New Age guru and self-help author, who'd written several popular books in the last decade— *Your Erroneous Zones, Pulling Your Own Strings,* and *The Sky's the Limit.* Dyer's advice aimed to reduce stress and increase the enjoyment of life. So, like Bruce himself, I became a disciple, reading Dyer's books and listening to his cassette tapes. Throughout his career, Wayne Dyer would sell over a hundred million books on how to lead a satisfied life. Yet two of his marriages had ended in divorce and a third in separation. He had died of a heart attack at age seventy-five, and though it doesn't appear that he led a stress-free life, his advice had proved helpful to many, including Bruce and me.

Bruce invited me to attend one of Dyer's lectures with him—"You'll See It When You Believe it." Dyer preached that there's a reason for everyone you meet and that these people are put there—at that time and place—for a reason. He expressed a belief in the concept of synchronicity, as first proposed by Carl Jung, who defined the concept as "the simultaneous occurrence of two meaningfully, but not causally connected, events." Dyer considered himself spiritual but not necessarily religious. He believed that God is the conductor of the symphony of life and that we are all interconnected. In his own words, "I am convinced that this phenomenon (synchronicity) is omnipresent in my life, and there are no accidents of any kind."

It was an interesting idea, given by an excellent speaker, yet unlike Bruce, I was not yet convinced. But that would soon change.

In early May of 1988, Bruce and I scheduled a weekend retreat at a resort in Palm Springs to resolve some of the issues in our partnership. I didn't like confrontations and was concerned I'd become angry if I couldn't convince Bruce to see things my way. Wrath and pride were alternating as my chief sins, although all seven had impacted my behavior. Several weeks after Easter, it was a time of renewal, rest, reconciliation, repentance, and joy for a devout Catholic, but I'd experienced none of these—which wasn't surprising. Instead, stress-induced hypertension, headaches, neck stiffness, lower back pain, and insomnia haunted me.

On the Tuesday evening before the retreat, I sat in my Mercedes-Benz in the driveway of my ocean-view home, listening to the waves crash on La Jolla Shores, experiencing severe mental anguish. Then, as if guided by a cosmic, compassionate presence, I gazed at the stars—polar-white against a cloudless dark sky—and peered through the blackest hole into the universe, silently crying out:

"God, if You are up there, all I want is inner peace. Please help me."

I don't know why I chose those particular words. But I certainly wasn't prepared for the sequence of events about to unfold.

Chapter 25   Don't Worry, Be Happy

A DEEP VOICE FILLED the Mercedes as I drove the short distance from my office in the Village—La Jolla's downtown—to my home in the Shores on Wednesday evening. It sounded like someone was beside me in the passenger seat, but the source was a cassette tape in the stereo system, an authoritative voice with an air of compassion.

I'd bought the tape at Warwick's, established in 1896, the oldest family-owned bookstore in the United States. Walking there during my lunch hour, I'd hoped to find an interesting tape for the long drive to Palm Springs, where I was meeting Bruce for the weekend. Warwick's rotating rack held cellophane-wrapped, book-sized boxes, one of which stood out, its wide red border enclosing bold black caps—LOVE IS LETTING GO OF FEAR. A red heart formed the O in LOVE, giving the box the appearance of a Valentine's Day card. It was May, not February, yet the subtitle intrigued me: "Twelve Steps to Greater Happiness." I'd never heard of the author/reader—Gerald G. Jampolsky, M.D. But if there was one thing I needed, it was happiness.

Jampolsky spoke in a raspy voice, like a male Janis Joplin. He told of his Jewish heritage, medical training, psychiatric residency, successful private practice, late-model sports car, and beautiful home. After a stressful divorce, he'd become an alcoholic and—like me—experienced debilitating neck and back pain. This had kept him from playing tennis, a sport he loved. Then someone had given him a spiritual self-help book. "I read one page," he explained, "and in that one page, I heard for the first time a little inner voice saying, 'Physician, heal thyself. This is your way home.'" Immediately, he'd experienced a sense of oneness with the world. There was no separation— only love—and a feeling that he was to serve God his entire life.

Wow, I was thinking. *What a Pollyanna!* But when I drove up my steep driveway and got out, I felt relaxed. Was it due to the stately Queen palms? The sound of the waves on the shore? Or the calming voice of Jampolsky?

In the tape's first ten minutes, he'd described his transformation from an alcoholic atheist to a man who'd found the peace of God.

After dinner, I listened on my Sony Walkman to more of *Love Is Letting Go of Fear*. The eighty-two-minute tape addressed familiar concepts, but the way Jampolsky explained them aroused my interest. Love and fear, he said, are mutually exclusive. Love is meant to expand. Fear retracts because it's based on comparison and competition. We all desire love, but without realizing it, we fear it because it can lead to rejection. We need to release this fear to feel love.

There was more. Forgiveness is the key to happiness. Giving is better than receiving. Accepting is preferable to judging. By giving unconditional love to others, we give it to ourselves, increasing the love within us and receiving love in return to find a middle ground. We must abandon "attack thoughts" in all conflicts.

As Jampolsky continued, the tenseness in my neck diminished. He argued that when we move away from negative emotions—fear, anger, jealousy, loneliness, annoyance, and melancholy—we will experience inner peace. Those words resonated, the very words I'd used the day before when I'd cried out in despair. Still, I didn't believe that life could be so simple. *You can't ask for something, then hear a voice telling you how to get it!*

But as I listened for the next hour, Jampolsky repeated the important principles: Forgiveness is critical. Withdrawal of attack thoughts is mandatory. Judging is damaging to others. Live in the present and forget the past. Instruct your mind to see peace rather than conflict. To live a life of love, let go of your fears and rid your mind of negative experiences. Don't worry about adverse events that might occur, but probably won't.

Just as Jesus told parables, Jampolsky emphasized his points with stories. One that I remember to this day involves a man who goes to an elegant restaurant, expecting a wonderful experience, but the waitress is abrasive, rude, and curt. The angry diner decides not to leave a tip. "I know you're upset," says a man at an adjacent table, "but her husband died two days ago. She's got five kids to support. She's overwhelmed by grief and fear." Filled with compassion, the diner left a large tip. His experience was the same, but he now felt peace instead of anger.

The most important concept I learned from Jampolsky came in question form: "Would you rather be happy, or would you rather be right?" That question hit home. I'd become an egomaniac, spending so much time proving myself right, as Margaret knew all too well. Now I faced a new test. I wasn't looking forward to my weekend meeting with Bruce because I wanted to reduce the number of our employees, but he didn't. The conflict promised to be stressful—something I didn't need. And so, on Thursday afternoon, leaving the Rancho Bernardo office early, I stopped by the La Jolla office on my way home to ask Bruce if he'd listen to the Jampolsky tape during his drive to Palm Springs. He was receptive.

The next morning, I was ten minutes late for work—being on time was never my strong suit. Concerned, my assistant Julie followed me into my private office.

"The new patient in Room 3, Mr. Bergstrom, seems anxious," she said. "He's been looking at his watch, asking when you'd be in."

I'd scheduled an hour for the appointment, so I wasn't worried about having time for a complete examination. As I continued to look at my mail, Julie explained that Bergstrom was an executive of a division of Hewlett Packard, headquartered in Rancho Bernardo. "Tell him I'll be right there," I said without looking up.

Five minutes later, Julie was back. Bergstrom was now pacing the floor and threatening to leave. Previously, I'd have said something like, "If he's in that much of a rush, he should leave. I don't want to treat an angry patient. After all, I'm booked solid for two weeks."

Remembering Jampolsky, however, I decided on a different approach. This man might be operating out of fear, not love. What could he be afraid of? That the examination or treatment would hurt? Be more expensive than he thought? Had he just bought a new house? Was he stressed by mortgage payments? Afraid to be late for work? I began to feel sorry for him, and an aura of tranquility descended upon me as I followed Julie down the corridor.

"Mr. Bergstrom," I said after Julie stepped out. "Sorry to keep you waiting." Then I told a white lie. "I was on the phone with another doctor about a patient."

His voice was stern. "I have to leave. I've got a meeting at HP."

"Now that you're here," I said, "just let me look at your x-rays. It'll only take a minute. I want to see if anything serious is going on." Then I added, "There'll be no charge for today."

"OK," he said and hopped into the chair.

Bergstrom now perceived me as someone who wanted to help him without getting anything in return. Examining his x-rays, I observed moderate bone loss around his posterior teeth. "Would you mind if I take a quick peek at your gums?"

Again, he agreed, and I used a soft touch to measure the loss of support for his teeth.

"You've got some problems," I said, "but they're not too serious. An accurate assessment will take about thirty minutes, so let's schedule another appointment when you have more time. Again, there's no charge for today."

"Well," Bergstrom said, "why don't you finish. My associate can cover for me."

I completed the exam, explained the problem and required treatment, and Mr. Bergstrom scheduled a series of appointments on his way out.

To be honest, I never regarded Jampolsky's concepts in any religious sense—that would come later—but from that day forward, I made it a habit to consider the emotional needs of my patients above my own, and my professional life became more peaceful.

* * *

I met Bruce in Palm Springs, and between a warm greeting over cognac and our after-dinner coffee that evening, we had the most pleasant meeting in our five-year relationship. The key was compromise—plus cooperation and camaraderie—all as a result of having shared the words of Dr. Jampolsky.

Back at home the following Tuesday, at 6:30 p.m., our doorbell rang—an unusual occurrence given the length and incline of the driveway. "I've got a present for you," Bruce said, grinning widely. He handed me an elegant bag containing a neatly-wrapped book. I invited Bruce in, but he declined as he was en route home for dinner. The book was a Bible-size, navy-blue paperback. Its title was A COURSE IN MIRACLES in gold capital block letters. The bottom of the cover said FOUNDATION FOR INNER PEACE. A week earlier, I'd cried out to an unknown God, "All I want is inner peace," and now I was holding it in the form of a book.

I'd never heard of *A Course in Miracles*, but Jampolsky had described it in *Love is Letting Go of Fear*. Helen Schucman, a psychologist at Columbia University—a woman of Jewish heritage but a religious skeptic—had written the book during a period of extreme turmoil in her life. She claimed it came to her through inner dictation from a divine source. Christian terminology permeates the text.

When I told some of our Catholic friends that I was reading *A Course in Miracles*, you would've thought I'd bought the erotic Victorian novel *Fanny Hill*. "It's New Age," they said, meaning *demonic, paranormal, diabolical,* and *cultish*. But I didn't care whether the book conformed to traditional Catholicism. I couldn't quote the Bible like my friends, but I knew one passage attributed to Jesus, something like: "A good tree produces good fruit, and a bad tree makes bad fruit. A bad tree cannot create good fruit." And the peace I'd begun to experience seemed like good fruit.

These friends' comments made me uncomfortable—until I remembered Saint Augustine. In San Diego, a high school is named after him. In

Florida, there's the city of St. Augustine. In search of a spiritual foundation after a life of debauchery, Augustine had followed Manichaeism, which combined pagan, Christian, and Gnostic roots. His classic book—*Confessions*, the first Western Christian autobiography—detailed this period in his life. His non-traditional approach to religion was the springboard to his conversion to Catholicism. But I had no aspiration to use *A Course in Miracles* in the same context.

In the following months, I read other books by Jampolsky and listened to his tapes to reprogram my brain to become more peaceful and less stressed. Jampolsky's voice spoke to me on my thirty-minute commutes between La Jolla and Rancho Bernardo. I still experienced tension, but my neck and back problems and my relationship with Margaret improved. I began to forgive, in my own mind, at least, many people from my past. But I could not free myself from my two strongest addictions—greed and ego.

Every month I would calculate my net worth, chuckling at the thought of Mr. Hathaway. After predicting my failure at Penn, he'd be surprised at my success: In 1978, I'd purchased several residential rental properties. In 1981 I'd become a partner in the Rancho Bernardo office building. The rent money—minus mortgage payments, taxes, insurance, and other expenses—supplemented my income. Estimating the potential market value of each property, I subtracted the mortgage balance to determine the equity—what I'd receive if the property were sold—adding these amounts to the balances in my various savings accounts and certificates of deposits.

It excited me to see my net worth increase. With hard work and reduced overhead following my meeting with Bruce, I didn't have to liquidate any real estate investments. I kept a list of state and national conferences at which I'd be speaking in the coming year, and would grow concerned if there was a gap of more than a month between engagements. I ignored the fact that frequent travel was detracting from my family life, and it began to exact a silent guilty toll.

As I reflect on this period today—rereading the above paragraphs—I realize the extent of my addiction. I was stressing about *my* real estate investments, *my* net worth, *but what about Margaret?* Her office management skills had been crucial to my early success, and her loving care of the boys and me was essential to our lives. I wasn't being fair to her, nor giving her credit for much of what I'd accomplished.

I also feel uncomfortable about how I treated Mom and Dad. They'd been struggling since the day they married, but I failed to comprehend their current financial difficulties. They'd moved from Connecticut to California, to a lovely twenty-four-hundred-square-foot home in an affluent section of Poway, just east of Rancho Bernardo. They had a large, lush, flower-filled backyard—a perfect home for their precious statue of the Virgin Mary. Then they'd downsized to a sixteen-hundred-square-foot home in the older Seven Oaks, fifty-five plus, community in Rancho Bernardo. There, they had a modest yard, with dry landscaping of gravel and desert plants to reduce mortgage payments and water bills. I knew Mom and Dad loved flowers, but why would they make such a move? Lost in my own luxurious world, I hadn't realized that money had become a problem for them.

In early August of 1988, a week after Margaret and I returned from a twentieth-anniversary Baltic Cruise to Amsterdam, Copenhagen, Stockholm, and St. Petersburg, I was visiting my parents when Dad asked me to hop into his aging Dodge station wagon and accompany him to the bank. The Dodge, which retained his special plates—JMJ653—functioned as his vehicle for construction jobs. At Downey Savings Bank, he withdrew some money and then showed me how to access his safety deposit box in case something happened to him.

"The key is in the glove compartment," he said, but I ignored his comment because he seemed very healthy. Then he added, "Your mother went to see her lawyer last week." Angry and distraught, he then changed the subject, leaving me feeling guilty. I'd never discussed with Mom her thoughts on divorce beyond our initial conversation.

"I want to tell you about something," Dad said. "Something I've kept to myself for the past forty-six years." His voice began to quiver. "Just before you were born, I decided to have you aborted."

Tears flowed down his face as he told me what had happened. He'd been outside the delivery room when Mom was ready to give birth. "The doctor backed through the swinging doors," he went on. "He wore an operating gown, cap, mask, and blood-stained rubber gloves. He said there was an unexpected complication, and Dad might have to decide between saving you or your mother." Sobbing outright now, Dad said, "I told him, if it came to that, to save your mother and let you die."

He knew Mom well, he explained, having lived with her for six years. But he didn't yet know *me*. So he'd chosen her. "Now she's divorcing me after fifty-two years! Please forgive me!"

I was stunned. "Of course, Dad. Of course."

No words could assuage his anguish. Dad had begun his life in the poverty of Mistretta, Italy, then immigrated to the "other side of the tracks" in Greenwich, Connecticut. He'd countered every adversity and sacrificed much to send me to Penn and Georgetown—private, expensive universities—so I could become a doctor. And he was asking me to pardon *him*?

Just days earlier, on our Baltic Cruise, Margaret and I had stood before one of Rembrandt's greatest paintings—"The Return of the Prodigal Son"—at the Hermitage in St. Petersburg, Russia. As we studied that life-sized painting, the docent, in broken English, explained how the artist had captured the pinnacle of Jesus' parable. It was, she told us, perhaps the most famous story of forgiveness known to humanity. The repentant son, who'd squandered his inheritance on wild living, kneels before his father in tattered clothing. The wizened face of the father exudes compassion as he embraces his son. His right arm and hand—slender and effeminate—express a mother-like nurturing, while the left, broad, muscular, and masculine, convey strength. It's as if the father is saying, "It's alright, son. We'll get through this."

But at this stage of my life, my ego simply would not allow me to seek forgiveness from my parents for my inattention to their needs. I'd been concerned only with my own, thinking I had years to mend my ways and show appreciation.

* * *

Two weeks after Dad's startling revelation, my son Mark, now a senior at the Bishop's School, wanted to visit Stanford before starting the laborious process of applying to colleges. The trip brought an unexpected opportunity.

We flew to San Francisco on Thursday evening, and in the morning, I drove Mark to Palo Alto for a campus tour and full day of activities. After dinner, exhausted but exhilarated, we watched TV, discussed the day, and agreed to leave for the airport right after breakfast on Saturday. I'd been reading another book by Jampolsky, *Good-bye to Guilt: Releasing Fear Through Forgiveness,* and wanted to finish it by the end of the trip. Meanwhile, Mark had various reading materials from Stanford to sift through.

We were at the gate forty-five minutes before boarding, and I'd just started Chapter 8, "Forgiveness Releases Me From My Past," when I heard a voice exactly like the one I'd been listening to on tape for the past four months. It was the raspy and compassionate voice of Jerry Jampolsky. *Was I hallucinating?* I couldn't be. I was relaxed and certainly hadn't been drinking. But where was this voice coming from? It was ten o'clock in the morning.

Looking up from my book in the direction of the voice, I saw a man who—judging from the gray hair on the back of his head—was in his sixties. He was talking on a payphone, his voice carrying to where I was seated. Setting my book aside, I listened for a few minutes. The man was complaining that a driver should have met him at the gate but hadn't shown up. I figured my curiosity would vanish the moment he turned away from the phone and I could see his face. Then I heard him say, "How's Bobby Martinez doing? I know they aren't giving him much longer." Jampolsky had a program that offered emotional support to children facing catastrophic illnesses. But this was too much of a coincidence.

"Ok," he said, finally. "I'll look for a new driver in thirty minutes." Then, hanging up, he turned slightly to the right and began to walk away.

I had to take the chance. "Jerry!" I called.

"Oh, there you are. I've been waiting for you."

It was him!

"No. I'm not your driver. You don't know me, but I know you." I held up his book.

Mark and I had thirty minutes left before boarding, the same that Jampolsky had to wait for his driver. Flattered, Jampolsky listened carefully as I blurted out the story about how I'd discovered his ideas. Then we discussed the interplay between love and fear.

The half-hour flew, ending with an invitation: "Why don't you and your wife attend our upcoming workshop at the Center for Attitudinal Healing? I'll comp your registration fees."

We shook hands, I collected Mark, and we headed to our gate.

* * *

The Center for Attitudinal Healing had existed for thirteen years in Tiburon, just north of San Francisco Bay. It offered psychological and spiritual support—at first for children, often with terminal cancer diagnoses—and, more recently, to patients with AIDS. A month later, Margaret and I, along with Bruce and Debbie Johnson, arrived there for a three-day workshop. I had to convince Margaret to go, not only because of the anti-New Age bias of our Catholic friends, but because we'd be mingling with AIDS patients. In the 1980s, this virus was little understood, except for the fact that it tended to infect sexually-active homosexual men. Little was known about transmission or treatments. Nonetheless, trained as a nurse and always supportive, Margaret agreed to attend. She felt compassion for the cancer-stricken children, but I wasn't sure what she'd feel about the patients with AIDS.

Twenty people had signed up for the workshops in which, through joint lectures, Jerry Jampolsky and his wife—Diane Cirincione-Jampolsky, Ph.D.—presented the principles of attitudinal healing. Bruce and I had become familiar with these principles, but they were unknown to Margaret and Debbie, who paid careful attention.

During a mingling session on the first afternoon, the organizers separated the spouses so we could meet individually with terminally-ill children. Chemotherapy had ravaged the hair of some of these kids, rendering them bald. Yet they were adorable and precious. I used black marking pens to draw with Ricky, a four-year-old suffering from acute lymphoblastic leukemia.

Posted on the wall were poignant drawings from previous sessions. They'd been positioned around an award-winning poster created in 1986 by the Jampolskys and artist Jack Keeler. It showed a lovable child with a mop of red hair, arms outstretched from a long yellow shirt, standing on stick legs among bright orange flowers. Above and below the child were the words: "I HAVE AIDS—Please Hug Me—I Can't Make You Sick." The poster had been adopted by the World Health Organization, which distributed it in one hundred forty-two countries. Subsequently, it was deemed the most effective AIDS educational tool in addressing the psychological, social, and emotional needs of AIDS patients.

One of the posted drawings, created by a child at a previous workshop, showed a battle scene with dead, egg-shaped cancer cells flat on their backs, feet outstretched, one on another, with little Cub Scout caps on their heads. Atop the pile stood a proud, smiley-faced victorious cell, a gun in its holster, holding a flag with huge letters—Good Cells. Another depicted a boxing ring, its corner posts connected by taut ropes. In the center, a long-legged, Good Cell with raised fists confronted a similar Bad Cell. The referee stood between them, but only the Good Cell had a fan—a little cell beating on a drum with a smiley face.

Love permeated the room. The unmistakable message was that we must work together to beat these diseases—whatever they might be. In an uplifting spiritual moment, we workshop attendees realized that life was terminal for all of us.

On the final afternoon, we were randomly assigned seats in a conference room with five round tables—each with two men and four empty chairs. The men were AIDS patients from the San Francisco area. The organizing committee provided us with a list of topics, someone at each table volunteered to be the leader, and everyone was encouraged to speak. We discussed the fear of death, childhood memories of feeling loved, and memories of estrangement from others.

I looked across the room at Margaret. Trained in the sixties to be wary about the spread of infectious diseases, she'd expressed the fear of getting close to an AIDS patient. In the mid-1980s, research on the AIDS virus was sparse. It had been named the Human Immunodeficiency Virus (HIV) in 1986, and its transmissibility was poorly understood.

We couldn't believe it when Jerry announced that our two hours were up. It was time to say goodbye. As everyone stood, it was readily apparent that warm relationships had developed. At our table, everyone shook hands, and there were pats on the back. Across the room, I saw Margaret giving a long hug to one patient, then turning to the other and doing the same. I smiled and felt a new sort of peace. The weekend had been a giant step for all of us.

Dr. Jampolsky passed away in 2020 at the age of ninety-five. More than one hundred thirty Centers for Attitudinal Healing exist worldwide—good fruit from the tree containing the principles of *A Course in Miracles*—even if in places that book is contrary to Sacred Scripture. For me, it was a stepping stone for my acceptance of Christianity as the true religion. Perhaps God knew I was not ready for the giant leap.

Chapter 26   Mobile Homes

FRANCIS CRICK ADDRESSED THE American Academy of Periodontology in October 1988. Mom divorced Dad the following month. The former was the result of positive action on my part. My avoidance impacted the latter.

Because I'd succeeded in preventing my parents' divorce in 1985, Mom blamed me for adding several more years of misery to her life. And three years later, when she actually went through with it, I had no idea how devastating it would be—for her, Dad, Margaret, me, and the entire family.

Mom not only divorced Dad, but she also sold their house, agreed to the distribution of their meager savings, and moved into a double-wide mobile home in Escondido, thirty-five miles northeast of La Jolla. Unfortunately, the statue of the Virgin Mary—a major bone of contention—was moved to a patch of grass behind Mom's mobile home, and I believe Dad was devastated by losing something that had meant so much to him.

"She threw me out of the house," he dejectedly told his friends, as if he was totally innocent of their marital discord.

Conflict, and a major alteration in one's status or position in life, are major causes of depression, but I was unprepared for the changes in Dad. He ceased to enjoy life. He stopped calling friends, never smiled, became sullen, and his once-powerful voice became a whisper. Seeing no alternative, Margaret and I invited him to move in with us, which he did, although he confined his activity to moping around the house.

Fearing for his well-being, I encouraged him to get out, go places, and meet new people, finally persuading him to attend a singles dance. I was surprised when he went, but I was even more surprised by the result. On that evening out, he met Doris Robinson, a joyful lady twelve years his junior, who loved to dance, as did Dad. Within weeks they moved together to a small apartment in Oceanside, a coastal town thirty miles north of La Jolla, twenty-two miles northwest of Mom in Escondido.

For years, Mom had depended upon Dad to do certain chores she didn't like. After the divorce, she routinely called him with her shopping list, and he'd deliver groceries to her doorstep. But Doris put an end to that, which angered Mom, increasing her resentment and unhappiness.

Despite initiating the divorce, Mom assumed little responsibility for its aftermath. Gone were the large family dinners—it was impossible for Mom and Dad to sit at the same table—and for the rest of us, "la famiglia e tutto" lost its meaning.

* * *

With two private-school tuitions to pay, annual dues for the La Jolla Beach and Tennis Club, plus season tickets to the San Diego Chargers, San Diego Opera, and La Jolla Playhouse, I immersed myself in my profession, working in two offices and lecturing at any opportunity, to supplement my income.

Old issues and memories still plagued me: *I was never good enough. Jay-Jay, Buddy, and Brian had laughed at my Hopalong Cassidy outfit. I launched that nail over the Raybestos Field backstop.*

Some believe pride drives poor self-worth and fear of shame. I struggled with my ego and the image I projected to the community. It didn't help that my thirty-year-old-ocean-view home needed serious renovation. Margaret didn't want to do the remodeling; if we did, she wanted Dad to do it. I loved Dad, but he had no idea what made a house in La Jolla elegant—especially one on a lot as desirable as ours.

La Jolla's recently organized Mainly Mozart Society annually attracted accomplished musicians from around the country to perform at concerts given by the Society's Festival Orchestra. In addition to paying for these concerts, I spent an extra twelve hundred fifty dollars each year as a member of the prestigious Club 1250, so Margaret and I could attend quarterly chamber music performances in some of La Jolla's grandest homes. Arthur Porras, chair of Club 1250, known for accessorizing glamourous homes in Beverly Hills, Hong Kong, Jakarta, and Rome, did the interior designs. Several of his houses had been featured on the cover of *Architectural Digest*.

Like my friend and colleague Alex Koper, I considered Arthur Porras a Renaissance man. He had an enthusiast's understanding of the arts, culture, and beauty, and exuded a general aura of sophistication. Obsessed with the need to impress, I gave in to my pride and hired Arthur as our interior designer, assuring Margaret that I had a budget in mind.

Arthur always chose the best materials in the planning stage for his homes. He selected a curvilinear slab of Breche de Benou marble from

France for ours. This multicolored gravelly structure, with shades of yellow, green, and pink, would become a custom-designed desk in my private office. For the same room, Arthur recommended cabinets of Bocote wood, imported from a particular forest in Central America. Exotic Bocote is known for its strength and beauty.

As time passed, I assumed that Dad was happy with Doris and that Mom had made friends in her mobile home park. But in 1989, I rarely saw them since we alternated their visits for holiday meals. Subconscious anger and resentment may have been the root cause of my estrangement. I believed my parents' divorce had adversely affected the entire family. For me personally, it was a betrayal of what I'd been taught since infancy.

* * *

If asked, Margaret might say that 1991 was one of the worst years of her life. First, her mother died from lung cancer. Soon after, I initiated the demolition and reconstruction phases of a significant renovation of our home, which necessitated a six-month move to a rental house, with much of the planning and packing left up to her. In addition, my parents weren't speaking to each other, making Margaret's role as daughter-in-law increasingly difficult.

In April, my sister's husband, Glenn, in his mid-fifties, died due to a surgical misstep during an operation to remove his gall bladder. Given the loss of her mother, Margaret now grieved for Janet as well.

Meanwhile, I lost myself in my daily surgeries and frequent lectures. Although I had approved the remodel cost, I left overseeing the renovation to Margaret, increasing her stress. Plans called for removing the sheetrock throughout the house so new wiring and plumbing could be installed. But the contractor kept encountering unexpected situations, necessitating expensive change orders with which Margaret had to cope when I wasn't available. Despite my budget, additional expenditures soon exceeded the value of the construction loan we had secured.

Once again, poor planning on my part had caused a financial disaster—we simply ran out of cash, spending more on remodeling than we'd paid for the home eight years earlier. I maxed out three credit cards, borrowing over forty thousand dollars at 18 percent interest. Not surprisingly, Margaret's resentment toward me increased, paling in comparison to that sparked by my trip to Japan years earlier—when I took off to purchase cameras and stereo equipment several weeks after Mark's birth.

On the surface, she remained calm; underneath, it was a different story. Bills were piling up, and the principles of attitudinal healing we'd embraced at Jampolsky's workshop were being tested to the brink of failing. I needed to change my attitude. My newly-acquired spirituality lacked depth. If only Dad had reviewed the construction contract and protected my interests, many problems could have been avoided. But I'd ignored him in the planning stage, and now my pride prevented me from asking for help.

Then, during the first week of June, Dad's girlfriend Doris was diagnosed with stage 4 colon cancer. Not wanting to become a burden to Dad, she moved out of their apartment. I didn't think to ask how he'd fill the void in his life. My agenda was overwhelming—an upcoming lecture in Victoria, Canada, at the end of June, and a week-long seminar for USC in early August at the Kapalua Bay Resort in Hawaii. Then I'd be on to San Francisco as one of the featured speakers at the Annual Meeting of the California Dental Association, which thousands would attend.

In November, Arthur Porras—knowing that the renovation of our home would be finished but that the custom-ordered living room furniture would not have arrived—asked if Mainly Mozart could use our massive living room for its chamber music program in December. Club 1250 would set up one hundred folding chairs for a concert featuring a violinist, cellist, and flutist. Arthur believed our high ceilings and panoramic ocean views would be perfect for a sunset concert. In addition, our two thousand-square-foot wraparound deck could easily hold the expected audience for wine and hors d'oeuvres.

During that event, my ego swelled when Arthur introduced me to the attendees—including the CEOs of some of San Diego's largest corporations—as the homeowner. I had no idea what Margaret might have been thinking, exhausted by the preparations. But I was certainly proud of myself.

* * *

On the following Tuesday, Dad called me at the Rancho Bernardo office. He sounded terrible, almost unable to talk because of a continual cough, sneezing, and hoarse voice. I asked if he'd seen his internist. He said he'd been to his cardiologist the day before, but there was no reason for antibiotics. He had a virus, and the symptoms would most likely dissipate.

Two days later, Dad was in intensive care at Tri-City Medical Center in Oceanside. After seeing my last patient, I headed north from my Rancho Bernardo office. The doctor-in-charge was Dr. Omar Elbaz, who came out to talk before admitting me into Dad's room.

Dr. Elbaz got right to the point. "Your father's critically ill. Pneumonia caused a septicemia, then septic shock. Given his age and overall health, he has a 50 percent chance of surviving." When I'd last seen Dad a month ago, he was vibrant and sharp. He'd just returned from a deep-sea excursion out of Oceanside Harbor, fishing for rockfish and sea bass. But, because rolling seas bothered my stomach, I hadn't offered to go with him.

"We have him on a ventilator, so he can't speak to you," Dr. Elbaz said. "He's sleeping, but you can sit by his side."

Dad was waking up as we entered, and the sight wasn't pretty. He had two IVs in his arms, and a breathing tube protruded from his mouth. One end of the tube went past his tongue and into his trachea, the other was attached to the ventilator. Two nurses stood attentively on either side of the bed.

When Dad saw me, he reached toward his mouth with both hands, attempting to pull out the tubing, which elicited a severe gag response. Immediately the nurses secured his hands to his sides with Velcro, but Dad pulled violently against the straps. Then, while one nurse held his hands, the other took a hypodermic needle, withdrew a sedative from a bottle, and inserted it into an IV line. Finally, dad stopped struggling and closed his eyes.

The skin on the back of his hand was thin, revealing bulging blue veins. A myriad of dark brown age spots showed through a sprinkling of light brown hairs. As a toddler, Dad had picked me up and thrown me into the air, only to catch me and rub his nose into my belly, turning his head left to right and back again, causing me to laugh hysterically, as he later did to our sons. These hands had built the largest home on Park Street in Stratford, Connecticut, aligned granite blocks in a Romanesque arch over the head of his Virgin Mary statue, and built my first office. Now they were old and weak. I placed the palm of my hand over the back of his. Surprisingly, he rotated his hand and squeezed mine but didn't open his eyes. Using my thumb, I massaged the fleshy part of his palm until he fell asleep. I couldn't bear to see Dad wake up—only to struggle again with the ghastly tube that prevented him from speaking to me.

When I left, Dr. Elbaz followed me out, and we talked some more. His main concern was organ damage. "Your father's labs," he said, "are showing alterations in his liver, adrenals, and kidneys. At times he appears confused and delirious, but it's too early to tell if he'll have any permanent cognitive impairment."

I left, and when I returned the following evening, Dad was awake, overjoyed to see that the breathing tube had been removed. Then I realized that Dad, though awake, still couldn't speak. On the front of his neck, in the region of his Adam's apple, a clear vinyl tracheostomy mask had been strapped in place. From its center, a corrugated plastic tube extended to the ventilator, feeding him oxygen and keeping him alive. When his eyes met mine, he managed a half-smile. I looked into his eyes and returned his smile with a burst of compassionate love. Dad no longer struggled as he had the day before. Holding his hand, I talked to him for forty-five minutes.

"They're really taking good care of you, Dad. I can't believe that Christmas is in five days. We're praying you'll be able to join us. Wouldn't that be great? Everyone would love to see you. They all send their best."

Dad didn't attend Christmas dinner, but I visited him that night, as I had every night, to hold his hand. It was the least I could do. Comforting him helped to assuage my guilt for having distanced myself after his move to Oceanside with Doris.

Dr. Elbaz said that Dad had lapsed into a coma earlier in the day, and that his chances for recovery, while slim, were not impossible. I sat with him for half an hour, then left, returning to hold his unresponsive hand in subsequent evenings.

* * *

Dr. Elbaz called on the day of New Year's Eve, his voice full of excitement. "It's amazing," he said. "Your dad just woke up. He's breathing on his own and in good spirits. Can you come over soon?"

I rushed to the hospital. The nurses had tilted the back of Dad's bed to a forty-five-degree angle. His color was better, and he managed a small smile when I entered. The corrugated plastic tube connecting him to the ventilator was gone. Instead, a plug had been placed into the tracheostomy mask. Dad's lips moved in the form of a greeting. He was saying, "How are you?"

He'd been on the edge of death for two weeks and asked how *I* was. I could run, walk, talk, and spend hundreds of thousands of dollars remodeling a multi-million-dollar house—without his help and guidance—and he wanted to know how I was!

The truth was, I was overwhelmed with guilt and remorse—that's how I was. Jampolsky's books stressed living in the moment, saying goodbye to guilt, forgetting the past, and not worrying about the future. But I was flunking the course miserably.

Without thinking, I blurted, "Do you want to see Mom?"

Dad nodded. I found a payphone and called Mom, asking if she could come to the hospital immediately—Dad was awake and wanted to see her.

Meeting Mom in the empty ICU reception room, I hugged her. She looked harried but better than the last time I'd seen her. Then the double doors swung open, and through them, an aide pushed Dad in a wheelchair. And as Mom stepped forward, Dad stood. He was 78 years old, had just come out of a coma, hadn't moved his leg muscles for two weeks, and was standing, shuffling his feet to meet Mom.

Studies have shown that several weeks in bed will cause muscles to atrophy. Yet Dad had stood up on his own power, walked, and hugged Mom for several minutes. Both were crying profusely. It was an unforeseen and unexplainable moment of healing, "a gift from God," as Margaret said when I described the scene to her later.

Fatigued, Dad then sat down in his wheelchair, and the aide pushed him back to his bed in the ICU. Mom and I embraced, exchanged some sentiments, and she left to return to her mobile home alone.

Chapter 27   Father Bill Wilson

JANUARY 1 IS A Holy Day of Obligation for Catholics—The Solemnity of Mary, the Holy Mother of God. Margaret and I were sitting in the first pew, so she could access the podium and lectern easily when she did the First and Second Readings.

As the elderly priest began his sermon after the Gospel reading, he occasionally lapsed into a heavy Irish brogue.

"Good morning and Happy New Year. For those of ya who don't know me, I'm Father Bill Wilson, and I'm an alcoholic. This morning I want to tell ya how to find God . . . *Really* find Him, not just *think* you've found Him."

I leaned toward Margaret and whispered, "I think we've stumbled into an AA meeting!"

Fr. Bill was the new associate pastor of All Hallows Church, which we'd joined when we moved to La Jolla in 1983.

"I come from where all the *real* alcoholics come," Fr. Wilson went on, speaking louder now. "And I want ya to know there's a difference between Irish alcoholics and all other types. As we Irishmen drink, we become the best bull artists."

The congregation laughed.

"When I visited Ireland last year," Fr. Bill continued, "I heard a story about a Texan who'd visited my hometown. He told a local farmer, 'Back in Texas, we call our estate a *ranch*, not a *farm*. If at sunrise I got into my car to drive around the borders of my property, at sunset I wouldn't have finished the trip.' The Irish farmer said, 'Is that so? I once had a car like that!'"

This time the congregation roared, and I leaned toward Margaret again. "This is going to be fun!" But I wasn't prepared for the serious nature of what followed.

"In my village," Fr. Bill said, "everyone was Catholic. As an adolescent, I was quite the sinner, into all kinds of shenanigans. Once, I went into church all by me-self and knelt in front of four rows of candles and a coin box. Ya know how it is—you're supposed to put in a coin and light a candle. I put in a coin and lit all thirty. I couldn't stop myself from mischief like this, so I decided to become a priest to save my soul."

Again there was laughter.

But the word "soul" made me consider my own. Ever since reading *Love Is Letting Go of Fear* and *The Course in Miracles*, I'd felt comfortable with the Christian concepts of forgiveness, acceptance, and love of one's fellow man. But I disliked the drudgery of the Catholic Church—the repetitive liturgies, face-to-face confessions, strict policies on birth control, and all the rest. I'd discovered the Church of Today in Mission Valley, located in an expanded storefront, and occasionally attended on my own. Although Christian in origin, it advertised "great messages, great music, great people, no weird stuff, and none of the guilt." That last idea especially appealed to me.

Margaret, who'd schooled our three sons in their Catholic education, tolerated my behavior. After attending Mass with her and the boys, I'd often drive twelve miles south to the Church of Today to listen to the entertaining sermons of Reverend Wendy Purcell, who brought a quasi-Christian, part-New Age message to a late Sunday morning service. Conveniently, I'd return home in time for lunch and the San Diego Chargers' one o'clock kickoff.

Loud laughter returned me to the present, to Fr. Bill's life story.

"After I became a priest, I lived in a monastery in England. At age 30, I went to study in Rome—at a university right under the Pope's nose." He paused and chuckled. "I dreamed of becoming a renowned professor. I studied all kinds of highfalutin' stuff that ordinary snobs wouldn't understand. And I would've been fine if it weren't for the big dining hall, with its long tables . . . and two enormous flagons of wine within arm's reach."

He paused again, looking the parishioners right in the eye. Then he grinned and said, "We were supposed to share—four to a flagon—but the weird fellow on my right didn't take any, and the one on my left took just a bit, like the guys across the table. So, for the first time in my life, I became polluted—dead drunk—finishing both pitchers so none would go to waste."

All eyes were now riveted on Fr. Bill.

"From that first time on," he confessed, "I got smashed, two meals a day. Each time the monk at the microphone read the holy stuff, he seemed like a great orator. Everything was funny, funny, funny! Like Alice in Wonderland, I went down the rabbit hole into a whole new reality."

Fr. Bill went on at length to relate how he'd become an arrogant, intolerant, obnoxious alcoholic. When he finished up in Rome, he returned as a teacher to the monastery in England, where he continued to drink, albeit surreptitiously. But the monks soon discovered his problem. The Abbot called him an "alcoholic" to his face, and the term infuriated Fr. Bill. He was soon dismissed from the monastery, and the Abbott said he'd blacklist him throughout the Catholic world so he'd never get back into academia. His dreams of becoming a professor had ended.

I leaned toward Margaret yet again. "This may be a long sermon, but it's worth it."

Fortunately, as Fr. Bill explained, the Bishop of San Diego, California— six thousand miles away—offered him a position as a diocesan priest, and he accepted, hoping for a fresh start. But after being assigned a parish, he turned to drinking "hard stuff," unbeknownst to his parishioners.

"I had a talent for standing in front of people and talking about loving God," he said, "how they should be tolerant, humble, and compassionate— all the things I wasn't. Basking in grandiosity, I'd come to believe that I could pull the wool over the eyes of these inferior beings."

For seven years, Fr. Wilson lived a double life, committing sins he was ashamed to admit to, living in what he called a "pigsty," like the one in the Parable of the Prodigal Son. He couldn't pray because he was either drunk or hungover, and he lost any relationship he'd ever had with God. He figured that when people discovered his brilliance and realized where he belonged—at a top seminary or university—he'd clean up his act. In the meantime, he told himself, "Let's forget the whole thing and have another drink."

One family at his parish—a mother, father, and five kids, ages five to twenty—felt sorry for him. He was obviously a lonely man, so they invited him to spend a week with them in a beach house in Ensenada, Mexico, seventy miles south of the International Border. But Fr. Bill continued to drink, covertly during the day and heavily at bedtime. One day, the mother and her husband had to leave for a doctor's appointment in San Diego, planning to return the following day. So, the kids were stuck with "Uncle Bill," who, not long after their parents left, poured himself a glass of bourbon and headed to his bedroom.

Fr. Bill reenacted the scene. "'Where do you think you're going?' the twenty-year-old said to me. He was a rather large young man. 'I'm going to bed,' I answered."

"'Not with *that* in your hand. You're nothing but a good-for-nothing *alcoholic*, and you're taking advantage of our parents' kindness.'"

"There was that dreaded word again—*alcoholic*." Fr. Bill said. "And it made me angry. Already drunk, I tried to walk by the lad to my bedroom, but he knocked the glass from my hand. I don't know what came over me, but I lost control, grabbed him by the throat, and squeezed with both hands. I would've killed him if the other kids hadn't jumped me."

Fr. Bill averted his eyes now, looking down. I could sense the pain of his revelation.

"In the morning, I drove to LA, where I was to speak at a conference the following day. After reaching my hotel, I wandered aimlessly. On a side street, I found a small Catholic Church. When I rang the rectory doorbell, an old priest came out. I said, 'Father, I'd like to go to confession.' And for the next half hour, I told him my sins, shameful stuff that made me feel more than ever like the Prodigal Son. The priest said, 'Why come to *me* with all this garbage?' 'I've come for God's forgiveness,' I said. 'I know that,' he replied, 'but *why me?*'"

"'I guess you're just in the wrong place at the wrong time.' That's all I could think to say. Then he said, 'What you must realize, Fr. Wilson, is that you have a disease. Take a drink, and it goes right to your brain. You think you can overcome it on your own, but you can't.'"

Looking into my eyes, Margaret instantly caught my attention—as if this message pertained to me. Did she think I was becoming an alcoholic because of my regular glass or two of wine with dinner? *Was I?* We returned our eyes to the pulpit. Fr. Bill had me mesmerized.

"That old priest screamed, 'Do you think you came here by some kind of fluke? Well, you didn't. You were *brought* here. *Brought by the Lord.* I'm a recovering alcoholic myself. I've been going to Alcoholics Anonymous for years. I'm the only priest in AA for many miles around, but you found me. I'm not going to ask you to say prayers for your penance. For your penance, you're going to an AA meeting—*tonight*—and I'm taking you!'"

"I went to the meeting and was introduced to a sponsor, Harry, a hardened man who'd spent years in a penitentiary for murder, a guy with a temper just like me. 'You wanna get better?' Harry said. 'Then you gotta read AA's *Big Book*. Start with Chapter 4.' When we met again a week later, Harry asked if I'd read Chapter 4—'We Agnostics.' I admitted I hadn't. 'It's not about proving there's a God,' he said, 'because you can't prove it to yourself—*you're too stupid.* You have to make an adjustment so *God* can prove it. And He only can do this if you make it possible. It's all there, in that chapter you didn't read!'"

Fr. Bill grabbed the sides of the pulpit and made direct eye contact again. His voice became softer, almost melodic, and he said, "So I read Chapter 4, which tells us we live in a wonderful world. We plant a seed and a flower grows, and that's wonderful. Birds lay eggs, they hatch, and new birds fly away. That's wonderful. Men and women get together and do what all men and women do, and new life is created. And that's wonderful. But you need to get the alcohol out of your system to see the wonder."

Again Fr. Bill's voice grew louder, as if to implant his words into our brains indelibly.

"That chapter taught me that many of us are on a treadmill. One minute you see wonder and think God exists, but the next, you see war, cruelty, and pain and are certain He doesn't. Then the cycle repeats. Faith in God has to become part of our DNA. Search fearlessly, and you'll find a reality deep inside where God can be found. When you do, you'll know God is a fact. You have to sense your powerlessness to overcome your addictions. It doesn't matter what you're hung up on—alcohol, drugs, possessions, sex, greed, whatever. Whisper to yourself, 'Are you there, Lord, or are you just the biggest mistake the human race has ever made?' Say, 'I hope you're there because I want to be truly humble. Please change me. *Change me!* I want to be changed.' God changed me," Fr. Bill said, "and I will forever be grateful."

Suddenly, I wasn't listening to a sermon in church—I was sitting in my Mercedes, under extreme duress, with back pain and neck pain, calling out and pleading, "God, if you're up there, all I want is inner peace. Please help me." I seemed stuck in that moment. Fr. Bill struck a chord in me.

Fr. Bill was nearing the end of his sermon, his voice strong and steady. "This isn't a head trip, people. It's a gut trip. You have to say, 'God, are you there? I *want* you to be. *Rescue* me! I mean it!' And you'll slowly begin to notice changes in your life."

Once again, I remembered sitting in my Mercedes, asking if God was, in fact, up there. The next day I'd found Jampolsky's tape at Warwick's. Then I met him at the airport and spent an unexpected weekend at his Center for Attitudinal Healing. All of which seemed like a dream now. *Were these just unrelated events, or had divine guidance been involved?*

Whatever the cause, since then, my neck and back pain had vanished. *Maybe it was the result of my change in attitude.* I no longer lay on the horn when cut off on the road. Instead, I forgave the driver, thinking he was afraid of something. I tried to be loving, and was the better for it. Fr. Bill's voice returned me to the moment.

"When I was a little boy," Fr. Bill concluded, "and returned home from the playground dirty and bruised, my Mum would clean me up, kiss me, and make me feel wonderful again. I knew she loved me. It's no different with God. After I started drinking, I didn't believe anybody could do for me what I couldn't do for myself. I didn't believe in God—until I hit bottom. In order to survive, I asked Him to help me, and He did. I believe in Him today." Fr. Bill paused and grinned. "And when you're in the job *I'm* in—it helps to believe!"

The congregation roared again, leaving me feeling I'd taken another step toward inner peace. Four years later, Fr. Bill would help me yet again when my mother lay dying from cancer in our home.

* * *

Later that day, as I sat with Margaret in the last row of the theater awaiting the start of *Father of the Bride*, I felt my pager vibrate. I didn't recognize the phone number but was on call for the office, so I excused myself and slipped out to the lobby.

"Dr. Sottosanti," said the somber voice of Dr. Elbaz, "your father passed away peacefully a little while ago."

A heavy gloom descended upon me. I returned to Margaret and motioned for her to follow. She could tell by my doleful expression that something was terribly wrong. Back in the lobby, I broke the news, my tears streaming.

During the drive home, Margaret rubbed the back of my neck, understanding my silence. "Sweetie," she said, "your Dad lived a good long life. His reconciliation with Mom yesterday was such a blessing."

"I thought he'd recover," I blubbered.

Dr. Elbaz said it was highly unusual for Dad to wake from his coma, breathe independently, then stand and walk. He said I was "lucky" to have witnessed his reunion with Mom. Of course, this couldn't have been a matter of luck, but I was reluctant to call it a miracle, though it smacked of divine intervention.

"*God may take his soul to heaven,*" I mused. "*If so, given his license plate, Jesus, Mary, and Joseph may meet him at the gate!*"

The comforting image brought me peace, and a small voice within me murmured, "Thank you, Lord."

* * *

Three years later, I held an impressive document in my hands. Across the top, in bold print, it said: "The Commissioner of Patents and Trademarks of the United States of America." The eight-by-eleven booklet impressed me with its weight and gold serrated sticker—the size of a Las Vegas casino chip—embossed with an eagle clutching an olive branch and arrows. Two red ribbons from the seal's border formed an inverted V. The symbolism was terrific. The colors were those of USC—cardinal red ribbons and amber gold. Proudly I read aloud to Margaret: *This United States Patent grants to the person or*

persons having title to this patent the right to exclude others from making, us-
ing, or selling the invention throughout the United States of America for the
term of seventeen years from the date of this patent.

It was dated November 22, 1994, and my name was listed as *inventor.*
I'd found a way to use calcium sulfate—similar to that found in sheetrock—
to stimulate bone growth. The patent was a potential goldmine, and I want
to explain how it happened.

Back in 1987, the *Journal of Periodontal Research,* in an article titled
"New Attachment Formation by Guided Tissue Regeneration" had cited
animal research studies that used a Gore-Tex membrane. This membrane,
produced by W.L. Gore & Associates, was made of a polymer of expanded
polytetrafluoroethylene, similar to that used for making rain gear. If used in
periodontal surgery, it could exclude unwanted cells, allowing bone-forming cells—known as osteoblasts—to enter a bone defect around a tooth to
generate new bone, thus stabilizing the damaged tooth. In theory, a surgeon
could create a bone-forming chamber and isolate it from cells that would
interfere by generating unwanted tissues.

But I noted some negatives. A second surgery would be necessary to
remove the membrane since it wouldn't resorb. And if exposed, the membrane could become infected. Purchasing two membranes, I experimented
with the procedure, and one did become infected. *"This is ridiculous,"* I
thought. *"Fourteen years ago, at the VA hospital, I used plaster of Paris to do*
the same thing on many patients, without post-op infections."

The U.S. Gypsum Company (USG) had a medical division, so I contacted them and obtained a vial of medical-grade calcium sulfate. It was
marked "For Experimental Use Only" since it wasn't being marketed and
hadn't been cleared by the FDA for a specific purpose.

Previous articles in the medical literature reported that calcium sulfate
was very safe, but only a weak bone-inducing material. However, I knew
it was biocompatible, did not support infection, and might be combined
with bone graft particles to improve their handling during surgery. Also, I
had clinical evidence that, if combined with the BMP (bone morphogenetic
protein) found in cadaver bone and processed by the technique introduced
by Dr. Urist (now available from many FDA approved human tissue banks),
calcium sulfate would accelerate bone formation by either providing calcium ions to the site or by its conversion to calcium phosphate—a precursor
of new bone. It didn't matter. I was quite sure it worked.

A year later, an article appeared in *Clinical Orthopaedics and Related*
Research—"Response of the mouse femoral muscle to an implant of a composite of bone morphogenetic protein and plaster of Paris." Dr. Yamazaki,
from Japan, with his co-workers, had placed composite grafts of plaster of

Paris and BMP into the bellies of mice, where they expected no bone formation. Instead, the combination induced much more bone growth than in the control sites containing just BMP. *Voila,* I thought. *It does work. My hypothesis is validated!*

Emboldened, I used this technique from 1988 until 1992, combining Urist-bone—now commonly known as demineralized freeze-dried bone allograft (DFDBA)—with medical-grade calcium sulfate from USG. My test patients suffered from severe periodontal disease and extensive bone loss around their teeth. Documenting the successful outcomes, I published three papers in the scientific literature, resulting in a deluge of invitations to present the technique at dental meetings throughout the United States. Meanwhile, I filed for two patents.

In 1993, the American Academy of Restorative Dentistry (AARD) invited me to speak for eighteen minutes on a Saturday in February at their annual meeting in Chicago. *Ridiculous,* I thought. *Eighteen minutes is barely enough to get started!* I was going to decline the invitation, but my friend Bob Allen—a La Jolla prosthodontist—said that the AARD was perhaps the most prestigious organization in all of dentistry. Founded in 1928, it had an invitation-only membership of the finest dentists in the country. To be considered for membership, an opening had to occur, usually due to death, and then you had to be nominated and approved by a two-thirds vote. According to Bob, if I did well in that eighteen-minute talk, I could be invited back for a forty-minute presentation the following year. Then I'd be a prime candidate for membership.

I was sent a list of presentation rules after I accepted the invitation. The most demanding one was that I had to finish my lecture at *precisely* eighteen minutes, aided by a green light, then a yellow and red, after which they would silence the microphone.

I arrived on a Friday night at the Drake Hotel in Chicago, at the intersection of the "Magnificent Mile" and Lake Shore Drive. The Drake is a grand Beaux-Arts hotel, with French architectural features that give it a massive, elaborate, and ostentatious appearance. It had opened on New Year's Eve, in 1920, for the entertainment of two thousand of Chicago's high society. Several hundred feet above the magnificent sidewalk entrance, gigantic pink, gothic, neon letters spell out "The Drake." It is Chicago's answer to the famous "Hollywood" sign that provides a stunning backdrop to Los Angeles.

The thirty-foot ceilings of the Grand Ballroom stunned me, as did the crystal chandeliers and wraparound balcony. Lush potted plants were scattered everywhere. The cavernous ballroom above the Rudy Molinaro

Accordion School in Bridgeport, the venue of my childhood Wiffle Ball games, was a quarter of the size.

I handed my Kodak Carousel slide tray to the audio-visual aide and headed to the men's room to check my hair, teeth, and tie. I had eighteen minutes to impress my audience and wanted everything to be perfect. I wanted to be invited back. My ravenous ego was subconsciously crying—*Feed me! Feed me!*—as it regularly did.

After a brief introduction by the program chairman, I began to speak to a packed house in the ballroom. I held a laser pointer in my left hand, a remote slide changer in my right, and kept one eye on the lectern's digital clock. With about a minute remaining, I realized that the lavalier microphone, clipped to my tie, allowed me to roam, so I moved to the edge of the stage. I was proud of my dark blue Armani suit, purchased weeks earlier at Neiman Marcus, and tailored for a perfect fit. It gave me the confidence to establish eye contact with members of the audience, as I stated—with just seconds remaining —"So, as you can see, medical-grade calcium sulfate is the key to practical and predictable bone regeneration."

There was a short break while the aide replaced my slide tray with the following speaker's. Bob Allen came rushing up as I descended the podium steps, so I prepared myself for his congratulations and a return invitation. But he leaned close and whispered the words every male fears to hear. "Your fly is open." The Academy of Restorative Dentistry did not contact me again. For a rare moment, I was crushed and humbled.

Chapter 28   Heaven on Earth

LATE IN 1993, JUST as my publications and lectures accelerated the demand for medical-grade calcium sulfate, USG signed an agreement with Lifecore Biomedical, a company listed on the NASDAQ Stock Exchange, to provide medical-grade plaster for use with Hapset—a new bone graft material. This product combined synthetic bone, known as hydroxyapatite (HA), with calcium sulfate. I didn't believe it would compete with my technique because HA contains no inductive proteins necessary to convert stem cells to osteoblasts. Instead, HA simply provides a trellis upon which bone can grow. Nevertheless, this relationship between USG and Lifecore ended my ability to purchase medical-grade calcium sulfate.

Fortuitously, my son Mark had recently graduated from the Wharton School at my alma mater, the University of Pennsylvania, with a major in marketing. Together we found an inexpensive source of calcium sulfate, hired an accredited laboratory to analyze it—to ensure that it was free from impurities—and sterilized it. Finally, we placed it in one-gram bottles and added a label—"Medical-Grade Calcium Sulfate Hemihydrate—For Experimental Use Only." Mark then formed the Edgemark Company, using a Del Mar post-office box address rather than a La Jolla one, for a degree of separation from me. So when asked the inevitable question at the end of my lectures, "Where can I buy medical-grade calcium sulfate?"—I referred the questioner to Edgemark.

Edgemark's sales began to rise as an increasing number of surgeons were pleased with the results they were getting. It was risky to encourage using a product that had not been FDA approved, but I saw this as a temporary measure. I relied on the individual responsibility of the surgeons who used it, hopeful my patents would be approved, after which I could adopt a conventional model for product development. Had Dad's occasional questionable behavior in pursuing his goals affected my own?

I brushed the question aside. Driven by my ego—and the knowledge that the product was safe—I forged ahead.

In March of 1994, Jim Bracke, founder and CEO of Lifecore Biomedical, contacted me to arrange a breakfast meeting in La Jolla. He'd heard of me from U.S. Gypsum and wondered if a joint business opportunity might be possible. I explained why calcium sulfate mixed with DFDBA was better than their Hapset product, and he said he'd be interested in signing a licensing agreement if my patents were granted.

Later that spring, I flew to Yonsei University in Seoul, South Korea, at the invitation of Professor Chong-Kwan Kim, to work with him and his team on a dog study. It was designed to test my claims regarding significant improvement in periodontal bone regeneration by using calcium sulfate with a bone graft. Initially, I hesitated to travel to Asia as tensions between the Koreas escalated. President Kim Il Sung had begun reprocessing fuel rods from a nuclear reactor, giving the country weapons-grade plutonium. Months later, former President Jimmy Carter would travel to Pyongyang to meet with the dictator and attempt to defuse the situation. Knowing that the Demilitarized Zone (DMZ) was only thirty-five miles away from my hotel, and that South Korea had discovered tunnels under the DMZ for a possible invasion by the North, I was wary but felt the risk was worth it. I needed a "proof of principle" study to demonstrate the validity of my technique, and we were successful.

I was thrilled when my patents were approved, giving me bargaining power within the industry. Subsequently, Lifecore licensed them, agreeing to pay royalties on any calcium sulfate products sold worldwide.

In 1995, Lifecore obtained FDA approval and launched Capset—a kit with a gram of medical-grade calcium sulfate to mix with a bone graft, which would then be used to fill a defect. In addition, an accelerating agent was included so that calcium sulfate would harden within minutes if the surgeon placed a "cap" protecting the bone graft, providing an effective barrier for guided tissue regeneration similar to Gore-Tex.

With Lifecore Biomedical's help, investigation of the benefits of calcium sulfate began appearing at major university research centers. In addition, Lifecore was very interested in Edgemark's customer list and purchased it from Mark, providing him royalties on U.S. sales for three years.

Italian fathers, whether due to genetics or culture, want to help their children succeed, and though I was too busy with my career to give my sons the time they deserved—something I'd do if I could live my life over—Mark's success was a partial fulfillment of that obligation.

* * *

One of my favorite songs is "Don't Cry for Me Argentina" from the musical *Evita*. Margaret and I had seen both the theatrical performance and the film, after which I'd hummed that tune for weeks. In 1947, Eva Perón, the wife of the Argentine President, had her "Rainbow Tour" of Europe, meeting with a number of dignitaries and heads of state, including Francisco Franco and Pope Pius XII. I only mention this here because, in March of 1996, supported by Lifecore Biomedical, I set out with Margaret on what my ballooning ego regarded as my own miniature version of that tour, with stops in Madrid and Rome as the highlights.

Sitting beside Margaret as the plane descended into Italy, I saw golden fields edged by green trees and blue rivers. We landed at Leonardo da Vinci International Airport, twenty-five miles from the center of Rome, where I prepared for my lecture at the *Congresso Nazionale Del Collegio Dei Docenti di Odontoiatria*—the National Congress of the College of Teachers of Dentistry.

If Dad had been alive, he'd have been proud—his own son addressing a congress of distinguished dental surgeons in the capital of the country he so loved. But that wasn't enough for me. Since Lifecore was paying my expenses, plus a fifteen hundred dollar honorarium, I'd convinced Margaret to travel with me, after the meeting, to the Villa d'Este on the shore of Lake Como. *Travel and Leisure* magazine recently cited the Villa as the most luxurious hotel in the world. My speaker's fee would cover much of the cost of a two-night stay.

The opulent Villa exuded Old World charm—from beautiful gardens and waterfalls to impeccable decor and hospitality. Its fountains, reminiscent of those at Caesars Palace, let me escape from all that plagued me internally, while I mingled with the world's nouveau riche. I could now thumb my nose at the American Academy of Restorative Dentistry, which couldn't see any humor in a guy with his fly open, Armani suit or not. As Dad would have said, "Give 'em the evil eye—the *occhio malocchio!*"

At this very hotel, in 1925, Alfred Hitchcock had filmed honeymoon scenes of his first feature film, *The Pleasure Garden*. Later, Elizabeth Taylor began her romance here with Conrad Hilton. As we entered the lobby, I marveled at the crystal chandeliers suspended from the intricate domed ceiling. Dad would have appreciated the latter, with its massive marble columns.

Two gentlemen greeted us as we stopped at the concierge desk—a Carrera marble structure in front of a staircase of polished stone. They were dressed identically in gray Harris Tweed blazers, navy-blue V-neck cashmere sweaters, white shirts, and blue-and-gray-striped silk ties. Their lapel pins displayed the crossed gold keys of the *Les Clefs d'Or*, a prestigious society of concierges who gain their "keys" through rigorous written and oral exams. From that moment on, I felt deservedly and appropriately pampered.

Forty-eight hours later, when the two concierges said, "Arrivederci," I felt like we'd glimpsed heaven on earth. Margaret enjoyed herself, but was less effusive than I, and happy to be heading home.

Where, all too soon, the realities of life resumed with a new intensity.

* * *

I remember the date well—April 22, 1996. Mom was a relatively healthy eighty-one-year-old. For the past four years, with our financial assistance, she'd lived in Wesley Palms, a retirement home in nearby Pacific Beach, a major improvement over her mobile home park in Escondido. She had a separate one-bedroom patio home, with more than enough space for her beloved statue of the Virgin Mary. It was a short walk to the five-story main building and dinner with friends.

Two weeks earlier, on Easter Sunday, she'd joined Margaret and me, along with our three sons, for our traditional holiday meal of lamb, manicotti crepes, spinach-and-artichoke casserole, and rainbow ice cream cake. Having attended Easter Mass at All Hallows, Mom was dressed for the joyous holiday in a matching skirt and jacket in a floral pattern, over a honey-colored blouse. A gold necklace with a large heart hung from her neck. She'd had her hair colored a strawberry blonde and styled in a wavy bob. Only her skin revealed her age. "How do you stay busy at Wesley Palms?" I asked. "You seem quite content."

Mom laughed. "Helping the old folks. Some are in their 90s, and two are a hundred."

We were all pleased to see Mom so happy. Besides a minor cough, she seemed quite healthy, albeit somewhat fatigued.

Then, several weeks later, Mom's physician, Dr. Ben Goldstein, a highly regarded pulmonologist, called me at my office. I'd consulted with him on several of my own patients and was well aware of his knowledge and compassion.

"Your mother's tests are in, John, and I'm sorry to say—she has stage 4 lung cancer." I was shocked as Mom had never smoked.

"What—what will the treatment involve?"

"Radiation and chemo would be horrific and wouldn't do much good. I'd bring her home for palliative care. The odds aren't good—less than a 10 percent five-year survival rate."

Within a few weeks, Mom had moved in with us. Our son Paul gave up his first-floor room and moved to the second-floor guest suite. We gave Mom his bed, from which she could look out a window at her statue of the Virgin Mary. "At least she has her faith," Margaret said. "She loves Jesus so much, says her daily rosary, and prays every morning and evening."

I was pleased that Mom and Margaret had this to share, although I dreaded the thought of watching my mother deteriorate. I couldn't bear to see her in pain, having difficulty breathing—or worse—coughing up blood. Although my faith remained shallow, I prayed for Mom's comfort.

Occasionally, I attended the Church of Today while Mom was with us. One Sunday, after early Mass at All Hallows, I convinced Margaret to attend the eleven o'clock service with me. Reverend Wendy Purcell had invited Mark Victor Hansen, co-author of the bestselling *Chicken Soup for the Soul*, for a forty-five-minute talk. Hansen was inspiring—Margaret and I laughed and cried throughout—and drew a standing ovation. Walking to the car, I asked Margaret what she thought. "I feel I've been to a great motivational lecture," she said. "But not to church."

"It's certainly different from All Hallows."

What I admired most about All Hallows was the sense of communion—not the wafer, understood by devout Catholics to be the body and blood of Christ—but the camaraderie afterward, over coffee and donut holes. At Margaret's urging, I'd agreed to join her for a series of weekly church meetings offered during Lent. They called them "Small Groups Bible Study." As a kid, I'd never read the Bible directly, but had heard the same passages during Mass, repeated every three years in the liturgical cycle. Bible study provided a chance to read select verses, understand them with a study guide, and meet with parishioners for discussion in someone's home. There were ten to a group, and in that setting, I pretended to be holier than I was for Margaret's sake.

One topic we discussed was the soul—how to ensure its transition to Heaven. At such times, enraptured by my earthly successes, I felt like I was listening to the distant chatter of the devoted faithful. I felt present, yet simultaneously separate.

Historically, I understood that the soul isn't regarded as part of the body. Instead, it's been defined as the sum of our mental abilities, character, and personality. But that idea seemed to oversimplify such a complex concept. *What's the meaning of life?* That, to me—first and foremost—was the most significant quandary.

I'd read Gary Zukav's *The Seat of the Soul*, a 1989 *New York Times* bestseller, in which he discusses "authentic power." The five senses limit our awareness, Zukav believes, but the universe, if we're open to it, allows us to grow spiritually into a "Universal Human," humanity's ultimate potential. The book was a bestseller due to Oprah Winfrey, who'd invited Zukav to her show more than thirty times.

Zukav believes the soul is immortal and knows what we should do. But we can't align it with our will if we rely on our limited perceptions. As a result, we lose control and succumb to arrogance or addictions. A sense of not belonging, a feeling of inadequacy, or a fear of the unknown can overcome our will. Addiction to substances, actions, people, or possessions becomes a substitute for troubling issues. For me, personally, the greatest issue was the fear of a meaningless death. Was my drive to win praise, accumulate wealth, and succeed beyond expectation the result of this fear? Or was it to fulfill the dream of my Sicilian father, who'd sent me to the finest universities to have his son be called "doctor" and be respected?

Zukav, I came to realize, differed from Fr. Bill. He believed you have to align your will with the truth, love, power, and beauty of the universe, then make correct decisions to overcome your shortcomings. Everything depends upon you. On the other hand, Fr. Bill believed that God, the creator of the universe, is the ultimate power. He sent His only son, in human form, to relay His message—that you must humble yourself, ask for His help, and love Him and those around you. The reward for doing so is His unlimited love, helping you overcome addictions and lead a more fulfilling life. One was a New Age message, the other the two-thousand-year-old message of Christianity. And I was caught, as ever, smack dab in the middle.

As a surgeon, I certainly understood addictions. Over a lifetime, they become like an accumulation of scar tissue in the body—the literal adhesions within us—causing abnormalities and pain, and preventing us from functioning in the way our bodies intend. Flip that idea and adhesions become a metaphor for our dependencies—on alcohol, smoking, drugs, gambling, sex, work, power, and the like. They cling tenaciously, preventing true love and inner peace.

I began to see that the New Age belief—that I have the power within to transform myself—was belief in a weak power. Fr. Bill spoke of a higher power, God, who had given him the strength to shed his alcoholism. The first step in Alcoholics Anonymous is the admission that we are powerless over alcohol and that our lives have become unmanageable. The second is the belief that a Power greater than ourselves can restore us to sanity. It's right there in the *Big Book*, as Harry, Fr. Bill's sponsor had said. Did I believe in such a power? It wasn't that I didn't. It's just that, if I was going to change my life, I needed proof. Just how much was the question.

* * *

While Mom was living with us, my lecture schedule promoting Capset was full. I worked with Mark, conducting workshops in various cities and speaking at major professional meetings. Lifecore had arranged for the First Annual Calcium Sulfate Symposium to take place in New Orleans on October 12, 1996. It was planned in advance to be on the day before the American Academy of Periodontology met for its annual meeting, since there would be thousands of periodontists in the city. The Calcium Sulfate Symposium validated my technique with its nationally recognized speakers. However, very few people realized that this innovative approach had sprung from a sudden burst of wind, generated by swinging doors blowing Urist-bone graft particles onto the clinic floor of the VA. I'd needed a filler material to add to the small amount of remaining bone particles, and there just happened to be a jar of sterile plaster of Paris on the shelf, and I'd decided to use it. If this was dumb luck, I'd been intelligent enough to realize its potential.

I returned home from New Orleans in good spirits. The small group Bible study had ended at Easter, after which Mark Jorgensen and his wife Billie, friends for almost twenty years, asked Margaret and me to join them and others for a course titled "The English Bible as Literature." Dr. Bill Creasy taught this course as a full-year offering at UCLA. However, wanting to reach more people, he'd formed Logos Bible Study in San Diego to take the message to the broader community. Although the course necessitated a five-year commitment, I understood that I could drop out at any time, and that missing classes for lectures and travel wouldn't be a problem. So I agreed to participate with Margaret. If nothing else, I would learn something about literature and history—two subjects I'd always enjoyed.

When Mom moved in with us, the Jorgensens gave us water obtained from a trip to Lourdes, the famous Catholic healing shrine at the foothills of the Pyrenees in France. The faithful had revered the site since 1862, when the Catholic Church accepted as credible the 1858 appearance of the Virgin Mary to fourteen-year-old Bernadette Soubirous. Bernadette claimed that Mary had told her to dig in a cave along the bank of the River Gave, exposing a hidden spring. Since that reported vision, thousands of pilgrims have declared they'd received unexplained physical or emotional healings after drinking and bathing in the waters of the spring. Some of these cases have been brought to the attention of the International Medical Committee of Lourdes. This group, established in 1883, consists of twenty international experts from various medical disciplines, and having different religious beliefs. Over the years, after an extensive review of medical records—including x-rays, photographs, examinations, and testimonies—seventy cases have been deemed by the Committee to be miraculous, the cure unexplainable. Lourdes—a remote town of only fifteen thousand permanent residents—averages five million visitors annually.

As Margaret reminded me, *The Song of Bernadette* had been on the *New York Times* Best Sellers List throughout 1941, before being made into a critically acclaimed film, winning four Oscars, including one for Jennifer Jones as Best Actress in a Leading Role. Mom had seen the movie, so the water had significance for her. I thought, *either many people are being deceived—even medical specialists—or something extraordinary is happening there.*

Each night before Mom went to sleep, I wet my thumb in the water and made the sign of the cross on her forehead, and it seemed to have a calming effect. Mom had been an anxious person throughout her life, and this disquiet had increased with age. When she asked why medication wasn't being given for her cancer, we explained that she was to focus on the breathing exercises first, and she seemed content to do so. Three times a day, she blew into the tube of a spirometer, raising the piston in its cylindrical chamber to a designated level. In November, we added San Diego Hospice as part of her care, but other than adding a small dose of Xanax at bedtime, nothing else was recommended. The goal was to have her pass away as peacefully as possible. Pleased that she was having no symptoms other than fatigue, we continued as directed. Mom's daily rosary and the statue of Mary comforted her.

Then, on Friday, December 6, after her breakfast and breathing exercises, Mom lapsed into a coma during her mid-morning nap. I touched her skin—it was warm—but when I shook her shoulder and shouted her name, there was no response. Her eyes were closed, her breathing almost imperceptible. She looked peaceful, as if having a pleasant dream.

An hour later, when Margaret and I looked in, Mom was still warm to the touch, lying in the same position as before. Through the picture window, the statue of the Virgin Mary could be seen in an elevated flower bed, her head tilted forward at the perfect angle for Mom's eye level. Her outstretched arms reached downward, palms toward the window. She stood on a globe, one foot on the head of a serpent. We'd placed the statue there the day Mom moved in. As Margaret said, it symbolized the image of "Our Lady of Grace," a popular portrayal of Mary.

"In 1830," she explained further, "Catherine Labouré, a Catholic nun in Paris, experienced a vision of the Virgin Mary."

"Sounds like *you*," I said, and Margaret laughed.

"This statue represents what she saw."

I didn't believe in spiritual visions, as there was no scientific evidence, but if they were a comfort for Mom and Margaret, how could I not be supportive?

Ever since my unexplained troubles with the "haunted" Mercedes, I'd been open to the idea that, if such a demonic realm could exist, might not an angelic or divine one also be possible? It seemed logical, though the existence of these ethereal realms challenged my belief in science as the ultimate determiner of reality, an uncomfortable psychological position.

When Mom remained in a coma, we called the All Hallows office to ask if Monsignor Fox, the elderly pastor, could give her Extreme Unction, the Last Rites of the Catholic Church. Anita Gholson, the parish administrator, said that Mgr. Fox was gone for the day, but she'd ask Fr. Bill Wilson. When she called back to say that Fr. Bill would arrive at 5:30, we asked her to tell him we'd like him to stay for dinner.

Since Mom was unconscious, Fr. Bill couldn't hear her confession or give her Holy Communion, but he recited the Apostles Creed, expressing, on her behalf, a belief in God. Then he recited the Lord's Prayer, dipped his finger in holy oil, and made the sign of the cross on Mom's forehead. It was similar to what I'd been doing with the water from Lourdes. As Fr. Bill massaged the oil onto her forehead, he said quietly, "Through this holy unction may the Lord pardon thee whatever sins or faults thou hast committed." Then we joined him in reciting a Hail Mary, before he concluded with a final blessing, *"In nomine Patris et Filii, et Spiritus Sancti,"* passing his hands over Mom's body in the sign of the cross.

After dinner, Father Bill looked deeply into my eyes and said, in his touching Irish brogue, "Ya know, John, I'm an ole priest, and I've given last rites to thousands, but I've not seen one as peaceful as your mum." He put his hand over mine. "The look on her face is angelic. It's unbelievable. I think the dear Lord is watchin' over her."

For the next two days, whenever I entered Mom's room, I found the corners of her mouth turned up in a smile. She hadn't moved—she was still lying on her back as if made of stone—but the warmth of her skin went through my fingers. "I love you, Mom," I whispered each time. There were no movements, only her chest's shallow, steady rise and fall. She was not in distress, and remained so until the third day of the coma, which was Sunday. She hadn't had any water since Friday, and it appeared that all bodily functions had ceased. It was just a matter of calling the mortuary when her skin turned cold.

After returning from church, as I walked briskly down the hallway toward my den, not stopping to check on Mom—I'd recently done so, I heard a firm, assertive voice call my name— "Johnny!" I froze, astonished, and made an abrupt about-face. "Mom, you're awake!" I exclaimed.

Sitting upright, she said, "Yes. I saw heaven." Her smile broadened. "It was beautiful!"

I was surprised, befuddled, ecstatic.

"There were flowers everywhere," Mom went on, "particularly roses. The colors were amazing!" She leaned back, placed her head gently on the pillow, and closed her eyes. But thirty minutes later, she called my name again. "Johnny, I'm hungry and thirsty."

This time she not only ate and drank but got out of bed and walked to the bathroom. Later, when I thought to ask her about heaven, she could remember that she'd been there but couldn't recall any details beyond the colorful flowers. I wished I had pursued it earlier.

Mom remained surprisingly lucid for several weeks, although fatigued, never coughing or complaining of pain. She persevered with her breathing exercises, and I blessed her forehead nightly with the water from Lourdes. And its calming effect continued.

Christmas morning, Mom joined us as we opened our presents by the tree. I was elated that she could share Christmas with Margaret and me, her three grandsons, and our cocker spaniel, Buffy, who sat at her feet as if she knew this would be Mom's last.

The next morning, Mom arose at eight o'clock, ate a breakfast of oatmeal and bananas, and engaged in conversation about my sister Janet and her family. Then she blew into the mouthpiece of her spirometer ten times, raised the cylinder to the proper line, yawned, and said, "I think I'll get back in bed and rest some more."

As she lay back, I adjusted her pillow and tucked her in. Before leaving, I looked out the window at the rigid smile on the white stone face of the Virgin Mary statue, winked once, and shook my head. Then I admonished myself for the foolish gesture.

An hour later, when I walked by Mom's room, she had not moved. She was still on her back, in the position she'd always deemed the most comfortable. Nothing had changed on a third pass, an hour and a half later. She had the same peaceful countenance and closed eyes, but there was a palpable stillness I hadn't sensed before. I touched her skin—it was very cold. The life force had departed. In its place, there remained a serene expression of peace, the same look of tranquility and acceptance that the wizened Fr. Bill Wilson hadn't seen in more than half a century as a Catholic priest.

Aided by her faith, Mom had been granted a peaceful death, something we all hope for, whether we acknowledge it or not.

Chapter 29   *In Vino Veritas*

My heartbeat was rapid, the ceiling obscured by darkness except for intermittent flashes from the overhead fire alarm. *What was going on?* I'd always been healthy, except for minor colds and sore throats. So why was my heart pounding? Why couldn't I sleep? I hadn't slept well all week. I was physically exhausted and couldn't turn off the adrenaline.

Suddenly, I was in my bed in Stratford, Connecticut, the voice of Basil Rathbone emanating from the transistor radio under my pillow. Rathbone had been a Shakespearean actor in London before starring with Boris Karloff and Vincent Price in the 1939 Hollywood movie *Tower of London*. Later, he became known for his readings of Edgar Allan Poe's macabre stories on late-night radio. His voice was sinister and sophisticated, ranging from high to low, stressing terminal consonants, pausing, then spewing words with increased speed, volume, and intensity. *Could a voice be Satanic?* I wondered.

An avid fan of Edgar Allan Poe, I'd read and listened to *The Tell-Tale Heart* many times, even had memorized some of the lines, and in my current state of heightened awareness, they came to me now. It was as if Rathbone was in my hotel room. I could hear his diabolical voice: "It was the beating of the old man's heart . . . The sound grew louder . . . The heart was beating so loudly that I was sure someone must hear."

But it was my own heart beating wildly. The night terror I'd experienced forty years earlier was being replicated and markedly enhanced at a time when Margaret, my love and comforter, was a thousand miles away. I'd always believed that, by sheer willpower, I could control my health with positive thinking, aerobic exercise, and a low-fat diet. As Poe's speaker insisted, "I have full control of my mind." Such was the height of my egotism. I believed I'd accumulated wealth, possessions, titles, awards, a devoted wife, and three fine sons—through my own talents and determination. I thought anyone with knowledge, wisdom, fortitude, perseverance, and understanding could have control over his own life. I knew I possessed those traits. But Margaret had reminded me that, to devout Catholics, these are gifts and virtues of the Holy Spirit. I'd neglected the most important ones—humility, piety, temperance, prudence, and fear of the Lord. "Fear of the Lord," she explained, "means having a profound respect for Him."

My hammering heart and increased anxiety were not improving. Was I having a heart attack? Ever since "Nurse Ratched" had made me sleep in a urine-soaked bed at the age of seven, I dreaded spending another night in a hospital. But I didn't want to die, either. I wanted to continue traveling to exotic places, enjoy our home overlooking the Pacific, and drive a new Mercedes-Benz every few years. I'd been building my Tower of Babel, like the Babylonians of old, who'd been captivated by their desire to become special people. Now I wondered if this was the beginning of my fall.

We gain insight as we age. A burst of reality illuminates a dark sky. As Friedrich Nietzsche wrote in *Twilight of the Idols*, "That which does not kill us makes us stronger." If I survived this heart-related incident, what might I learn? It had taken me years to realize that I might not be in control.

I angled my wristwatch on the nightstand to watch its luminous second hand make its rounds. My pulse was racing. Turning my palm upward, I pressed my wrist with my other hand's index and middle fingers and began to count. As a regular jogger, I had a resting heart rate of fifty-two beats. I wasn't prepared for the number as the secondhand completed its circle—one hundred thirty-five!

I panicked, as when trapped in Colorado's Marble Canyon. But I'd understood, then, the reason for my anxiety. On this early Sunday morning, March 16, 1997, I was alone in a king-size bed on the sixth floor of the Denver Marriott. Margaret had flown home to San Diego on Friday to be with our sons. I was scheduled to lecture all day Saturday to the Denver Columbine Study Group and return to California on Sunday.

As I waited for my pulse to slow, I relived the past week. Enamored by his success with my calcium sulfate technique, a periodontist friend from Colorado Springs had tempted me to accept a winter speaking engagement in Denver, including five nights for Margaret and me at his condo at the Breckenridge Ski Resort. Landing in Denver, I'd driven a rental car toward Eisenhower Tunnel, seventy miles west, to an elevation of eleven thousand feet. But as we approached, I could sense a burgeoning uneasiness. Ever since my Grand Canyon experience, I'd dreaded tunnels. This one was nearly two miles long—two lanes of cars doing sixty miles per hour, albeit in the same direction. A terrible accident occurred in a five hundred-foot-long tunnel west of Palermo, Sicily, a year earlier. A tanker carrying liquid petroleum exploded, killing five people and leaving thirty with severe burns. The Eisenhower Tunnel was fifteen times longer!

I was all too familiar with the stress of performing surgeries, not to mention managing a fifty-person business, and lecturing in distant cities, while meeting my obligations as husband and father. Surgery alone, though some practitioners might deny it, is demanding. We can be perfectionists, while our patients frequently present with unknown variables—extra bleeding from heavy aspirin intake, or heightened stress levels of their own, which makes sedation difficult. Some present with unusual anatomy, others with unrealistic expectations, adding to my stress.

Now, at the Marriott, that tension seemed minimal compared to the anxiety coursing through my body in the months since Mom died. I was familiar with the classic stages of grief in Elizabeth Kubler-Ross's book *On Death and Dying*. I'd been in the first stage, denying Mom's death was affecting me, filling her void with work, more work, travel, and speaking engagements. Dad had told me that my birth had been difficult for Mom. I'd been a large baby, nearly aborted to save her life. According to Kubler-Ross, depression precedes acceptance. My life had been so filled with activity that I hadn't noticed subtle changes in my sleep patterns and moods. So Breckenridge promised a needed escape. Margaret and I would share a marvelous week of skiing.

The idyllic village had been founded during Colorado's Gold Rush. Its Main Street was the state's largest historic district, evoking the days when hopeful miners left the Great Plains for altitudes as high as their expectations for instant wealth, whereas I'd proudly accumulated my own wealth over time. Each day of skiing ended with a final trip down Four O'clock Run—three-and-a-half miles long— followed by a mellow glide to the car. Then came a hot shower at the Conner's condo and dinner at the Briar Rose Chophouse and Saloon. One night I'd ordered the filet mignon with truffle butter and a bottle of 1994 Grgich Hills Cabernet Sauvignon. *What on earth, I asked myself, could be better than this?*

I now realized my current condition at the Marriott began with being at Breckinridge's altitude—ninety-six hundred feet. I was accustomed to sleeping at a meager two hundred feet above sea level in San Diego. The Rocky Mountain elevation caused insomnia, and my last three nights had been fretful. Margaret had warned me that three-quarters of a bottle of wine each evening was part of the problem, but my taste for great wine—I was a glutton for wine—had been stronger than her pleas for my well-being. "Besides," I'd said, "if you drank your share, it wouldn't be an issue."

"So now it's my fault!"

It was obvious that our relationship was suffering. I rationalized that Margaret loved Mom and simply felt her loss, which explained her explosiveness. But I was ignoring my own contributions—my ego, busyness, drinking, and refusal to share my feelings. The need to share feelings was one of the key concepts at our Marriage Encounter Weekend. But that had been twenty years ago. *Men,* I liked to think, *prefer to keep their feelings private.*

"We're on vacation," I explained. "I'd never do this at home."

Margaret had frowned and said nothing.

After five days at Breckenridge, I'd driven Margaret to the airport and then straight to the Marriott, hoping for a good night's sleep before my all-day Saturday lecture. But again, my night was restless, even at a reduced elevation of fifty-two hundred feet. Several cups of strong black coffee at breakfast increased my adrenaline, making me alert and energetic, so standing and delivering my morning and afternoon lectures was not a problem. The problem came when I tried to unwind to get some sleep before my early-morning flight to San Diego. The anxiety in my life had been increased by daily caffeine, along with excessive alcohol on weekends. I wondered if my drinking had become detrimental, as it had been for Dad.

As I lay awake at the Marriott, an hour passed timelessly, my thoughts careening as wildly as my heartbeat. My mouth was dry, chest tight, arms and hands tingling— possible signs of a heart attack. I needed to get to a hospital.

Phoning the desk, I asked the clerk to call a taxi. He said the Denver Medical Center was not far away. I hated the thought of being a patient but had no choice. My childhood experience was only part of the issue. The other was that I didn't want to yield control. I felt I was the master of my own destiny. I often bragged to friends that I could meditate to slow my pulse and reduce my blood pressure. But it wasn't working now. Not once did I think of prayer.

The cab pulled out and headed for the hospital. "Faster," I said to the driver.

Minutes later, at the emergency department entrance, the cab stopped at the curb, and an attendant assisted me inside. After a brief check-in, they rushed me to a treatment space bounded by a wall and three curtained partitions. They placed me on a gurney— its back propped at an angle. Various monitors, IV poles, mobile cabinets, and rolling stools filled the small space. It was like being in my own office, except that I was the patient—an abhorrent thought.

Entering abruptly, an ER nurse drew blood, administered an EKG, recorded my vital signs, and rolled me to the nearby radiology department for a chest x-ray. "Your BP's two hundred twenty over one hundred twenty," she said. "You're sure you're not having any chest pain?"

"Just a bit of tightness," I said. She looked concerned.

Awaiting the results of the lab tests and x-ray, I tried to relax. Before long, Dr. Reed Andrews, a kind man about my age, drew the curtains, walked in with my chart, and smiled. "You're not having a heart attack, Dr. Sottosanti," he said. "You're having a panic attack."

I was relieved, but only slightly. "What's a panic attack?"

"They're very common for about 3 percent of the population." He paused. "What's going on in your life?"

I told him about my mother's death, the stress at work, the coffee, the alcohol, and the sleepless nights of the past week.

"Do you carry medication when you travel? For anxiety and insomnia?"

I didn't, but he said I should. He handed me a light blue oval tablet and a cup of water. "You'll feel better in less than an hour. I'm giving you one milligram of Xanax. It should settle you and let you sleep. And I'm giving you a prescription for tablets of a lesser dose—enough for a few days. After that, you should see a physician in San Diego for a follow-up."

After being released, I returned to the hotel, called the airline, changed my flight to Sunday evening, and slept soundly. The flight home was uneventful. But I had no time to recuperate back in San Diego. My schedule had been set well in advance.

* * *

Four days after returning from Denver, I delivered the Annual Peter Fedi Periodontics Lecture at the Midwest Dental Conference in Kansas City, a marathon six-hour talk at a major dental meeting. Fedi had been a revered periodontist at the University of Missouri-Kansas City. The lectures had begun in 1991, with a committee choosing candidates from around the country. Proud of the honor, I felt compelled to work late each night, preparing my lecture at the expense of my family. I felt Margaret's silence to be supportive, yet could sense her resentment.

The night before that lecture, a Xanax tablet let me sleep well, and strong coffee allayed my residual grogginess in the morning. It was a successful trip, and I returned the following Friday excited about that evening's dinner plans. Several weeks earlier, without telling Margaret, I'd made a reservation at George's at the Cove restaurant for a wine-tasting dinner sponsored by Grgich Hills winery. I hoped the surprise would assuage her resentment.

Born in Yugoslavia, Miljenko "Mike" Grgich had received international recognition at the famous 1976 "Paris Tasting." There'd been a blind tasting of white Burgundies from France and a few Chardonnays from Napa Valley. After sniffing, tasting, and appraising a series of wines, the French judges had been astonished when the scores were tallied, and the title of "the finest white wine in the world" went to the Chateau Montelena Chardonnay, Mike Grgich, winemaker. A year later, on the Fourth of July, 1977, Mike, and his sister, Mary Lee Strebl, of the Hills Bros. coffee family, began Grgich Hills Winery.

Arriving at George's, Margaret and I descended the steps to our table and learned that Mike himself—now famous as the man who'd introduced the world to California wines—would host the evening, describing the wine paired with each course. From his first words, spoken with a heavy Yugoslav accent, it was easy to see that this seventy-three-year-old man—in a dark blue blazer, light blue shirt, paisley tie, and black beret—was a charmer.

"My father taught me how to develop feelings for wine," he began. "He told me that wine can be an art, and art comes from your heart." He paused and grinned, exposing a mouthful of crowded, wine-stained teeth that no one but a dentist would have noticed.

I considered myself a connoisseur of wine. When we moved to California, I'd stopped drinking hard liquor and beer, and turned to wine. I liked the taste and appreciated the fact that, if you drank too much, you were an "aficionado," not an "alcoholic"—a term both Fr. Bill Wilson and I loathed. I didn't consider my weekend imbibing a problem.

The meal was lavish. We started with grilled octopus with mustard vinaigrette, interspersed with charred eggplant, fennel, roasted garlic, and squid-ink potatoes—all served with a generous glass of 1996 Grgich Hills Estate Grown Dry Fumé Blanc. The straw-colored wine had an aroma of apples, papaya, and pineapple. I savored every sip and drained the glass, holding it vertically to get the last drop. Following the salad, a small portion of local yellowtail fish was served with a wine that was familiar to me—1995 Estate Grown Chardonnay, fermented in French oak. I drank it slowly, savoring the peach, honeysuckle, and vanilla. Bruce Johnson and I often ordered it during our business retreats at Palm Springs.

The final course was a fillet of beef, with creamed corn, grilled asparagus, roasted peppers, and curried lamb jus, accompanied by my favorite Grgich Hills wine—1994 Cabernet Sauvignon Napa Valley. This rich wine bore a sandalwood scent, plummy fruit flavors, and a hint of chocolate, tannins, and minerals. The delight I take in recalling such meals shows how far gone I was into my own world. I assumed Margaret was lost in there with me. But that wasn't the case. Instead, I was the one addicted to wine and a glutton for elegant food.

Before each course, Mike Grgich described the wine, then roamed the tables, engaging in spirited conversations. He spent twice the amount of time at our table than any other. Repeatedly, however, he ignored me, preferring to converse with Margaret. This caused flashbacks to Robert Goulet staring past me in Las Vegas, and Lawrence Welk doing the same at the San Diego airport, ignoring my stupid question to ask Margaret if she could sing, for he wanted her on his TV show.

I looked closely at Margaret now. How could she not be enjoying this sumptuous evening and the personal attention of Mike Grgich? Aging gracefully, she'd retained a movie-star appearance—high cheekbones, blue eyes, broad smile. *She's so beautiful,* I was thinking, as she chatted with Mike. *So how could she be so ornery at times?* I ignored my part in her behavior.

Our marriage had unresolved issues. I'd never apologized for my two-week pleasure trip to Japan after Mark was born. I'd disregarded Margaret's religious views on birth control, not really understanding them, feeling that the rhythm method removed the spontaneity from our sex life. I'd spent money extravagantly, particularly on remodeling the house, while she watched the budget and the house finances, no doubt saving us from bankruptcy. Yet I'd never thought to compliment her on this. I figured all marriages had problems. Why should ours be any different? Still, faced with taking the sexy Candace Farrell to a motel or bringing her home to meet Margaret, I'd made the correct decision. I loved Margaret and wanted her to ignore my faults. But it would be years before we could resolve such issues. Until then, we tolerated them. Mike Grgich was flirting with my wife, but I ignored them as I sipped my wine—a late harvest vintage that went well with a warm chocolate tart topped with ice cream and salted caramel sauce.

"I'll drive," Margaret said as we left. And she drove us home in silence.

Chapter 30   Mountaintop Transformation

AT BREAKFAST, WHEN MARGARET called me "John" instead of "Honey," I knew I was in for it.

"Why do you drink so much? You know what happened to Dad. He couldn't give it up, and it ruined his life."

I was adamant. "As I said in Colorado, if you'd just drink your share—"

"I won't be blamed for your drinking, John!"

At that moment, Jerry Jampolsky's voice echoed in my head: *Would you rather be happy, or would you rather be right?* I changed the subject, but coolness followed as I finished my omelet, coffee, and toast—yet another breakfast prepared for me by Margaret. Then I left my dishes on the table and retreated to the marble-topped desk in my study. We hadn't concluded our discussion of what had happened at George's. I'd long since forgotten about spousal communication. What good would it do? I wasn't going to apologize. I was too stubborn.

Fortunately, attending Dr. Bill Creasy's Bible study with Margaret began to help our relationship. As Bill cited books from the Old and New Testaments, I was surprised by how much of the New had been prophesied by the Old. His vast knowledge and charismatic lecture style brought Abraham, Isaac, Jacob, Moses, the Apostles, and Jesus to life, making them real to me. Still, there were questions I had to resolve. For example, how to reconcile the Bible with Darwin.

I learned of Christ's teachings on love, forgiveness, and compassion through Dr. Creasy's Bible readings. Subsequently, my hard exterior, encrusted with layers of pride and other sins, softened over time. At this point in my life, although I knew of the Seven Deadly Sins, I'd never understood the meaning of "sloth." Then I encountered this Christian definition: "Sloth is a desire for doing things your way instead of following the will of God." This, in my case, was all too true.

But the process was painstakingly slow if I was being converted to a true believer in Christianity. I wasn't ready to surrender my agenda to anyone, even if it was possible that this someone had created heaven and earth. I paid him lip service, unthinkingly reciting "The Apostles' Creed" at every Mass: "I believe in God, the Father almighty, Creator of heaven and earth, and in Jesus Christ, his only Son . . ."

I firmly believed in the popular Zen notion: "When the student is ready, the teacher will appear." And maybe that is why, in February of that year, when our good friend, Mark Jorgensen, asked me to join him in April for a weekend retreat called a *Cursillo*, I agreed to go. He said the men would attend for the first weekend, their wives for the second. His wife, Billie, would be asking Margaret, and the Jorgensens would be our sponsors. "The goal of the weekend," Mark said, "is a closer relationship with Christ."

To be truthful, I wasn't thrilled to give up three days of my life for a spiritual endeavor, but Margaret was eager, and it might further our relationship beyond Bible study.

Sixty miles east of La Jolla, the Whispering Winds Catholic Camp and Retreat Center is nestled in the Cuyamaca Mountains at forty-six hundred feet. Driving up in Mark's car after an early dinner, I felt in my pocket for my pillbox of Xanax. After my heart-pounding experience in Colorado, I no longer believed I fully controlled my life, and the thought of sleeping at a higher elevation, in a room full of twin bunks filled with snoring men, disconcerted me.

Getting out of the car, I was met with the aroma of pine, oak, willow, and manzanita. The camp had constructed separate dorms for men and women through generous donations. The large meeting room, with an adjoining kitchen, could accommodate a hundred people. Outside was a stone fire pit and rows of benches. A grotto in the woods held a statue of the Virgin Mary.

Mike Daniels, the tall, handsome rector and leader of the retreat, welcomed me. "We're at your service, John, to provide you with a meaningful weekend. Forty men have donated every Friday night for several months to make this weekend special for you and your fellow *cursillistas*. These weekends began in Spain about fifty years ago. They're a proven method to convert a lukewarm Catholic into a fervent one."

Shaking his hand, I heard my inner voice saying, *I wish you luck.*

It was a highly-structured weekend. We began with the Stations of the Cross, walking with candles and stopping at individual pines to read from printed prayer sheets. Each tree trunk held a large scene from the final three days of Christ's life on earth, from the First Station—"Pilate condemns Jesus to death"—to the Fourteenth Station, "Jesus is placed in the tomb." The most difficult one for me was the Eleventh, depicting a wooden cross on the ground and a muscular Roman soldier holding Christ's arm. A red tunic covered his armor, and a fan of red-dyed horse-hairs adorned his galea helmet. An equally powerful man wielded a small sledgehammer, poised above a nail at the juncture of Christ's palm and wrist, from which blood flowed profusely. The mouth of the bearded Christ was opened wide in an apparent scream. I found it challenging to look at this scene. *I thought that either this actually happened, or it's all a gruesome, massive deception that has endured for two millennia.*

After breakfast in the morning, each of us stood, gave our name, and told where we lived. Our hosts, men from the San Diego community—without pay or other rewards—had volunteered to cook our food, wash our dishes, and clean our bathrooms. They stood and cheered after each intro-duction. One well-groomed, intelligent-looking man smiled and said, "Hi. I'm Ronald McDonald from Escondido." We all laughed. Was this a stunt? Then he grinned and sat down.

Next, we split into groups, seven per table, to hear several *rollos*, or talks, by speakers relating events that demonstrated how the Lord had changed their lives. One man, a successful San Diego businessman, told how drugs had ruined his life. He'd been contemplating suicide when he found the *Cursillo* movement. Subsequently, he overcame his addiction and embraced sobriety. Such witnessing made me uneasy. *Why would any-one make himself so vulnerable by sharing such a story with total strangers?* It reminded me of Father Bill Wilson, admitting his alcoholism during Mass. *Might love for others be present in their hearts?*

On Sunday morning, Rector Mike informed us that we were to spend an hour outside, but first, we had to stop at a table by the door for a large paper bag with our name on it. Sitting in the shade of an oak tree, I opened mine to find small religious gifts—rosary beads, prayer cards, and a small metal crucifix. But what really impressed me were the many handwritten notes from people all over San Diego County, written specifically to me. "Dear John," one said, "we don't know each other, but I was given your name. The entire week-end I'll be praying that your *Cursillo* will be meaningful, long-lasting, and bring you a sense of peace as you grow closer to the Lord."

There was that word again, "peace." I'd been looking for peace my en-tire adult life.

After filing through the lunch buffet line, I chose a seat at a table in the crowded room opposite Ronald McDonald from Escondido. Introducing myself, I mentioned that in June, I'd be vacationing with my family in Italy.

"Going to Medjugorje?" he asked.

My devout Catholic friends had told me about Medjugorje in Bosnia and Herzegovina. Each year a million pilgrims visit the site where, since 1981, purported apparitions of the Virgin Mary had recurred to six children. I didn't know exactly what an apparition was, but apparitions of the Virgin Mary had made Lourdes famous, and the Jorgensens had given me holy water from Lourdes, with which I'd blessed Mom. Intrigued, I'd looked up a definition: "An apparition is an image of a person seen by one or more individuals. It is often ephemeral, appearing and disappearing, with ghost-like attributes." I didn't know if I could believe in apparitions.

"Why?" I replied to Ronald McDonald. "What does Medjugorje have to do with Italy?"

"It's a short flight from Rome to Split in Croatia. Then two hours by bus to Medjugorje. My wife and I never go to Italy without visiting."

Ronald McDonald then explained that, several years earlier, he'd gone to Medjugorje at his wife's request, and it had been the most incredible trip of his life. "At Mass at St. James, during the consecration of the Host, as the priest held high the wafer, the most amazing thing happened." Suddenly this soft-spoken man waxed effusive. "A plain wall above and behind the altar became transformed, as if a projector was beaming a movie in vivid color. I saw Christ hanging from a cross, and blood was dripping from His crown of thorns, the wounds of His scourging, the nails on His wrists, and the wound in His side. I heard him cry out in agony, 'Father, forgive them, for they know not what they do.' Then it faded and disappeared."

This quiet man, who'd had no qualms about eliciting laughter as "Ronald McDonald from Escondido," looked deeply into my eyes and began to weep profusely, his tears dripping onto his blue shirt and the table by his plate. These were genuine tears—from the hazel eyes of a humble man. When they ceased, I felt uncomfortable, either from my concern for him or my shame as an unbeliever. It was a startling moment. A quarter of a century later, I can close my eyes and see it all again—it was that dramatic.

At dinner, a trio consisting of a bass fiddle, guitar, and piano entertained us with traditional *Cursillo* songs. During a break, Woody, the tall, portly bass player, happened to walk by my table when I said, "I can't take notes. I've misplaced my reading glasses."

"Take mine," Woody said. "I don't really need them," and before I could refuse, he reached into his shirt pocket, put them on the table, and vanished. Such was the love and compassion evident on that mountaintop, expressed by men who, in the city below, were as aggressive, competitive, and successful as I was.

Early Sunday morning, singing female voices awakened us. They belonged to our wives, who'd driven up the mountain with their sponsors.

Then Margaret attended an outdoor Mass with me, during which, holding hands, we listened to testimonials from the new *cursillistas* as to what the weekend had meant to each of us. I wasn't as eloquent as the rest, but managed to mutter something about my visceral reaction to the Eleventh Station of the Cross. Leaving the mountain and the men who'd contributed to such a spiritual experience was difficult.

* * *

On Monday morning, I returned to my stressful world. When Mark Jorgensen arrived the following Sunday at 6 a.m. to drive to Whispering Winds so I could serenade Margaret, I told him I'd been experiencing such severe stomach pains that I was heading to the hospital. Disappointed, but concerned, Mark left wondering what was happening to me.

The diagnosis, this time, was severe gastritis—inflammation of the lining of the stomach. After several hours in the Scripps Memorial emergency room, they gave me Maalox and an antacid prescription. And once again, I was urged to reduce the stress in my life. I agonized over missing Margaret's last day on the mountain and hearing her explain what the weekend had meant for her. Even though our relationship had been suffering, I loved her and admired her faith, which provided a stable framework for her role as a wife and mother.

Fortunately, by mid-morning, I'd sufficiently recovered to attend Mass at All Hallows. Ironically, one of the readings that morning, from the "Book of Proverbs," Chapter thirty-one, pertained to wives. This book from the Old Testament, written *circa* 970 to 931 BC, had been attributed to the wise King Solomon. The reading began with the tenth verse: "A good wife who can find? She is far more precious than jewels." I will paraphrase the remainder of the reading. Her husband can trust her. She brings good things into his life. She provides for her family. She manages the household and adds respect to her husband's image in the community. One verse, near the end, had special meaning: "Charm is deceitful, and beauty is vain, but a woman who fears the Lord is to be praised."

I left Mass knowing that I was a fortunate man.

Margaret had demonstrated her household management skills during the remodeling of our ocean-view house on Calle Chiquita. We hadn't trusted our general contractor because of the "change orders," exorbitant extra costs that came when he encountered something unexpected. Because of my workload and professional travels, Margaret had to make immediate decisions. She'd been raised in an Air Force family of six children, and with her dad away so much, her mom had been very frugal, a trait Margaret had inherited. This remodeling added significant stress to her life. When she selected a painting contractor, I considered him second-rate and named another we should hire. "But that guy's so charming and good-looking," she said. "I won't put myself in that situation. We're not hiring him!"

Her honesty startled me, and I thought of Candace Farrell. I wasn't as strong as Margaret, and with Candace, I'd come precariously close to ruining my life, if not condemning myself to eternal damnation, according to that famous passage from the "Book of Matthew": *If your right eye causes you to sin, pluck it out and throw it away; it is better that you lose one of your members than that your whole body be thrown into hell.* That's serious business, even to a doubting Thomas. Most people know the line from The Lord's Prayer: "lead us not into temptation." Matthew takes the idea further. And if it was true two thousand years ago that we should avoid temptation, it remains even more so today. Margaret knew enough to recognize situations that could lead her astray.

* * *

After lecturing to the Wisconsin Society of Periodontists in April and the Oregon Society of Periodontists in May, I took Margaret, and our sons Wayne and Paul, to Italy for a week, renting an apartment in a sixteenth-century stone farmhouse with terracotta floors and wood-beamed ceilings. Our rental looked out on a vineyard and sunflower field in the commune of Greve in Chianti, situated partway between Florence and Siena. Florence boasted Michelangelo's *David* and Botticelli's *Birth of Venus*, but I preferred the small and romantic Siena because the beautiful medieval buildings were far less crowded.

After climbing the five hundred steps of Siena's Torre del Mangia and exploring the Piazza del Campo—one of the great medieval squares in Europe, famous for the Palio horse race around its perimeter—Margaret requested we visit the shrine of the House of Saint Catherine of Siena. I had no interest in this famous Catholic saint but agreed to go. Now a museum, the house has several chapels and a large kitchen with a fireplace into which Saint Catherine—then Caterina Benincasa— reportedly fell during one of her ecstatic trances, only to emerge unharmed by the blazing fire. She slept on a hard floor with a stone as a pillow. In her severe asceticism, she lived for years with only the Holy Eucharist for sustenance. The stories of her mysticism intrigued me, although I didn't consider them particularly plausible.

Many believe that Saint Catherine had been gifted spiritual visions, the ability to heal, and levitation because of her extreme piety. I didn't believe in her levitation—a gravity-defying rising of the human body off the ground—because the legend had come from the written word of her confessor, the Dominican priest Raymond of Capua, who'd never witnessed the actual event. He wrote, instead, that Catherine's mother had seen her daughter going up and down a staircase so rapidly that her feet no longer touched the steps. This story reminded me of Dad, and how Italians love to embellish their stories. However, what impressed me was that, with no formal education, Catherine had become a counselor to many heads of the most prominent Italian city-states, helping return the Papacy to Rome after it had strayed to Avignon, France. Her many writings are so profound that she was named a Doctor of the Catholic Church. Only four women in history have received that honor.

After visiting all the major tourist sites in Florence and Siena, on the advice of our guidebook, *Fodor's '97 Italy*, we motored into the Tuscan countryside. Our goal was the Abbey of San Galgano, twenty-five miles southwest of Siena, built in honor of Galgano Guidotti, who'd been declared a saint four years after his death in 1181. Here I expected to spend a short time among the ruins of the thirteenth-century Gothic monastery, which had been sacked by *condottieri*, roving mercenaries, who'd driven the monks away. And yet we lingered. The ruins—their beauty, grandeur, size, and history—amazed me. In this obscure rural valley stood roofless cathedral walls, a massive, empty rose window, and multiple columns and capital stones. Standing in the middle of the church, on well-trodden grass, amid ancient walls and arches crafted by medieval stone masons, I gazed into the blue sky and white clouds and found myself wondering: *Is Heaven truly up there, in the far reaches of space, in an expanding, never-ending universe? Was this universe an accident, as some of my scientific friends claimed, or the work of an infinitely intelligent, omnipotent, transcendent designer unknown to finite minds?*

I had no idea what the others were thinking. However, I knew that if this profound question still bothered me at dinner, several glasses of a great Super Tuscan wine, like a Tignanello or Sassicaia, would mellow my troubled thoughts before joining Margaret in the warm bed back in Greve.

The entrance fee to the Abbey included a hilltop visit to the Hermitage of Montesiepi, famous for the legend of San Galgano and his fabled sword. A twelfth-century knight, Galgano Guidotti, born and raised in the nearby county of Chiusdino, had lived a ruthless and hedonistic life until the Archangel Michael, sword in hand, appeared to him in two visions, causing him to renounce the material world for the spiritual. On

Christmas day, 1180, after Galgano smashed his sword against a large rock on the hilltop—a symbolic gesture of repudiation—that boulder is said to have swallowed the blade to the hilt.

The circular chapel, made of concentric, alternate layers of white stone and terracotta, holds a boulder protected by Plexiglas, from which protrudes a sword's black metallic guard, grip, and pommel. Nearby are the mummified hands of a thief who, according to legend, tried to remove the blade from the stone but was immediately attacked and devoured by wolves. Apparently, those hands had prevented any future thievery. Struck by the similarity of the legend to that of England's King Arthur, I learned that some scholars believe that this part of Arthur's story was borrowed from San Galgano folklore. Did I believe the San Galgano legend? Not really. Reminded once again of my father's stories, I surmised that a clever twelfth-century Italian had used a file to create a groove deep enough to secure the handle in the stone. But strong glues weren't available in Europe until the sixteenth century. Strange.

Four years after our 1997 visit, the research of Professor Luigi Garlaschelli, of the University of Pavia, validated many aspects of the legend. Examining metal filings from the handle, he determined that both the design and metal were consistent with the timeframe of the legend. Using a radar scanner, his team determined that the one-piece sword extended three feet into the stone. Garlaschelli carbon-dated the mummified hands to the same period (circa 1180).

As we flew home a few days after visiting San Galgano, I gazed out the window over the Atlantic. A dense layer of clouds, with peaks of luminescence, obscured the ocean, and their beauty and the distant horizon seemed to underscore my insignificance. I was flying above a world I knew, in a universe, I didn't. Until recently, my response to the ultimate question—the meaning of my life itself—had been that of an uncompromising, agnostic scientist, a follower of Eastern religions who practiced meditation and mindfulness. Now I felt myself slowly becoming a true Christian, open to the possibility that an omnipotent and omniscient God had sent his Son to die for us on a wooden cross, with the promise of eternal life to those who believe in him.

Chapter 31

The DNA of Truth

His hairline receded to the apex of a shiny dome. His thick gray side hair was combed downward, overlapping the tops of his ears. He had an expansive forehead and shaggy white eyebrows above piercing blue eyes. His face was tapered, his thin nose pointed, and he spoke with a formal British accent. Nattily dressed in a dark sports jacket, pinstriped shirt, and crimson tie, he was none other than eighty-one-year-old Francis Crick, the 1953 co-discoverer of the structure of DNA, described by friends as "bold, brilliant, and elegant," and he was sitting in a dental chair at my office, late in 1997. I'd just completed his annual periodontal examination.

After informing Crick that his condition hadn't progressed, I hoped to engage this worldly man in an intellectual conversation, having allotted extra time in my schedule, and hoping his would allow it as well. I hadn't expected what followed.

"Have you and your wife been traveling?" I asked.

"Odile hasn't been feeling well," he replied, "so we've no plans at the moment."

Fresh from the Cursillo retreat, plus visits to the home of Catherine Benincasa and the embedded sword of Galgano Guidotti, I said, "That's too bad. I'll pray for her."

"Dr. Sottosanti," Crick said, with a pleasant smile and boyish grin, "I very much appreciate the thought, but I don't personally place any credence in prayer. Oh, there's some benefit to be derived from religion. One needs to understand what's called 'biochemical theology.' I believe when people pray, there may be an elevated level of a neurotransmitter, like dopamine or serotonin, which creates a sense of well-being."

"Have you always felt that way? You grew up in London, right? Was your family affiliated with the Church of England?"

Crick said that his family, indeed, had attended Sunday services, but as a teenager, he lost interest in religion because science seemed to disprove it. Moreover, their preacher had been a bore. When he was young, Crick's parents gave him a book titled *The Children's Encyclopedia*, which contained much history and literature, but by the age of fourteen, he was only attracted to science, an emphasis at the boarding school he attended. He'd grown to resent religion, which he saw as contradicting science. It became an obsession with him, and he became a devoted atheist.

Crick spoke with his hands in front of his chest, his palms and fingertips touching, almost prayer-like, which seemed ludicrous considering the subject of our conversation. As he spoke, his fingers fluttered, often interlocking, to the beat of his voice. His left ring finger sported a flat black onyx ring. My gaze returned to his animated face as he relayed a fascinating story.

"Back in 1960," he recalled, "I accepted an honorary fellowship at Churchill College—the largest college at Cambridge. Shortly thereafter, an alumnus donated money to build a chapel in the middle of the campus, and the College Council agreed to accept it. The College had always claimed to be one of the most forward-thinking academic institutions in the world. Ever since Darwin's *On the Origin of Species* a century earlier, discrediting the claims of traditional religions, the College had always been based on science. But now I saw it returning to the Dark Ages with this idea of a chapel on campus."

He paused briefly, then continued earnestly. "I was so upset I resigned my fellowship! Winston Churchill himself wrote to me asking me to reconsider, explaining that no one need enter the chapel unless they wished to, and it would be open to all faiths, even atheists, for a place of prayer, worship, or relaxation. I wrote back—I even remember the date, October 12, 1961—and told Churchill I was enclosing a check for ten guineas as a down payment for the College to build a bordello. For the comfort of many."

Ten guineas, at the time, were worth about fifteen U.S. dollars. But even had Crick sent a check for ten thousand, I couldn't have been more stunned.

"I believe students, faculty, and alumni would support such an establishment," he went on, "particularly with carefully selected ladies and a suitable Madam, who, once the institution had become traditional and popular, most likely would be granted a seat at the High Table."

It was only later that I learned about the long table at the College, the "High Table," that is reserved for fellows and their guests. It sits on a riser in the same large room used by the other students, whose tables are set below at right angles.

Crick laughed resoundingly, the crow's feet at the corners of his eyes deepening into furrows, his smile exposing aged-darkened teeth. He'd been described as charming, garrulous, with a lively sense of humor and infectious laugh, and I now understood why. He said that Churchill had returned the check, and they reached a compromise. An ecumenical chapel was built for those "who worship or are in doubt," on the outskirts of campus. Therefore it was not really part of the College. He smiled with pride—an attribute to which I could well relate.

"It was a chapel *at* Churchill College," he said, alluding to the truce with Churchill, "but not *of* Churchill College." It seemed a minor point to me, but to Crick, it seemed monumental.

I was surprised that Crick remembered the actual date of his letter, but then I thought: *When the co-discoverer of DNA, one of the greatest scientific minds in the world, writes a cynical letter to perhaps the most famous statesmen of the twentieth century, it's a date worth remembering. Should I let this opportunity pass?* Here was a rare opportunity to engage in a debate with a worthy adversary.

I'd met Dr. Gerald Jampolsky in the boarding area at the San Francisco airport, all because I called out to him. He had no idea who I was, but I was proud of my assertiveness, and it led to a life-changing experience. Dare I do so now?

"Why do you think you became so anti-religious?"

"Because it's all so untrue. Take the Bible. Much of it was written thousands of years ago when people knew little about the universe. They had no conception of our planet, its size, or its relation to the sun, the moon, and the stars. They had to fabricate stories that gave them a sense of peace."

"Can you give me some examples?" I said. I wondered if he'd mock the seven-day creation story, Noah's ark, or Jonah being swallowed by a whale only to escape and walk to the city of Nineveh.

"Let's begin with Adam and Eve," Crick said. "I learned about them as a child, and I'll never forget how embarrassed I became when I mentioned to a medical student friend that women have one less rib than men because God took a rib from Adam to make Eve. My friend smiled, then let go with an unrestrained belly laugh."

Crick smiled broadly, and I followed suit.

"If anything in the Bible is false," he continued, "then everything else in it must be doubted. My friend later told my other friends what I'd said, and they ridiculed me for weeks. I've never felt more simple-minded in my entire life!"

He grew serious, his elbows set on the arms of the dental chair, his right hand curled into a loose fist, as his left stroked its knuckles. I didn't want to stare at his hands, but that large onyx ring was like a hypnotist's watch.

"I'm sorry that happened," I commiserated, remembering the raucous laughter of my childhood friends—Jay-Jay Rackiewicz and the Smith brothers—as I leaped from the bushes in my all-black Hopalong Cassidy outfit, with a tall, broad-brimmed hat, pistols drawn and pointed, shouting "Bang! Bang! You're dead!" That moment has stayed with me for forty-five years. Now I'd learned that even one of the most famous people in the world had been wounded for life by the inconsiderate actions of others.

Humans have such fragile egos, I thought. *Wouldn't it be wonderful, as tough as we would like to appear, if, in circumstances like this, we could return to the arms of someone that loves us unconditionally—like our mothers!* As Fr. Bill Wilson said: "When I was a little boy and returned home from the playground, dirty and bruised, my Mum would clean me up, kiss me, and make me feel wonderful again." *Would belief in a compassionate God—Jesus Christ and in His mother, the Virgin Mary—provide immeasurable solace in times like this?* I didn't have that level of faith, but Margaret, and others I admired greatly, did.

I snapped out of these thoughts at the sound of Crick's voice.

"It was humbling," he said, "and it made me determined to get rid of any residual beliefs, so I could get to solving the problems that prevent us from understanding what the world is really all about."

He became more animated now, hands chest-high, fingers curved and interlocked, pulsating to the beat of his words. Occasionally, his right hand would swing laterally to emphasize a point. I was pleased that this famous man, known for his vitality, intellect, and wisdom, was giving serious attention to our conversation.

"You must understand, Dr. Sottosanti, that the world changed forever when Darwin published his great work explaining evolution through genetic mutation and natural selection. That one book decimated the gibberish of Christianity."

Crick looked into my eyes compassionately, placed his hands on his knees, leaned forward and politely said, "This certainly is no affront to you. There are two billion Christians in the world—almost a third of the world's population, so you're in good company."

"Regarding many of the stories in the Old Testament," I said, "I believe many are allegorical and figurative, to teach theological principles, not to be taken literally."

"It's not just the Old Testament," Crick said. "The New Testament is filled with stories of a man born of a virgin, walking on water and rising from the dead. All those things are scientifically impossible."

I paused, gathering my thoughts to regain my confidence. *Time,* at the end of 1999, would publish a list of the top "100 Persons of the Century," headed by Albert Einstein, "the preeminent scientist in a century dominated by science," and the *TIME 100 Persons of the Century* would include Francis Crick.

Emboldened by several years of Bill Creasy's Bible study classes and trips to the library to reconcile the Bible with Darwin's theory, I said, "Dr. Crick, if God didn't cause the Big Bang, who or what did?"

His response was immediate. "It's not easy to convey the whole story of how it started, but we know life emerged and then evolved. Attempts have been made to elucidate the causative factors of the Big Bang, and I believe one day they'll be explained. It's a notoriously difficult subject, you understand. Somewhere around thirteen billion years ago, there was matter—protons, neutrons, electrons, and the like—and there was an explosion which caused an expansion of the material that existed at the time."

"Wasn't that theory proposed by George Lemaitre, a Belgian Catholic priest?"

"Yes." Crick tapped his fingertips together. "But he was also an outstanding scientist, mathematician, and professor of physics. He wasn't lost in superstition and thoughts from the Dark Ages."

"I believe God caused the Big Bang," I said, "since something had to. Even Aristotle believed in a Prime Mover setting the universe in motion."

"My own view," Crick countered, "is that everything was in place for the occurrence of a rapid expansion of extremely dense material, and this ultimately led to life on Earth today, in all its beautiful and wondrous manifestations. Many may think God designed it, but Darwin showed it all came about by evolution."

"It's a fascinating subject," I said. "According to a recent article in *Scientific American,* the universe has a mathematical basis. More than twenty constants— like the force of gravity and the speed of light—needed to be determined and set into place, or we couldn't exist. If the force of gravity were infinitesimally weaker, the basket-ball-sized mass—containing everything needed to create the universe—would have shot out into space with a velocity preventing the formation of our solar system. On the other hand, if the mathematician set the constant stronger, the ball would have collapsed within itself, and increased density and darkness would have remained."

"You've certainly done your homework, Dr. Sottosanti. But proving the existence of God is notoriously difficult, if not impossible."

I slid my doctor's stool a few inches closer. "But Dr. Crick, who was the mathematician if not God?"

He laughed. "We'll never know because it can't be scientifically proven—it happened so long ago. Your theory doesn't prove that God or a creator exists. Scientists are trying to find the answer as to how the first cell formed. Life, as we know it, began with a few simple molecules and then evolved into the macromolecules of complex organisms. There's a theory that a 'prebiotic soup'—of carbon dioxide, hydrogen, nitrogen, water, methane, and ammonia—existed on Earth billions of years ago. Then some form of electrical energy, lightning or some such thing triggered the creation of simple organic compounds. From that, life emerged. We don't yet know how, but I think we one day will."

"I believe there's more truth in the Bible than you think," I said. "I've always had an interest in astronomy. Obviously, a 'day' in the Book of Genesis is just a period of time. In the beginning, God said, 'Let there be light,' but the light separating night from the day didn't appear until the fourth day. We know in its earliest days, the Earth was covered by dense gasses and cosmic dust. As they cleared and oxygen increased, sunlight reached the surface, and that could have happened on the fourth day."

"You may be right about that," Crick acquiesced.

"And on the fifth day, life began in the oceans. Doesn't science agree that life started in the sea?"

Crick had been looking out the window behind me as I spoke, but then his eyes riveted on mine. "Some of it may be true, but the Bible's full of dreadful stories about a menacing God—like turning Lot's wife into a pillar of salt, and killing innumerable people, even children, for a variety of insignificant reasons. Abominable things were done to Job and his family."

"As I said, some of those stories are allegorical, and the language is figurative. But in the Old Testament, God punished his people because of their wickedness. Things changed with the appearance of Christ. Christ brought salvation to mankind."

"Where's the evidence that Christ was born of a virgin? Or turned water into wine? Or walked on water?"

"Obviously, there is none, but as C.S. Lewis said in *Mere Christianity*—and I'm paraphrasing now—'A man who was merely a man and said the sort of things Jesus said would either be who he said he was, the Son of God, or a raving lunatic.' Would you call someone who preaches love, truth, courage, justice, patience, compassion, forgiveness, restraint, mercy, respect, and humility, *a madman?*" These terms rolled off my tongue from a combination of what I'd learned from Jampolsky and *The Course in Miracles*, Bill Creasy and his Bible study classes, and *Mere Christianity*, which Margaret had chosen for our Catholic book club.

"I will concede," said Crick, "that a few ancient Jewish historians say Jesus existed, but we don't have any proof of his performing miracles, except for very limited accounts written by his followers years after he died. You can't base your whole life on that."

"I don't," I said. "My wife is the religious one in our family, but when I see her Christian values displayed so lovingly to our children and to me, I can't disregard them."

"No doubt, Dr. Sottosanti. No doubt." Crick showed no signs of impatience, and it occurred to me that he might actually be enjoying our discussion.

"Besides," I said, "the fact that Christianity spread so far in such a short period of time could be considered miraculous. The twelve Apostles—many of them were simple fishermen, speaking only Aramaic—traveled to distant lands and preached Christ's message to foreigners, and converted them. Some were tortured, stoned to death, beheaded, and even crucified upside down on a cross, rather than renounce Christ. Don't you think that's unlikely unless they believed that Christ was the Son of God?"

"But Dr. Sottosanti, a charismatic personality can cause people to do strange things, even kill themselves. Just months ago, thirty-nine members of Heaven's Gate—a cult right here in San Diego County—committed mass suicide because of a madman's belief in a biblical prophecy, so they could reach an extraterrestrial spacecraft following the Hale-Bopp comet."

"You're talking about mass suicide," I countered. "This can occur in a religious setting, but such suicides usually occur within a short time. Years after Jesus died, his apostles were separated from each other, and could have saved their lives with a simple recantation of their beliefs. But they didn't."

"Give me another example of evidence that Jesus existed."

"Take the resurrection. If this didn't happen, then one could easily say Christ was just a great prophet. I'm sure you've heard of the Shroud of Turin—claimed to be the burial cloth of Christ when He was laid in the tomb."

Our book club had visited the Shroud Center of Southern California, which has a full-scale high-resolution reproduction of the Shroud. The Center weaves together a remarkable story of faith, scripture, history, and scientific evidence. Its museum tells the ancient story of the 14' 5" x 3' 7" linen cloth convincingly, including evidence that small metal balls, recovered in archeological digs, attached to the strands of Roman whips, match in size and shape the wounds appearing on the image of a scourged body on the Shroud.

"In 1898," I said, "an Italian amateur photographer, Secondo Pia, developed photographs he took of the faint images and stains on the surface of the Shroud. Looking at the negatives, he discovered the lightest areas of the image appeared dark, and vice-versa—exposing a clearer likeness of a man whose body and face could now be seen in great detail. There were wounds on the four limbs, one on the side of the chest, and various bleeding points around the crown of the head."

"But that whole hypothesis was debunked by a carbon dating test in the late 80s, which showed the cloth to be a medieval forgery."

"I'll get to that in a minute, but first, I want to tell you about STURP—the 1978 Shroud of Turin University Research Project, comprised of an international team of scientists and image experts—Christian and otherwise. They conducted many scientific investigations on the cloth and determined the image was of a real human form that had been scourged and crucified. It was not created by paints, dyes, or chemicals."

Not wanting to belabor the subject, I didn't mention that the scientists had found that the dark stains in the areas of the wounds actually contained human hemoglobin and bilirubin.

"So, how do you think the image was created?"

"Some believe it was caused by a sudden burst of radiation at the moment of the resurrection, affecting only the very surface of the linen fibrils. Dyes and paints would have penetrated deeper. I realize this seems preposterous, but I'm just recalling what I've read."

"Carbon dating is a very accurate measure of age," Crick said, "so I'm still convinced it's a medieval forgery."

"Well, we know the Shroud had been in a fire in the Middle Ages, but nuns repaired it with new linen patches interwoven with the old. Many believe the strips used for the test were taken from a patched area."

He tapped his fingertips together again and smiled. "I'll rest my case on the carbon dating. The Shroud of Turin is a forgery, masterfully crafted in the fourteen century."

"But if we ask today's scientists, allowing them all the equipment available, to recreate all the properties embedded in the Shroud, like 3-D imagery, they still can't do it."

"Science evolves, Dr. Sottosanti. What it cannot prove today will be a simple matter in the future."

I looked at my watch, stood, and said, "Let's agree to disagree."

Crick stood slowly, smiled warmly, and offered his hand. "Cheerio, Dr. Sottosanti."

We shook hands, and he followed my assistant out.

Is it possible to be a scientist and still be religious? Nicolaus Copernicus, Gregor Mendel, Roger Bacon, and Georges Lemaitre, among others, were all Catholic priests.

Chapter 32   My Pisces Problem

CONTROVERSY HAS SWIRLED AROUND the discovery of DNA by Watson and Crick for years, clouding it in accusations of misogyny, deception, and, perhaps, dishonesty. Following my discussion with Francis Crick, I learned about these charges at the La Jolla Library.

In 1951, Rosalind Franklin, with a Ph.D. in Chemistry from Cambridge, worked as a researcher in a laboratory at King's College in London, a place where women were not held in high esteem. Without her permission, her colleague, Maurice Wilkins, showed James Watson and Francis Crick Franklin's x-ray diffraction research—a technique wherein x-rays are scattered by the atoms of a crystal to determine their structure. This gave Crick and Watson information crucial to constructing the double helix model of DNA. What they were shown has become widely known as "Photograph 51." They rushed to publish their article in *Nature* on April 25, 1953, leaving Franklin's name off the paper, not giving her credit for providing a key piece of the puzzle they claimed to have solved.

Was this willful chicanery? I didn't know, but I wondered if Captain Wally Grossman, a devout Catholic—the man who'd fought for the truth to surface at the Nellis Air Force Base Dental Clinic to protect our military personnel—would have participated in a similar event. I thought of Margaret and her belief that truth and honesty were one and the same; and of the Sicilian woman who wouldn't let a photo be taken of her with Dad and me without her husband being present so he wouldn't see her cavorting with strange men while he was laboring in the fields of Mistretta. In my own life, I'd encountered a number of unusually honest people who were very devout Christians. *Was this coincidental or consequential? Why did my own behavior vacillate—from exemplary to objectionable and virtuous to sinful?*

This question had lingered in my mind since my debate with Francis Crick on the existence of God because I'm not really the person I led him to believe. Born in March, I'm a true Pisces, with the astrological sign of two fish, one above the other, swimming in opposite directions, which suggests indecision. As a result, I'm often ruled by gut reactions.

It's as if I'm an actor in a play titled *Life,* and each scene has two scripts from which I must choose. One is a "theo-drama," a term attributed to the Swiss theologian and Catholic priest Hans Urs von Balthasar, in which God is the protagonist, and I'm subordinate to His will. He's the creator, and I'm the creature, and my aim is to please Him. If not, there'll be consequences. In an alternate reality, often referred to as the "ego-drama," my will is in charge, its ravenous needs dictating my behavior. I am subject to it and helpless to challenge it as it cries out, "Feed me! Feed me!" It devours what I give it and screams for more, whether it's cars, homes, alcohol, vacations, money, awards, or other enticements and sensual delights.

Several months after my interaction with Dr. Crick, I brought home from the office the 1998 *Sports Illustrated* swimsuit issue. My rationale was that the patients in the reception room should not be subjected to such smut—our office is too professional—but I, personally, had no problem with it. Reclining in a chaise lounge, looking at the ocean—and alternately at Heidi Klum on the cover—I heard the French doors open behind me.

"John," Margaret said, her formality announcing there was something serious on her mind. "We need to talk."

I looked up from Heidi Klum.

"Do you remember you promised we'd sell this house after Paul left for college?

I really didn't. "Why sell one of the best views in La Jolla?"

"There are many reasons!" Margaret retorted. "The house is too big, the upkeep is too expensive, and the stress I experienced dealing with the contractor is part of the problem. I'm not sure he was honest, and this house reminds me of those unhappy times."

She was earnest, and I just listened.

"Then there was the cost of the remodel. You followed the advice of that high-end designer and never consulted Dad or me. Instead, you went ahead without a budget and ordered everything he recommended. We nearly went bankrupt! Can you imagine anyone in their right mind paying 18 percent on maxed-out credit cards?"

"We paid those off in a year."

"But we had to refinance, with a much bigger mortgage. So every month when I write that humongous check, I wonder where the money's coming from."

"Lifecore pays that bill."

"Will those royalties continue indefinitely?"

"No," I had to admit. "Not really." Although the income wasn't guaranteed, Lifecore's calcium sulfate sales, mainly from Capset, had continued to rise as I continued to speak at major scientific meetings. In 1998 alone, I'd accepted engagements in nine states, plus one in Mexico. So I hoped that international sales would continue to grow. But that would necessitate more trips abroad.

"You're gone so much," Margaret complained, "that you don't even realize what's happening here. The neighbors are complaining about our bushes and trees. They say they're blocking their view."

I knew this but hadn't realized that the neighbors were troubling Margaret. After the remodel had been completed, Dr. Jim Brown, a retired orthopedic surgeon who lived on the hillside above us, had called to ask if I'd come to discuss a "view issue." When I did, he led me through his gorgeous contemporary home, with its panoramic floor-to-ceiling windows, an unobstructed view of the sandy beach and ocean, and then down some steps to his vanishing edge swimming pool.

"I'd like you to sit in my favorite recliner," he said, "so you can see the view from that level." I sat down. "Your new chimney breaks the horizon line, where ocean and sky meet."

I could see the problem. Jim offered to pay for changing the dimensions, and I consulted my contractor. But city codes prohibited lowering the chimney's crown closer to the roof, and our relationship with the Browns was never the same.

* * *

As the months passed, an emergent melancholy washed over me like small waves hitting La Jolla Shores. At other times, it came with the intensity of a winter storm on Coast Boulevard at high tide. Besides our expensive mortgage and Margaret's desire to move, other stressors existed—long hours at the office, preparing and delivering frequent lectures, and managing two offices with many employees. In addition, an impending renewal for the lease on the La Jolla office loomed. My younger partner, Dr. Bruce Johnson, expected we'd renew for another five years, possibly ten, for a better rate. That responsibility and commitment, plus a new loan for office improvements and equipment, seemed stifling. Hadn't I asked for inner peace years ago, gleaning it through Jampolsky's books and *The Course in Miracles*? Yes, but it hadn't lasted.

Although I'd relinquished the religion of my childhood in college, my marriage to Margaret continued to impact me. A living example of the fruits of her loving the Lord, she prayed for my conversion, as Mom had. And I realized that, over the years, I had experienced—or been blessed with, as my Catholic friends would say—"unlikely events." Not necessarily miracles but events with spiritual overtones.

Years ago in Connecticut, I'd been given extraordinary strength to lift several hundred pounds of snow and ice while trapped at the back stairs of my parents' basement, short of breath, in a room full of deadly smoke. Then there was Dad's one-in-a-million numbers racket "miracle," corroborated by Mom, who didn't fabricate stories. I'd witnessed his two-hour recovery from a terminal septicemia, allowing him to reconcile with Mom just before his death. Later, when suffering from terminal cancer, Mom had lapsed into a deep coma on a Friday, with a pleasant smile on her face, and received the last rites from Fr. Bill Wilson. Then, on Sunday morning, she was suddenly "resurrected," calling out, "Johnny, I saw Heaven." And then she described the place.

If healthcare professionals, researchers, and university academics heard me speak of these things, they'd think I'd escaped from a psychiatric ward and was simply posing as a surgeon. But my recent elections to the American College of Dentists and the Pierre Fauchard Society—the two most respected dental honor societies in the U.S.—attested to my credibility. In addition, I'd been married to the same woman for thirty years, which is evidence of stability and dependability. I'd performed complex oral surgeries in San Diego for twenty-six years and never once had been sued. As Jack Heimerer, the malpractice defense attorney for the California Dental Association insurance program, told me at a meeting, "Not many surgeons can make that claim. Congratulations!"

Still, I'd found the doctrines of the Catholic Church too complicated and difficult to follow. In 1992, the eight-hundred-page *Catechism of the Catholic Church* had been issued, containing teachings handed down from Christ and the Apostles through Sacred Scripture—the New and Old Testaments—and Sacred Tradition—beliefs and practices revealed by God that the Church had affirmed. Protestants believe that what isn't in the Bible isn't true. But the Bible was compiled from existing texts and scriptures in 393 A.D. at the Council of Hippo. Until then, in the years after Christ's death, sacred scripture did not exist. The Apostles and their thousands of disciples had spread the faith through the spoken word, as Jesus had instructed them to do.

I found New Age religions simpler to understand. "Teach only love," I'd heard Jampolsky say, "for that is what you are." I loved that statement. Another was, "We can learn to love ourselves and others by forgiving rather than judging." Like Jampolsky, my New Age mentors, such as Dyer, Zukav, and others, spoke of God and Jesus in an ephemeral way, mingling Him with terms like "inner voice," "unconditional love," and "power of the universe." They said love was our true essence but rarely discussed adversity or evil or how to combat it. It's not simplicity, I finally realized, that's important. Truth is what matters. And I found myself wondering just what that truth is.

At our previous Thursday evening Bible study, Dr. Creasy had read the famous passage in which Jesus overturned the tables of the moneychangers and drove them with a whip from the Temple in Jerusalem. Jesus was no weakling, Dr. Creasy stressed, but someone who had defined sin and enforced the law—just like my Sicilian father had done when I disobeyed him.

Ever so slowly, I began to see the New Agers—although their well-intentioned teachings *had* helped me—as promoting an array of beliefs to have universal appeal. They spoke with certainty, telling us that we are one with God, have to discover our divinity, and that "universal truths" exist to be discovered by those who seek them. They believe such truths can be found through an "altered consciousness" achieved by meditation, breathing techniques, crystals, chanting, or spirit channeling. If one doesn't work, you try another. The implication was that all spiritual paths lead to God. So why couldn't people just get along? Mainstream religions, they said, are too narrow and rigid, preventing an understanding of the totality of the spiritual realm. As a result, they keep you from experiencing true love and laden you with guilt. I'd heard it all, again and again. Such ideas left me thinking about Hitler, Stalin, and Mao Zedong, who had murdered millions. Had their evil intent been realized earlier, before they built their power structures, these deaths could have been avoided. *You just can't love your enemies,* I realized. *Sometimes you have to stop them.*

As an undergraduate, I'd read William Golding's classic novel, *Lord of the Flies,* which depicts the inherent evil of mankind. It shows that, in an attempt to gain personal power, human beings will resort to savagery, immorality, and pure evil. The author used British schoolboys stranded on an island, the only survivors of a plane crash, to illustrate the "beast" within all of us. Without the laws of a benevolent society to govern and control them, they resorted to mayhem and murder. Their rescuer was the commanding officer of a warship, who, despite the civilization that had built his ship, had been trained to inflict death on others. It was a sad commentary on human nature. But I felt that Golding might be correct, and maybe Satan was the demonic force behind it.

Christ, through his words and actions, and those of the Apostle Paul and others, gave us rules, claiming that the obedient would enjoy everlasting life and the disobedient would be punished. It's easy to dismiss the latter—but what if it's true? Do heaven and hell exist? Are there spiritual realms beyond the here and now?

The palpable darkness associated with my "cursed" Mercedes-Benz was inexplicable, as were the 1917 apparitions of the Virgin Mary in Fatima, Portugal, approved by the Catholic Church as "worthy of belief." The three young children who witnessed the six appearances of the Blessed Mother never recanted their stories, though repeatedly interrogated by civil and Church authorities and threatened with bodily harm and incarceration. Our Lady of Fatima, they said, had shown them a vision of hell—a "sea of fire" with "demons and souls in human form." Lucia, the oldest of the three, who was only ten, later became a nun, devoting her life to helping others. The other two died as children, as the Virgin had predicted.

"OK, Sotes," I told myself. "Let's get real here. Eternity is forever, so if you're gonna believe there's no afterlife, you'd better be certain."

But there could be no certainty. Which is why Blaise Pascal, the seventeenth-century mathematician, Catholic theologian, and philosopher, had posited a wager: Bet on an afterlife, follow God's rules, and if Heaven exists, you'll be rewarded. If not, you'll have lived a good life. You can't lose—unless you bet there's no hell, and there *is*. But, then, if you've disregarded Christ, your fate is too horrendous to contemplate.

* * *

The American Academy of Periodontology appointed me to its prestigious Continuing Education Oversight Committee (CEOC), planning speakers for its national meeting. Being on the CEOC meant four all-expenses-paid trips to Chicago each year, held at the luxurious Ritz-Carlton near the AAP's office at Water Tower Place—the best place to be in the city. Yet, the thought of helping other periodontists, and ultimately their patients by virtue of this volunteer position, gave me much comfort and pleasure.

With all this success, I wondered why I felt so troubled when I thought of Margaret wanting to sell my dream home. There was the expensive mortgage and the tension with the neighbors. I felt pressure from Bruce to sign a new office lease and loan papers for necessary improvements. I wanted to be in control, but I felt the opposite. Then a TV series brought sudden clarity to my thinking, a rerun of a 1988 documentary *Joseph Campbell and the Power of Myth*. After watching it, I bought the book, *The Power of Myth* by Joseph Campbell with Bill Moyers and read it several times.

Moyers, the renowned journalist and political commentator, had interviewed Campbell, a literature professor at Sarah Lawrence College.

An expert in mythology, Campbell believed "follow your bliss" was a way to set aside the belief that you must achieve certain things in life and live in a certain way to attain socially-approved goals. Instead, following your bliss frees you for the life you've always wanted. And so "follow your bliss" became my new mantra because it offered me hope from the desolation I'd begun to experience.

Putting it into practice, I ended my partnership with Dr. Bruce Johnson, on friendly terms, in June of 1998, giving him full ownership of the Rancho Bernardo practice. In exchange, I retained the La Jolla practice, which I immediately sold to Dr. John Lofthus, an associate who'd been working for me for six years. As I liked to be the top dog, becoming an employee of Lofthus was a blow to my ego, but it was liberating to be relieved of debts and responsibilities.

Our son Mark was now engaged to Martha Howton, a beautiful, brilliant woman. They planned their wedding for August 1998. A longtime La Jolla resident, Martha had been raised in the Episcopalian faith by loving parents who'd achieved much success in the business world. Like Mark, she was a graduate of the Bishop's School. She'd received a bachelor's from Yale, a law degree from the prestigious University of California Hastings College of Law, and was on the partnership track at one of San Diego's highly respected law firms.

Margaret wanted Mark to have a Catholic wedding, and Martha agreed to accommodate her. With Margaret as her sponsor, she registered for the process by which one officially becomes a Catholic, attending weekly Rite of Christian Initiation for Adults (RCIA) sessions. This spiritual journey culminated in an Easter Vigil Mass, where Martha, for the first time, received the Holy Eucharist in the Catholic Church. Episcopalians do not believe in the Catholic understanding of transubstantiation, in which the bread and wine become the body and blood of Christ after their consecration by an ordained priest. Which left me wondering: *Did I?*

Was I really a Catholic? People close to me thought so, yet I didn't believe in two of the most important Church sacraments—confessing my sins to a priest, an act known as reconciliation, and accepting the Eucharist as the actual body and blood of Jesus Christ. I hadn't been to confession since my senior year in high school when I'd gone at Mom's request, yet confession was always available at most Catholic churches on Saturday afternoons. Moreover, how could a surgeon, scientist, and researcher believe what allegedly happens during Mass? That when the priest says, "Take this, all of you, and eat of it, for this is my Body, which will be given up for you," it becomes the actual flesh of Christ?

Although I'd been questioning the validity of New Age religions, I wasn't convinced that the Catholic Church, or any traditional Protestant religion, for that matter, had all the answers. With more than two hundred Protestant denominations in the United States, there is much disunity and disagreement among them, let alone among the thousands of "Bible churches," each with its own interpretation of Scripture. Although the Catholic Church might not be perfect, at least everyone knows its beliefs.

Regardless of which religion I followed, Catholic or New Age—and I swung between the two—my Pisces problem persisted. My ego-drama was playing on Broadway, while my theo-drama was still in a community theater. To reduce stress, I alternated between the meditation techniques of Deepak Chopra (lotus position, palms up, repeating my mantra, "Om Tum Namah," which I'd been told never to disclose) and the repetition of the Hail Mary prayer, found in the Catholic Rosary. Neither helped for long. I hadn't realized that egoism and true spirituality were mutually exclusive.

On the evening of August 21, 1998, after a rehearsal dinner for Mark and Martha's wedding on our ocean-view deck, with more than fifty friends and relatives attending, we watched a perfect sunset—a red glow across the horizon. Before dropping from sight, the sun lit the underbelly of the cirrus clouds just above, affording some of us a glimpse of its elusive green flash. After Nature's stellar performance, how could I agree to sell this house?

The following day Mark married Martha at All Hallows Church on the summit of Mt. Soledad, overlooking the Pacific. The priest, Mark, and Martha were silhouetted by the sunshine streaming through the church's massive rear windows. It was a perfect day, and Martha was glowing. Overlooking the scene, high above the altar, a resplendent life-sized statue of the resurrected Christ was suspended by wires, hands extended outward, not in the form of crucifixion, but in a gesture of triumph, welcome, and forgiveness. His wooden cross was behind Him so no one could miss the message—the victory over death and the promise of a heavenly eternity for the righteous. Contemplating the symbolism, I could hear the words of Dr. Creasy as he read from the book of John: "I am the resurrection and the life. The one who believes in me will live, even though they die."

The next day, to Margaret's delight, I called the top real estate agent in La Jolla, a woman known for selling expensive homes.

Chapter 33   Taxing Deductions

THE AGENT WAS AGHAST when I told her how much I wanted for the house.

"That's twenty percent over market value," she chided, but I knew that a custom home on a lot pointed towards the ocean in such a way that the houses on either side could not be seen—with dramatic coastline views to the north and south—was a rarity. So, I found another agent willing to ask my price.

The house had been for sale for seven weeks, through Thanksgiving, Christmas, and New Year's, when Mark Jorgensen called. "Any offers?" Mark could be intuitive when I needed help—especially spiritual help.

"No," I said glumly. "Hardly anyone's looked at it. I may have to lower the price."

"Before you do," he said, "listen to what I just read about in the *National Catholic Register*— an old custom dating to St. Teresa of Avila."

Apparently, in the sixteenth century, St. Teresa had encountered difficulty finding land for a new convent, so she'd asked the nuns to bury St. Joseph medals, and they soon found the land. The word spread, and small statues eventually replaced the medals. The practice continues to this day. Skeptical, but willing to try anything, I went to a Catholic religious store and was surprised to find St. Joseph Statue Home-Sale Kits. They consisted of a four-inch white plastic statue, a prayer card, and an instruction sheet for only five dollars.

"St. Joseph," the female clerk explained, "is the patron saint of workers, the family, and the dying."

The instructions said to bury the statue upside down, so the house would sell faster because St. Joseph would want to escape from the ground more quickly. "But," the clerk went on, "Catholics aren't superstitious, so upside down or not, it doesn't matter. What's important is that you pray to

St. Joseph every day, asking him to sell your house since he's the protector of the family and wants to help."

Feeling ridiculous and looking up the hillside to make sure the retired orthopedic surgeon, Dr. Jim Brown, wasn't peering down at me, I buried the statue in our yard and then read from the card in the kit: "Dear Saint Joseph, protector of families, I implore you to bring me a buyer who will love and cherish this home." Then, cynically, I added, "And have the money to pay top dollar."

Three weeks later, while I was lecturing in Vail, Colorado, my real estate agent called. "We have an offer," she exclaimed, "and it's a good one, nearly the full price, and I believe there's room to negotiate. The guy loves the view, but he'd like an extra bedroom. So I suggested he convert your den."

Oh, no, I thought, envisioning a sledgehammer smashing my French Breche de Benou marble desktop and my cherry-stained Bocote wood cabinets from Central America. I hadn't realized how much my ego was invested in that home. But St. Joseph had spoken.

Most people would say that burying a statue to sell a house is silly, yet in 2007, eight years after we sold that house, the *Wall Street Journal* published a piece: "When It Takes a Miracle to Sell Your House." It cited the story of Cari Luna, from a Jewish family, who'd converted to Buddhism and had been meditating daily. When multiple attempts to sell her house failed, she turned to St. Joseph, ordering a kit online and burying the small statue in her yard. The house soon sold, and before the new owners moved in, following the directions in the kit, she dug up the statue and placed it in a prominent position in the office of her new home.

With cash from selling our ocean-view house, we purchased a townhome in the north end of La Jolla, in the gated condominium community of Blackhorse Farms. To assuage my disappointment from losing our ocean-view property, we took the residual money from the sale and made an offer, contingent upon the approval of a mortgage, on a vacation home in the mountains east of Los Angeles. The place was at an elevation of seven thousand feet, on the shore of Big Bear Lake—Southern California's largest freshwater lake—within a forest of Jeffrey, sugar, and lodgepole pines.

Although we'd traded one house for two, the value of our former La Jolla home was more than the combined value of the two new properties. So, after the escrow closed, I sold my year-old Mercedes-Benz S-Class sedan and bought a four-wheel-drive Ford SUV and a twenty-four-foot pontoon boat. Margaret objected to the boat until I told her we'd have grandkids one day and could take them fishing. Wanting grandchildren as much as I did, she agreed.

* * *

In early September of 1999, as I reclined on the chaise lounge in our small backyard at the Blackhorse townhome, I was enclosed by three ivy-covered walls. Despite less financial pressure now, I wondered about the source of my persistent subclinical melancholy, which I'm sure my patients, professional peers, and friends never suspected. I didn't discuss it with Margaret, but she may have known. I'd been reading *The Southern Cross*—San Diego County's Diocesan Catholic newspaper—which Margaret kept in a small basket in the bathroom of our master bedroom, intrigued by an article on the Seven Deadly Sins. According to *The Southern Cross*, these sins could cause discontent, even despair. The timing was uncanny. Was this another "unlikely event?"

I learned the ninefold fruits of the Holy Spirit from Bible study—love, joy, peace, forbearance, kindness, goodness, faithfulness, gentleness, and self-control. According to Dr. Creasy, during Bible study, you can obtain inner joy from a genuine belief in the Christian message that helps you respond to life's difficult situations without disturbing your inner peace. This state of ecstasy, he explained, could be achieved by study, prayer, and obedience, leading to a deep relationship with Christ—something I definitely lacked. Dr. Creasy emphasized that happiness can be superficial and fleeting—like when your favorite sports team wins an important game but disappears when it loses. In contrast, joy is profound happiness. Joy resides in the depth of the soul, in the inner recesses of the heart, and has a calming effect on the mind. It is an essential path to meaning and purpose.

To be in harmony with the Holy Spirit, one must avoid sin as much as possible. When I lived in Las Vegas, with temptations everywhere, I'd assessed my life as it related to the Seven Deadly Sins. And I'd come up woefully short. It had been many years since that self-evaluation. However, I'd memorized those sins years ago, using a mnemonic device I developed in my anatomy class at Georgetown—PEWSAGL—Pride, Envy, Wrath, Sloth, Avarice, Gluttony, and Lust. The pew, of course, was easy to remember as we sat in one in church. Now I revisited that list, in no particular order, with examples of sin from my life.

Pride: I loved awards. I'd received two Special Citations from the American Academy of Periodontology, the first for acquiring Francis Crick as our keynote speaker for the 1988 Annual Meeting. The second came when the meeting returned to San Diego in 1997—for securing Ken Blanchard, author of *The One Minute Manager*, as our speaker and the Beach Boys as the entertainment for our evening gala. I also received an award, framed with USC's cardinal and gold colors, for heading the Annual Periodontal

Symposium for twenty-five consecutive years. Still, my pride was insatiable. My goal was to fill the entire wall in the den of our new condo with framed citations, and I was well on my way.

Avarice: By selling my ownership in two offices and reducing my surgical days from five to three, my income fell substantially, but I supplanted it by investing actively in the stock market, becoming obsessed with the daily Dow Jones Industrial Average. Unfortunately, I invested more than was prudent. On August 31, 1998, when the market dropped five percent, its cumulative losses from mid-July were nearly 20 percent. We had sufficient money in the bank to meet our needs, but my mood was depressed for weeks. I had no control over the DOW and remained depressed until the averages increased.

Envy: Each time I descended La Jolla Shores Drive from our condo into the village, I would glimpse the view I'd relinquished, picturing Jim Brown in his poolside lounger, watching the sunset while grumbling about my chimney. It was more than a two-hour drive to Big Bear to experience open spaces, a view of the lake, and the smell of tall pines. Yet, I believed I deserved that ocean view in La Jolla.

Lust: For an entire week in late July of 1999, I'd lectured several hours a day at an oceanfront hotel in Nice, France, for the Los Angeles-based Association of International Dentists. The organization had invited Margaret, paying her expenses as well as mine. Reclining on our lounges at the Hotel Beau Rivage's private beach club—the hotel memorialized by the Matisse painting "My Room at the Beau-Rivage"—I'd looked up from my magazine as three beautiful, young, topless women walked by, tiptoeing to avoid the sharp rocks. It reminded me of the bare-breasted beauties in the Folies Bergere I'd seen twenty-five years earlier in Las Vegas. Margaret ignored them in both places, but my concupiscence—as the Church calls it—was intact.

Gluttony: In the spring of 1999, Margaret had accompanied me to Chicago for a CEOC meeting. On the evening we arrived, Margaret suggested a quick meal at the nearby Cheesecake Factory. But I knew Charlie Trotter's in Lincoln Park, a Michelin-starred restaurant, was just a short cab ride away. My eight-course, fixed-price evening meal cost one hundred forty dollars, and the wine added another eighty dollars to the bill. Margaret ordered the less expensive vegetarian option with tap water.

Sloth: I'd always been lazy, but the Catholic definition of sloth, "spiritual laxity," deepened my guilt. I appeared to be a church-going, weekly communicant to most people, but it was all a charade. I was committing a sacrilege since I never went to confession, which the Church required at least once a year.

Anger: Jampolsky's book on *A Course in Miracles*—with its message "Would you rather be happy, or right?"—had reduced the incidence of anger in my life, so I thought I'd conquered that sin. I no longer honked my horn at drivers who cut me off or became upset with patients annoyed at my tardiness. But I was wrong, as would become apparent in the "perfect storm" of temptations that soon descended upon me, over which I had little control, causing me to project my anger toward Margaret.

This onslaught began with a brochure from the Straumann Group, a dental implant company. Its "World Symposium," scheduled for October of 2000 in Switzerland, was to be held in Lucerne, on the shores of a deep lake surrounded by steep mountains.

The next day, in *The Southern Cross*, I read that Severino Poletto, the Archbishop of Turin, would be opening a "Shroud Exposition" in Italy on August 12. It would end in October—the day before the Straumann meeting began. The Shroud of Turin, with its image of a crucified man believed to be that of Jesus Christ, was displayed publicly no more than once or twice a century. This would be only the fifth public exhibition since 1898 and the longest in its documented history. I'd cited the Shroud in my debate with Francis Crick, but that had been just for argument's sake, not out of religious fervor, as I didn't know much about the famous relic or whether or not to believe its authenticity.

Then I went to shroud.com, a website created by Barrie Schwortz, a Jewish image expert and "Documenting Photographer" of the 1978 team of scholars and scientists that had examined the shroud. Schwortz had joined the team expressly to discredit the shroud's authenticity, believing that fourteenth-century forgers had created the image. But his effort had fallen short. After days of examining the cloth and taking several thousand photographs, he helped formulate the team's conclusion that the image was that of a scourged, crucified man. No pigments, paints, dyes, or stains were found on the linen fibrils. The source remained unsolved.

I was amazed. Here was a devout Jewish man who had for the past twenty years dedicated much of his life, talent, and own money to validate a religious artifact of the crucifixion, possible evidence for the resurrection of Jesus Christ. He understood that radiation or electrical energy—other plausible explanations—weren't available in the Middle Ages in sufficient strength to produce a comparable image.

Turin, Italy, and Lucerne, Switzerland, were less than two hundred miles apart! Margaret and I could see the Shroud, with my professional dental corporation covering much of the trip. I wanted to see this famous relic, and the wheels in my head started turning.

The next day, Brian Kane, from Lifecore Biomedical, called my office, offering an all-expenses paid trip to Brazil to speak for six hours at a conference in São Paulo on October 26. He didn't mention Margaret. The American Eagle company would be my sponsor. All I had to do was show slides of their dental instruments and discuss non-surgical therapy. I could also lecture on bone regeneration, spreading the word about Capset to South America. Telling Brian I'd get back to him, I immediately began scheming to convince Margaret that I needed this trip. I'd offer to bring her, knowing she'd decline. Given the weight of her increased responsibilities, the trip was too long—maintaining two homes, tending to our ailing dog, Buffy, and her volunteer work at church.

Margaret figured the trip would take five days, but I wanted ten—enough for three countries on two continents, with two days to recuperate on the beach in Rio de Janeiro, a place I had always wanted to visit, before flying home. Margaret objected to the unnecessary extension.

"And we don't have a nice beach in La Jolla?"

"We do, but I'm going to Rio—whether you like it or not!"

Margaret was no match for my powerful addictions. I couldn't control my anger. How could she not want me to see Rio? All I knew was that, when it came to my latest review of the Seven Deadly Sins, I had once again failed miserably in the face of a trip that would only exacerbate them.

* * *

On Thursday, October 20, "following my bliss" and putting the stress of La Jolla behind me, I flew to Milan on American Airlines, arriving the next morning. Taking a cab to a small hotel near the Duomo di Milano, the centuries-old Milan Cathedral, I dropped off my luggage and walked to the Piazza—the massive square in front of the Duomo—to see its gothic edifice. That evening I ate at an indoor sidewalk café in the Galleria Vittorio Emanuele II, a four-story beaux-arts masterpiece. Beneath its domed glass and steel ceiling lay the luxurious boutiques of Versace, Prada, Louis Vuitton, and others. I dined on chicken cacciatore with a fine garlic and tomato sauce while sipping a glass of 1994 Marchese Antinori Chianti. I also feasted on the alluring fashionistas strolling by with their purchases, my gluttony and lust intact.

In the morning, I took the train from Milano Centrale—by volume, the largest train station in Europe—to Turin, where, from the far side of the piazza, I could see the marble Cathedral of Turin and its red-brick bell tower. Above and behind it rose the elaborate dome of the Guarini Chapel, the

Chapel of the Holy Shroud, an ornate seventeenth-century structure built to house the famous cloth. It had closed in 1997, however, due to a suspicious fire that could have destroyed the shroud had it not been for the heroic efforts of local firefighters. The shroud had then been moved to the Cathedral, where I joined a line leading to a doorway in the rear. As we entered, an attendant whispered, "Go in silence and in prayer." Heavy, burgundy curtains with rippled pleats hung before the altar on my right, and a horizontal cutout within those curtains surrounded the framed Shroud of Turin.

The line moved slowly. All eyes were riveted on the famous yellowing-linen-burial cloth, encased behind bulletproof glass, in a large wooden frame, with a four-inch black matte. The relic seemed to emanate an aura of holiness.

Eight triangular patches covering the burns of the fire in 1532 were quite noticeable. Many Catholics blamed the fire on the Calvinists because of intense political and religious friction between them. The shroud had been folded at the time, encased in a silver box in a church in Chambery, France, where the intense heat had caused molten silver to drop on one corner. When the cloth was unfolded, the burn was seen to have penetrated through its many layers. Two years later, Chambery's Poor Clare Nuns repaired the damage by sewing in the patches to mask the holes.

Devoted believers filled the pews on my left. Many fingered rosary beads while staring at the shroud. As I turned to follow the line exiting by the central nave, an older man, sitting on the aisle of the third row, abruptly stood, genuflected, and left, inadvertently bestowing upon me a perfect seat. For the next half-hour, I stared intently at the shroud, studying two faint images of a man lying lengthwise. On the left was a frontal view—a six-foot image of a man with a bearded face, his hands crossed at the groin, his feet extending to the edge of the fabric. On the right was the same image but from the rear. What startled me in both images were the vivid blood stains. None of the photographic reproductions I'd seen had shown them so pronounced. There were significant bloodstains on the left wrist, which overlapped the right, and on the area of the ankles, and on the right side of the abdomen. These matched the scriptural account of the crucifixion, during which a Roman soldier had thrust his spear into Christ's side. Blood was on the man's head, along the forehead, in an apparent dripping pattern, possibly created by the crown of thorns.

I knew that the stains were found to be human blood—group AB— which is rare in the world's population but more common in people from Palestine. At a Shroud Symposium in Turin in March of 2000, Professor Baima Bollone, a forensic medicine teacher for more than forty years, had presented evidence that the blood contained unusually high quantities of bilirubin, which increases when a body undergoes extreme stress. He believed the elevated bilirubin level accounted for the persistent reddish color of the dried blood, which had always been an enigma for many.

The entire body had been scourged as if by a Roman *flagrum*—a whip with tiny metal balls attached—and the stains on the tops of both arms were remarkable. I could imagine a man attempting to avoid a whipping, raising his arms to shield his face, thus absorbing the blows. My eyes teared up, as they had on September 25, 1978, when I flew over the San Diego crash site of the PSA flight because the situations were similar—innocent people suffering untimely deaths.

On the return train ride, I sat solemnly, eyes closed, lost in thought. Either the man in the shroud was the scourged and crucified Christ, or someone else—a murder victim of a medieval forger who placed the body in the cloth to simulate that of Christ. *But who?* I needed to know the answers. I was beginning to believe the former was correct because, as I had told Francis Crick, if we ask today's scientists, allowing them modern equipment to recreate all the properties embedded in the Shroud of Turin, like the 3-D imagery, they still can't do it.

On the train to Lucerne the next day, I could focus on the villages, rolling hills, and waterfalls tumbling off the distant mountains. The meeting I attended at the new world-class Lucerne convention center—an architectural masterpiece—paled compared to the wonder and mystery of the Shroud of Turin. Nonetheless, the conference, associated hotels, and airfare would suffice as a tax deduction come April.

Chapter 34

Surviving Rio

My flight to South America was long and tedious, giving me additional time to ponder the enigmatic cloth. Was it an excellent forgery or "the real McCoy?"

I spent most of my first day in Brazil in my room at the upscale Hotel Oscar Freire, near the Reboucas Convention Center. There was no time for sightseeing—I had work to do. With the procrastination of an actual sloth, I'd put off preparing my lengthy talk for the conference, the thirtieth annual meeting of the *Sociedade Brasileira de Periodontologia*. Dr. Thomaz Silva, the conference chair and my host, had left me a message in the room. He would pick me up out front at 8 p.m.— in a black Mercedes-Benz sedan—and take me to dinner. I noticed the coincidence, but perhaps, I was getting used to them.

Arriving on time, the middle-aged Dr. Silva greeted me with a slight Brazilian accent, his charming smile and warm personality an immediate comfort.

"A pleasure to meet you, Dr. Sottosanti."

"Call me 'John,'" I said, extending my hand.

"And I am 'Thomaz.' I hope you are hungry. We are going to the Jardineira Grill, an all-you-can-eat steakhouse, for the best *churrascaria* in all of São Paulo."

Cruising down the busy *Avenida dos Bandeirantes*, Thomaz turned into the parking lot, and we left the car with the valet. The scene reminded me of my haunted black Mercedes-Benz sedan, rammed from behind at the entrance to Lawry's in Beverly Hills. Inside, we were promptly seated opposite a massive buffet—everything from salmon, octopus, and cod to polenta, salads, and desserts.

"Ever had a *caipirinha*?" Dr. Silva said. "Our national drink—sugarcane liquor with lime."

I shook my head. The drink contains nearly 40 percent alcohol, and it hit me hard. Thomaz picked up a coaster—red on one side, green on the other—and pointed to the *passadores* in white shirts, black ties, and beige aprons. "They love to serve you the best meats in the city." He set his coaster green-side up, I did likewise, and a *passadore* arrived with a large skewer, direct from the barbecue grill, to slice thin pieces of grilled beef onto my plate. Various other cuts, like pork and lamb, came next.

After the *caipirinha*, followed by several glasses of Argentinian malbec, the evening began to blur before my eyes.

"I know of a great party," Thomaz said as we left the restaurant. "It's just starting, with lots of gorgeous single women. Would you like to join me?"

I wasn't wearing a wedding ring, and—just as when Candace Farrell had asked for a motel near my office—I could hear a devil in one ear and an angel in the other. Margaret was 6,000 miles away, no doubt still fuming that I'd ignored her wishes about taking this trip. I was drunk, and I hesitated.

"It's—it's late," I managed to say finally, mustering sufficient sensibility to decline the temptation. "I gotta be at the Convention Center in nine hours—ready to teach all day."

* * *

I began my morning lecturing on non-surgical techniques for treating early-to-moderate periodontal disease. But to a room full of surgeons, the topic was mundane. In the afternoon, I presented surgical cases, with slides projected on the large screen, demonstrating generous amounts of new bone growth due to combining calcium sulfate with bone grafts.

"Those cases are fantastic," a young periodontist said, approaching the podium immediately after. "Too bad you didn't start with those this morning."

Always worried about my image and performance, the comment disheartened me—I could have prepared something more interesting for the morning—but I figured the sunshine on the beach in Rio would resolve that problem the following day.

On Friday, the eighth day of my trip, on the hour-long flight to Rio de Janeiro, I attributed this unnecessary junket to a late mid-life crisis, plus the unsettling realization that I was getting older. With a sense of my mortality, I wanted to experience everything before I died. I hadn't entirely accepted that this life is a precursor to an eternal one.

Frommer's Brazil guidebook listed the Onda Mar Hotel on Copacabana Beach as a good value, a hotel used by Brazilians who shun the expensive tourist hotels such as the Copacabana Palace, "the Crown Jewel of Rio," one of the great beach hotels of the 1920s. These two nights were on my own tab and not tax-deductible, so the Onda Mar would have to do.

As I entered, I greeted the clerk behind the mahogany counter.

"*Bom dia*," I said, smiling. "I'm Dr. Sottosanti. I have a reservation for two nights. I requested an ocean view."

"*Bom dia*." The clerk didn't smile in return. "I put you in a nice room on the ninth floor. You will like it. We fixed the elevator yesterday."

I glanced at the tight circular staircase—dimly illuminated by a small central skylight high above the lobby—wondering if I'd made a mistake. My hunch was confirmed as the elevator opened, revealing a space large enough for me, my shoulder bag, and my suitcase. Had Margaret been with me, she wouldn't have fit, something I'd have to remember to tell her.

As the elevator closed behind me, I experienced a wave of claustrophobia, which still plagued me periodically ever since being trapped in a cave in the Grand Canyon. The *elevador*, as the clerk had pronounced it, groaned as if rebelling against my weight, then slowly moved upward. I was relieved when the door finally opened on the ninth floor, adjacent to the top of the narrow circular staircase, not far from my room.

Entering, I set my things on the bed, rushed to the large window, and pulled up the blinds. Sunlight flooded the room from a cloudless blue sky, shining below me on one of the most famous beaches in the world. My mood spiked. The ocean was cobalt blue on the horizon, then sapphire, turning turquoise where the white waves lapped the two-mile stretch of yellow-gold sand. Beyond the bay, the thirteen-hundred-foot granite and quartz Sugarloaf Mountain jutted skyward. It was one of the most dramatic coastal views I've ever seen.

And we don't have a nice beach in La Jolla? Margaret had said.

The answer was yes. And no.

The sunbathers—dots in the sand— were enjoying the brilliance of the eighty-degree day. Unpacking quickly, I headed down to join them in a bathing suit, tee shirt, and running shoes, darting between cars on the *Avenida Atlantica*, a major beachside thoroughfare with three lanes in each direction. Pausing to catch my breath on the median, I danced the rest of the way across. My goal was the wide Copacabana Beach promenade, famous for its stunning *calçada Portuguesa*—the longest limestone mosaic walkway in the world. Its wave pattern of black and white stones runs the entire length of the view I'd seen from my room.

Dodging walkers, joggers, and food vendors, I ogled several beautiful young women in thong bikinis—attire first worn in 1977, as the locals claimed, at this very beach. I had to chuckle at the name they gave these thongs—*fio dental,* because they resembled dental floss. Here was another example of my persistent concupiscence, the church's euphemism for "lust."

C'est la vie, I told myself, not knowing the equivalent in Portuguese.

The Veloso Bar, where the world-renowned song "The Girl From Ipanema" had been composed, was in nearby Ipanema Beach, but the bar had recently been transformed into the sizable *Restaurante Garota de Ipanema.* The famous song was based on a local seventeen-year-old beauty who would come in daily to buy cigarettes for her mother, causing the male customers to whistle. Two men, in particular, noticed her—Antonio Jobin, who wrote the music in 1962, and the Portuguese Vinicius de Moraes, who wrote the lyrics. They'd been inspired by her youth, sex appeal, and white bikini—a modest outfit compared to the *fio dental* of today.

I made a reservation for 8 p.m.

The nighttime attendant at my hotel said it was a forty-minute walk to the restaurant, which would have been fine in daylight, but darkness, as my guidebook warned, increased the chances of being mugged. "Return by taxi," the attendant advised, marking a tourist map with the best route. I slipped a hotel business card from the counter into my pocket.

At the busy intersection by the crowded *Restaurant Garota de Ipanema,* tourists were arriving from the beach for dinner. Memorabilia of the famous songwriter and lyricist decked the walls—newspaper and magazine articles, photos, and a giant framed paper blowup of the original notes and words, which had supposedly been penned on a napkin. The waiter sat me against the wall at a table for two, directly under a white t-shirt with black letters, *Garota de Ipanema.* I immediately planned to buy one when I left.

But I don't remember leaving.

Feeling lonely, I downed a *caipirinha* on an empty stomach, followed by a similar drink, a *caipirissima* made with rum. All the other tables contained animated couples or groups. The walk had left me thirsty in the heat and humidity as it had been a sweltering October day. In broken English, the waiter recommended *feijoada,* the Brazilian national dish. The black beans, he explained, were soaked in water overnight, cooked in a thick clay pot, and served with rice, smoked sausage, and red peppers. I ordered the dish and a tomato-and-onion salad with olives, chickpeas, and pork. As long as I was in Ipanema, I figured I should eat and drink like the locals.

Despite my fuzzy memory, I recall thinking that the *feijoada* was delicious and that the rice would soak up the alcohol. But its spiciness only increased my thirst. I had nothing to do but order another drink, a vodka *caipiroska* this time, and a glass of Argentinian Malbec.

I don't remember anything else.

. * * *

I woke up in my bed—thirsty, head pounding—with vague memories of a taxi ride. The room was dark; slivers of light bounced at the edge of the blinds. Some kind soul must have found the business card in my pocket and put me in a cab.

Jumping from the bed, I opened the shade, and the sunlight nailed me. Sunbathers already lined the beach. The digital clock said 9:14 a.m. Oct 28, 2000.

Drinking hastily from a bedside bottle of water, I made a quick trip to the bathroom, put on my Bermuda shorts, which lay crumpled on the floor, and a t-shirt, not the *Garota de Ipanema* one I'd wanted, but a touristy one. And when I opened the door to the hall, I received one of the biggest shocks of my life.

Pungent black smoke filled the hallway, slightly illuminated by a small skylight above.

Then the stark realization that I was on the top floor, with no fire escapes or accessible exits, induced a panic. I slammed the door, ran to a window, opened it, and took a deep breath of air off the Atlantic. Then, forgetting all the hotel-fire information I'd gleaned in my travels—like "hold a wet washcloth over your nose and mouth"—I entered the hall, knowing I had to negotiate nine floors on that winding staircase in one breath. I strained to see the steps. If I tripped, the fall could be fatal.

The dense smoke became lighter farther down, but I was breathless by the third-floor landing. I needed air, took a short gulp, and ran down the remaining steps into the lobby, coughing and choking.

I found the day clerk speaking to a fireman. Another firefighter was wrapping a hose into a roll. They looked at me but continued their conversation. I became irate.

"Why was there no alarm? Or a call to my room?" It was the angriest I'd ever been.

The clerk shrugged.

"I want my money back—for both nights—or I'll call the police!"

Silently, the clerk went to a drawer, opened it, and handed me cash in Brazilian Real. But when I took my wallet from my shorts to tuck the money away, the cash I'd put in the night before from an ATM was gone. I couldn't tell if I'd been robbed at the restaurant, by the cab driver, or by someone at the hotel. Someone had obviously helped themselves to the money but left the credit cards. Given the murder rate in Rio, I knew I was lucky to be alive.

Shaken, I packed my things and caught a taxi to the Copacabana Palace, checking in early to allow myself time to shower and shave. I needed to calm down. I wanted a safe diversion to recover my wits, so I made plans for Rio's number one attraction—the cog railway to the twenty-three-hundred-foot summit of Corcovado Mountain, to the famous statue of Christ the Redeemer.

According to my *Frommer's* guide, a cog railway has a toothed wheel on the underside for traction, stability, and safety on steep grades. This one, constructed in 1884, was powered by a steam engine. Electricity had been added in 1910, littering the mountainside with unsightly poles and overhead wires but making the ascent faster and quieter. In my present circumstances, the irony of going to meet Christ the Redeemer was not lost on me.

The famous hundred-foot Art Deco statue sits on an enormous stone pedestal. Built by the French sculptor Paul Landowski between 1922 and 1931, it shows Christ with outstretched arms as if extending a blessing over the people of a city known for "sin, sex, and samba"—people in need of His help, myself included. It seemed like a giant reproduction of the risen Christ hanging over Mark and Martha's wedding at All Hallows Church—except this one was all white.

Exiting the railway car, I climbed to the observation deck. The lush Tijuca rainforest spread out below. The entire coastline extended hundreds of miles to the north and south. I could see the crescent row of skyscrapers on Copacabana Beach and the vast blue Atlantic beyond.

Turning, finally, to look up at Christ, I was struck by His welcoming and comforting nature, with a face like that on the Shroud of Turin and the statue at All Hallows.

None of the artists of the first few centuries knew the physical appearance of Christ— the Bible contains no descriptions—so depictions of his face varied. Most excluded a beard until the Eastern Orthodox Pantocrator image, resembling the Shroud's face, appeared in the late sixth century. But the origin of that image remains a puzzle. So in preparation for Turin, I'd focused on researching the Shroud's authenticity—because, if it was related to the Resurrection and Crucifixion, it might convince me to change my lifestyle and give up some or most of the "seven deadlies." Believing in Jesus as God was much more tenable if he actually died and rose again on the third day.

Many believe the Greek Pantocrator image came from "the mandylion," also known as "the image of Edessa," a city in central Turkey. The Edessa/mandylion image was first mentioned in 593 A.D. by a Syrian scholar who wrote that a miraculous or God-made image of Christ's face on a cloth had been discovered. When paraded around Edessa before the

Persian attack of 544, it saved the city. That cloth, now revered, was moved to Constantinople in the tenth century, a city sacked during the Fourth Crusade. Later, it appeared in France, presumably brought by a Crusader. If Edessa's famous cloth and the Shroud are one and the same, then the Shroud of Turin can't be a fourteenth-century forgery because it existed seven centuries before the carbon-dating results claim.

The drone of a low-flying aircraft jolted me from my reverie, and I climbed down the steps to catch the next train from the mountain. I needed to prepare for an early morning flight to San Diego. Meanwhile, I was left wondering: *Had God brought me here to contemplate His face on a statue days after scrutinizing the same face on a cloth in Italy?*

Margaret might think so. The trip was worth it if I could convince her of that.

* * *

With stops in Miami and Dallas, flying to San Diego took most of the following day. En route, I experienced a gamut of feelings. My relationship with Margaret had been strained by my obstinacy over this trip when she thought I had more important things to do at home. We'd had several phone conversations, but they'd been brief and emotionless.

Margaret fetched me at the airport, and as we drove to La Jolla, our words were few, and the tension was high. I wasn't ready to say, "I'm sorry," as I knew I should have. The next day I remained late at the office, answering all the correspondence that had arrived in my absence. For two nights, we went to bed in silence, without talking or touching, until sleep overcame us. Our huge California King bed was cold from more than the approach of winter.

On the third night, I stared at the ceiling, knowing I loved the woman beside me, who'd supported me in every way possible for over thirty years. Margaret was aware of my addictions and endured them. But now I wondered if she still loved me. The thought brought tears to my eyes.

I was deeply sorry for my sins and wanted to change—it was an epiphany of sorts, a rarity for me—but, enormously exhausted from my selfish trip, I felt overwhelmed and altogether powerless.

Closing my eyes, I pictured my astrological sign—those two fish swimming in opposite directions. I was at the mercy of the currents of life, pushing me one way toward my mortal desires and another in search of divinity.

Chapter 35   Bella Isabella

SELLING THE OWNERSHIP INTEREST in my private practices allowed me to reduce my workdays from five to three, freeing up discretionary time to review my investments, read for enjoyment, and stay current with the advances in my profession. Engaged in such, I was at my computer on Tuesday, November 7, 2000, when the phone rang. My son Mark was calling, and he sounded unusually serious and sad.

"We saw the doctor today, Dad," he said. "We may never have a baby."

Mark's wife, Martha, had miscarried more than a year earlier and suffered another miscarriage recently, but I was hoping that the third time would be the proverbial charm.

"Evidently," Mark explained, "after the egg was fertilized, some hormonal irregularity caused the embryo to detach from her uterine lining. The doc didn't say we won't have a baby, but he did say it's unlikely."

"Maybe he's wrong."

The news hit me hard. How often, growing up, had I heard the phrase *la famiglia e tutto*? If I could do anything to help Mark and Martha have a baby, I would do it. But, of course, there wasn't. *Or was there?* At that moment, I had no idea, but that would change.

Following my Cursillo weekend on the mountain, Mark Jorgensen, my spiritual mentor, invited me to join a small group of men who wanted to maintain the spiritual "high" we'd experienced by meeting weekly for breakfast. The group included Mike Daniels, the rector on our weekend. There was room for only one additional member, and I was honored to be asked.

Before my son's disheartening call, I'd contacted John Bowen—a man I'd met on the Cursillo weekend, who remained a friend—to have lunch. John said he was available any time since his wife Judy was walking the Camino de Santiago in Spain and would be gone for six weeks.

"It's the ancient pilgrimage route across northern Spain," he added, "a 500-mile trek— from the French border to Santiago de Compostela near the northwest coast—where St. James is buried in the Cathedral."

Wondering why a devout Catholic woman would leave her husband for six weeks to walk across Spain alone, I ordered some books on the Camino de Santiago. One of those books, *Iberia,* by James Michener, includes a chapter titled "Santiago de Compostela," which chronicles the history, beauty, and grandeur of the people, cities, and cathedrals along the Camino de Santiago. "Any reader," Michener wrote, "who has come with me so far through the Iberian Peninsula should be prepared for a pilgrimage across northern Spain to the sanctuary at Santiago de Compostela, the finest journey in Spain and one of the two or three best in the world."

According to Catholic tradition, after the death, resurrection, and ascension of Christ, James the Apostle was the first of the Twelve Apostles to be martyred. He'd preached the gospel in Spain, then returned to Jerusalem, where he was beheaded by order of King Herod Agrippa in his campaign against Christians. James' disciples brought his body by boat to northwest Spain and buried it seventeen miles inland in a field at the former site of a Roman cemetery. Nearly eight centuries later, one night, a hermit traveling in the area witnessed a bright star hovering overhead. Following the instructions of his local bishop, he dug in the field at the center of the light and discovered the remains of the Apostle James. Word quickly spread across Spain, a chapel was built, and pilgrims from all over Europe began walking to the site.

Soon after, Spanish soldiers fighting the Muslims—who'd conquered much of the country—reported seeing Saint James on a white horse, swinging a mighty sword, slaying the Moors. This depiction of Saint James "Matamoros," or "Moor Slayer," united and emboldened the Christians. Their battle cry became "God save St. James!" and turned the tide of war.

Pilgrimages to Santiago de Compostela increased dramatically. Construction of the present cathedral began in the late 11th century, with expansions continuing for hundreds of years. By 1999, pilgrims averaged one hundred fifty thousand annually. Most walked, but some rode bicycles, and a few rode horses. In the Middle Ages, Church authorities established a distance requirement for all pilgrims. At the outset, they received a *credencial,* or pilgrim's passport, to be stamped in churches and hostels along the way, then presented to authorities in Santiago de Compostela. If the passport was accepted, the pilgrims were granted a *Compostela,* a certificate of completion—a very coveted reward.

Michener's *Iberia* convinced me that this was a trip to consider. My next go-to book was *The Pilgrimage Road to Santiago* by David M. Gitlitz and Linda Kay Davidson. It gives a detailed journey, east to west, through each town along the way, with information on the history, legends, architecture, flora, fauna, saints, and religious iconography. Through Gitlitz, I learned of the Spanish priest Juan de Ortega (1080-1163), who'd become stranded after a violent storm on his return from a pilgrimage to Jerusalem. De Ortega prayed to Saint Nicholas of Bari, a patron saint of sailors, pledging to—if he survived— dedicate his life to helping pilgrims along a treacherous part of the Camino de Santiago. When he returned safely, he chose for his home a desolate area in the treacherous *Montes de Oca*, east of the city of Burgos and approximately a third of the way along the Camino, the site of his eventual tomb. In the mid-1400s, when the Church opened Ortega's sealed coffin, they detected a pleasant odor, like that of roses, and out flew honey bees—long considered a symbol of fertility. Word spread quickly that women who wanted children should pray to Juan de Ortega.

Queen Isabella of Spain, who later financed the voyage of Christopher Columbus across the Atlantic, gave birth to a daughter in 1470 and named her Isabella. But for the next five years, she was infertile. She and her husband Ferdinand desperately wanted a son, but she miscarried when she became pregnant in 1475. Having learned of Juan de Ortega, she prayed at his tomb in 1477, and ten months later, in June of 1478, she gave birth to a boy, naming him Juan in honor of de Ortega. Returning in 1479 to pray for another child, she was rewarded with the birth of her daughter Juana. I made a mental note of the saint and the location of his tomb in the town named for him.

Months after my conversation with John Bowen and a week after my son Mark's distressing phone call, Mark Jorgensen invited Margaret and me to his home for a healing Mass for our Cursillo buddy, Mike Daniels, who'd been recently diagnosed with stage 3 non-Hodgkin's lymphoma—a very serious and life-threatening condition. After Holy Communion, we gathered at a makeshift altar and prayed for him, placing our hands on his back and shoulders while a priest recited healing prayers.

The next time I saw Mike was the first Friday after New Year's, sitting across from me at a table for eight at the International House of Pancakes in La Jolla. At our Cursillo Weekend three years earlier, he'd been a tall, handsome, square-jawed, thick-necked man with the physique of an NFL linebacker. Now Mike appeared pale, weak, and discouraged. When asked what had been happening in his life, he lifted his baseball hat to reveal a shiny bald head—the result of a month of chemotherapy.

Feeling sorry, I asked if he'd heard of the Camino de Santiago. I was thinking of making the pilgrimage in hopes of having a grandchild.

"You mean that long hike in Spain?"

"Wanna do it with me? Walking takes six weeks, but we can do it in two by bicycle."

Mike looked at me in disbelief. "Are you kidding? I'm so weak I can't even walk around the block. You gotta be crazy!"

"It's early January," I countered. "The trip isn't till June. We can start training in Mission Bay, where it's flat, and gradually add miles and hills till we're ready."

Sitting beside me was Curt Dose, a six-four, athletic, ex-Vietnam fighter pilot, who promptly chimed in. "I'll do it."

We left breakfast with Mike still denying any interest in the trip, but a few days later, a mutual friend, Carlos Arbelaez, told Mike he'd also be joining us. Born in Bogota, Columbia, and college-educated in the States, Carlos was now co-owner of a tuna fishing fleet and such an endearing soul that he was difficult to refuse. Mike consented, and I set our first training date for a few trips around Fiesta Island at Mission Bay the following Saturday.

Subsequently, we trained every Saturday, then added Tuesdays, Thursdays, hills, and miles, and by May, we could bicycle from my house in La Jolla, have lunch in Oceanside, 25 miles away, and return. I'd found a small company online—Cycling Through the Centuries—that would provide hybrid bikes, most meals, van support, and luxury hotels for the entire two-week Camino de Santiago. The company timed the trip to end on a Sunday, so we could attend the Pilgrim's Mass, which John Bowen had told me not to miss.

* * *

On May 27, 2001, we flew to Pamplona, Spain, and met Maggie Deffense, owner of Cycling Through the Centuries. A middle-aged American with tightly-curled blonde hair, a delightful personality, and tremendous knowledge about the Camino, she introduced us to her two workers, young Tour de France-type cyclists. One of these assistants would leave early in the morning, chalk the route with large arrows at every turn, then return to drive one of the support vans while Maggie drove the other. The second would be the "sweeper," the group's last rider, to ensure no one was left behind.

The two vans took us up the mountain to the nine-hundred-year-old village of Roncesvalles. At an elevation of three thousand feet and thirteen miles from the French border, it had only twenty permanent residents. Our hotel, built in 1725, had recently been converted to a comfortable accommodation bearing the village's name. There we were fitted to our bicycles and given our Pilgrim's Passport. The attendant thrust a metal stamp onto an ink pad and marked each of ours. Carlos, who'd bought a new digital video camera for our adventure, recorded the event.

Before dinner, we attended the standing-room-only Pilgrim's Mass at the Colegiata de Roncesvalles. This thirteenth-century church had the largest organ in the province of Navarre, which accompanied the choir. The presiding priest, one of four, read a long list of countries represented by the pilgrims who would begin their journey the following day. At the end of Mass, he blessed us and asked the Lord to keep us safe all the way to Santiago de Compostela. At dinner that night, Maggie presented us with a white scallop shell bearing the red cross of Santiago to be worn around our necks. On the Camino, that shell would confer pilgrim status on us, ensuring that the locals would give us respect and greet us with *"Buen Camino."*

"You'll be making great sacrifices on this trip," Maggie said. Her somber tone left me wondering what they might be. *But if sacrifices are necessary to produce a grandchild,* I told myself, *so be it. La famiglia e tutto!*

Carlos became our unofficial videographer, and the following morning he decided to interview me before we departed. "What's your goal for today, John?" he asked.

"To keep out of the van is my goal. I want to ride across all of Spain without any help." I was adamant about this because I'd bargained with God, silently praying *I will ride the entire trip for You, Lord, if You will give Mark and Martha a baby.*

We began our pilgrimage along the Irati River, where Hemingway had fished when he wrote *The Sun Also Rises,* then continued through Pamplona, where the annual running of the bulls attracts a million people to the Festival of San Fermín, made famous by Hemingway's novel. Our first religious stop was at the mysterious Church of the Eunate, fifteen miles southwest of Pamplona, a small, stone, octagonal structure built around the year 1200. It sat amidst sunflower fields in the wide-open countryside, with no population center nearby. One theory for the odd location is that the site had served as a burial place for pilgrims who perished along the way. It was now a Catholic chapel, *Santa Maria de Eunate*—a perfect place to sit in prayer and meditation and renew my questionable bargain with the Lord: *I will ride five hundred miles, stay out of the van, and You will deliver a baby, Lord. Are you listening?*

There was no answer.

We spent the night in the pleasant village of Puente la Reina, known for its picturesque, six-arched Queen's Bridge. Built in the 11th century for the benefit of pilgrims crossing the green water of the Arga River, it led to the medieval town of Estella, which Gitlitz had highlighted, quoting the twelfth-century *Codex Calixtinus* pilgrims' guide: "where bread is good, wine excellent, meat and fish are abundant, and which overflows with all delights." Unfortunately, our brief visit, almost a thousand years later, left no time to confirm the description.

During a picnic lunch a few miles west of Estella, under a gigantic, gnarly, one-hundred-fifty-year-old olive tree, Maggie informed us that we were behind schedule, with a long ride ahead of us—twenty miles of gradual uphill climbing to the town of Laguardia in the famous Rioja wine country. Her final words troubled me: "Enjoy your ride. Around four o'clock, the vans will fetch you and your bikes for the drive to the hotel, so you'll have time to shower before the wine tasting at six. Dinner will follow." These were words I did not want to hear.

Actually, the Bodegas "wine fountain" that we'd encountered leaving Estella—which Maggie herself had recommended—put us behind schedule. The Bodegas vineyard dates to the 12th century. In 1991, the winery had built a "fountain"—allowing pilgrims to taste free wine. A bilingual sign said: "We are pleased to invite you to drink in moderation. If you wish to take the wine with you, you will have to buy it." We drank using our scallop shells as tablespoons as no cups were available. This took much time since almost everyone in our group imbibed.

Learning that the van would pick us up, I feigned another trip to the buffet table, tossed my paper plate into the garbage bag, and headed for my bicycle hidden behind a group of trees. Soon I was pedaling furiously, head down. I had the address of our hotel in Laguardia on the map Maggie provided. Seeing me leave, Carlos followed suit, and we worked our bikes as fast as possible up the gentle but endless hills of La Rioja, past green fields and groves of olive trees—some dating to Roman times. Acres upon acres of vineyards laden with tight clusters of small dark purple grapes flanked our way.

Several hours later, I heard the unmistakable sound of Maggie's van behind us. She tapped the horn several times, and Carlos and I pulled over.

"Let us finish, please," I pleaded.

With a stern, motherly look, Maggie glanced at her watch and said, "If you insist. It's only ten more miles. But don't stop for photos." Looking at Carlos, she added, "Or movies."

It may only have been ten miles, but they were all uphill. Arriving at the hotel tired and thirsty, I quickly showered, dressed for dinner, and took my place at the table at the one empty seat—Carlos had arrived minutes earlier—just as the waiters were serving the entrees.

Halfway through my bowl of *langostinos*, I felt a stabbing leg cramp and kicked up my foot, hitting the underside of the dinner table and knocking over two bottles of wine, staining the starched white tablecloth red—a sacrilege in the wine region of Spain. But I believed that keeping my vow to the Lord justified it. Regardless, I was embarrassed.

The next day we had a relaxing, short ride to Santo Domingo de la Calzada, home of the famous Spanish "Miracle of the Chickens," as summarized in Gitlitz, *Iberia*, and several other books I'd read. The account goes something like this: In the mid-14th century, a German couple and their seventeen-year-old son stopped for lodging at a small inn. The innkeeper's daughter wanted to seduce the lad, but he refused because he'd been raised in the Christian faith. Annoyed, she stuck her father's silver wine goblet into his luggage before the family departed.

Once the theft was discovered, the local magistrate sent several constables after the party and brought the lad back. According to the local law, a noose was placed around his neck at the gallows. Since they tied his hands in front, he could pray and petition the saintly, deceased Domingo de la Calzada for assistance. His request was answered—he survived several attempts to lynch him—so the frustrated constables ran to the magistrate, who didn't believe the news. "If you did what you said," he argued, "that boy could no more be alive than these chickens I'm about to eat." At this point, the rooster and hen sprang to life, jumped from the platter, restored their white feathers, and began to sing and dance. Out of respect for what they believed was a miracle, the locals placed these chickens in a cage in the Cathedral, and for the last six centuries, their offspring have been honored there.

As I entered the Cathedral, the faint smell of ammonia distracted me from the beauty and grandeur of the Gothic interior. Then, hearing an unusual sound, I looked up to see a small gilded chicken coop with ornate vertical brass bars and fleur-de-lys embellishments. An elderly Spanish woman entertained her companions by cajoling the rooster and hen to cackle in response to her enthusiastic efforts to imitate them.

Although the interior of the cathedral was beautiful, a carnival-like atmosphere prevailed. Keeping the legend alive was a way of attracting tourists to this modest town of 6,500. I had a healthy appreciation for miracles but couldn't fathom roasted chickens sprouting new white feathers. *These Spaniards are crazy*, I concluded.

Yet the following day, I would experience the most profound event in my entire life, for which "a miracle" is the only explanation I have. Upon returning from Spain, I told very few about what had happened. If it were not for my reputation of stability, honesty, and rationality among my friends, family, and colleagues, I would have been ridiculed, as I'd been as a young boy in Stratford, Connecticut. But I'm getting ahead of myself. Before this miracle came a series of unexpected accidents.

At breakfast, before we embarked on the fifty-seven-mile route to Burgos, Maggie, in a jolly mood, reviewed the day's journey, which would be long and arduous, with cloudy skies, drizzle, and challenging headwinds. At the start of the ride, the sweeper suggested to Carlos, Mike, Curt, and me that we might want to ride in a single file. The leader would shelter the wind, then drop to the rear, the others rotating in turn. "It's called drafting," he said. "They do it on the Tour de France all the time. The closer your front tire is to the biker ahead of you, the better the benefit."

An hour after leaving Santo Domingo de la Calzada, approaching the small village of Bellorado, it was time for a break. The flat plain had become rolling hills. Carlos was following Mike, and as the wind increased, Carlos's front wheel inched closer to Mike's rear wheel. Maggie's yellow van was in a parking lot off to our right. Hearing her familiar yell— "Water, bananas!"—Mike touched his brakes, Carlos's wheel touched his, and they both went sprawling. Mike was fine, but Carlos sustained a large scrape on his knee, which Maggie washed off, applying iodine from her ever-ready medical kit, as Carlos gritted his teeth and winced. Then Maggie added a square bandage to cover the wound.

Most of the group believed the highlight would come at the end of the day, with our entrance into the fabled city of Burgos—the home of El Cid, the Spanish national hero revered for his conquest of Muslim-ruled Valencia in 1094. But for me, my definitive destination was the coffin of San Juan de Ortega. Beneath its lid, I imagined honey bees swirling in the darkness. We would have lunch in the tiny village near his tomb.

As we headed into the foothills of the *Montes de Oca*, the blue sky, fluffy cumulus clouds, became a dense, rippled layer, at times descending upon us like a light fog. We were climbing through wheat fields now, then up and down hills of pine and oak. Then the fog lifted as rapidly as it had descended, and the long road ahead rose gently—in a straight line—to a small village on the hill's summit. On previous hills like this one, Carlos and I would race to the top, so I looked at him, he returned my gaze with a grin, and we dashed ahead, chins on our chests. Feeling particularly strong that morning, I opened a generous lead on the narrow asphalt road, then pulled to the center and raised a clenched fist in triumph.

Less than fifty yards from the first buildings at the summit, I noticed an older man who resembled my Grandpa Russo in his later years. He had a stubbled gray beard, wore a flat black cap, and fixed his eyes on mine. Suddenly he waved his arms frantically, signaling me to move to my right. At the top, the road narrowed to a single lane, touching the corners of two stone buildings while curving to the left. Seeing the old man, I steered to the right, but behind him came a speeding white truck. I could see MACK plainly visible across its grill. I could also see the angry face of the driver, glaring furiously as he sped toward me. He had to have seen me. The sun peeked through the clouds directly overhead, lighting my red cycling jersey.

There were just three feet between the truck and the stone building that I hit. My shoulder took the blow. Knocked from my bike, I landed on my back and could see the truck's rear tires passing within inches of my head. Alert for more traffic, Mike and Curt hoisted me to my feet and moved me to safety beyond the curve. My right elbow and left knee were burning. A small crowd gathered, five or six people from the village of less than a hundred. I looked for the old man who'd saved my life, but he wasn't there. He'd disappeared as mysteriously as he'd appeared.

In a yellow tee shirt, black bike shorts, and a white scallop shell around his neck, Mike stood beside me as I surveyed my wounds. Everyone wanted to know what had happened.

"The truck came right through the middle of the street!" Mike yelled. Carlos translated while videoing the scene. As I rotated my arm to show the camera my bleeding elbow, a second MACK truck zoomed by. "Just like that!" Mike yelled.

When the truck's roar receded, Mike continued talking to the locals. "He hit the building just as the truck reached him." Carlos now turned his camera to my bleeding knee.

Since the sting of my wounds—commonly called "road rash"—was more significant than the chance for infection, I let Maggie clean them when she arrived with her alcohol and iodine but left them unbandaged to the air. Then we hopped back on our bikes and pedaled off.

The strange appearance of the man I nicknamed "Gramps" has remained with me these many years. But that is not the miracle to which I was referring.

* * *

As we gained elevation, climbing through pine-and-oak forests and meadows of heather and broom, I imagined wild animals and thieves hiding behind trees, ready to pounce on unsuspecting pilgrims. Just that situation attracted Juan de Ortega to the area in the 12th century, earning him sainthood for his bravery, compassion, and sense of justice. Passing through the tiny village of Villafranca Montes de Oca, we were seven miles from his tomb.

We stopped next for a photo at an intersection where long white arrows pointed in opposite directions. One way led to Barrios de Colina, closer to Burgos and a hot shower. The other went to "S. Juan de Ortega," where Maggie had said we'd meet for lunch. Seeing that name on a sign now—not in the books I'd read—energized me. Mike, Curt, and Carlos followed as I biked straight ahead into that one-street village of fifteen permanent residents. At the end of the street stood a four-story Romanesque church of tan and white stones, with a rose window high over the front door. To the left, a bell tower extended thirty feet above its red tile roof. Famished, we all decided we needed to eat before doing any exploring.

At the Bar Marcela, I ordered a *bocadillo*—bread, ham, tomatoes, and strips of roasted piquillo peppers—drizzled with olive oil. Mike placed his order, then left the table and didn't return until after his food had arrived. Then, sitting down, he looked directly at me and said, "Drop your sandwich and go down to the church—*now*—before others arrive. It's empty now."

"Why?"

"I've been to Lourdes and bathed in its healing waters," he said. "Lourdes is one of the holiest places in the Catholic world. But I've never felt the presence of God as I just did in the tomb of San Juan de Ortega."

He was intensely serious, so I took one last bite and stood up.

"Skip the upper church," he said. "Go immediately down the steps to the tomb."

Exiting into the brilliant sunlight, I skirted an old monastery where we'd later get our passports stamped and entered the church. A curving stone staircase of a dozen or so steps descended to a black iron gate that was partially open. There was nothing beyond it but all-encompassing darkness. I hurried down, pushed through the gate, then paused to wait for my eyes to adjust. Votive candles—some lit, some not— were scattered about the room. The dank darkness caused me to pause further, a sound decision because I realized I was on an elevated concrete platform with steps to the crypt five feet below. Only a black iron railing prevented me from falling.

I felt an immediate need to kneel. There was something special about this place. It brought a sense of peace and sacredness, along with warmth, love, and the presence of God. It was a sixth sense, one I'd experienced only once before in my life—in the Newman Chapel at the University of Pennsylvania, after praying for several desperate hours, unable to study, after receiving a "Dear John" letter before finals, from the girl I thought I loved.

With total disregard for the exposed wound on my left knee, I knelt, without pain, on the damp, moldy concrete. I'd always hated to kneel, ever since the nuns of the Baltimore Catechism at Saint James Church in Stratford—the very church where Margaret and I were married—had insisted I must. Maybe, as a kid, my bony knees and sensitive skin had made me rest my buttocks on the edge of the pew. The nuns thought I was irreligious and were not far from wrong.

Now, fifty years later, clasping my hands prayerfully and resting them on the three-foot iron railing, I surveyed the room below. Several yards away, a medieval stone coffin was in the middle, about eight feet long and three feet wide. Beyond it, suspended on a whitewashed wall, was a plain, dark-brown wooden cross. The vertical beam was about six feet long, with a four-foot horizontal crosspiece. Because of its precise construction, I thought it might not be from the 12th century. Above it was a short, gray, curved oak branch forming a partial halo, calling attention to the cross, the dominant feature in the room. I sensed that this branch must have come from the saint himself, giving the crypt a feeling of his presence.

It was surreal. Words can't express the intensity of my emotions—but peace, love, strength, and certainty were among them. I felt the need to pray, so, like in the chapel at Penn many years ago, I repeated the only three prayers I knew—the Our Father, Hail Mary, and the Act of Contrition. Then I silently added, "God, I'm asking for your help. Please give me a grandchild. Let Martha become pregnant and deliver a healthy baby." I repeated this several times while focusing intently on the white coffin.

As I raised my eyes to the wooden cross above the crypt, what happened next astonished me. The words I wrote in my travel diary that night were the only words I recorded on the entire trip, helping me to remember ex- actly what happened in the tomb. As I prayed, I suddenly saw a small blazing cross—about eighteen inches tall and twelve inches wide—perfectly centered and superimposed upon the large wooden cross. At first, I thought of it as a cross of flashing lights. I couldn't believe I was actually seeing small flames— but that's what they were—without smoke, heat, smell, or sound.

After a few seconds, that one cross divided into two of the same size. One moved to the right, the other to the left of the original cross, which remained in the center. The process was like the mitotic cell division of a fertilized human egg, with one major exception. After fertilization, the egg splits into two nearly identical "daughter cells," and the "parent cell" disap- pears. But with the dividing crosses, the "parent cross" remained where it had been, and I saw three identical blazing crosses. But not for long, for those new crosses also divided and moved laterally. Now there were five against the far wall. Sequentially, the outer crosses divided and separated, and so there were now seven that remained. The process was rhythmic, as if in sync with a metronome. Every two seconds came another division until there were seven flaming crosses.

Though mesmerized, my rational mind stood fast. *How could this be?* I must have somehow set in motion a mechanized, Disney-like illusion, as in the beloved Disneyland attraction, *Pirates of the Caribbean*, in which, when a boat reaches a certain point in the audio-animatronics, the viewer is transported into another world. *What clever Spaniards*, I thought. *These crosses are being projected from the wall behind me!*

Turning, I expected to find an aperture in the wall through which an apparatus projected images of blazing crosses, but the wall was solid!

My scientific mind kept searching for an explanation. *It must be a weird reflection on my glasses from the light of the candles!* But as I reached to remove my glasses, I realized I'd left them in the back pocket of my cycling jersey since I needed them only for reading. I had no further explanation. Other than God.

What was the meaning of these seven flaming crosses? For lack of any other reason, I felt that the Holy Spirit had granted me a spiritual vision— a gift from God, a moment of grace. Yet I was so undeserving. *If anyone deserved such a vision*, I told myself, *it was Margaret.*

Dr. Bill Creasy had said that the number "seven" has great significance in the Bible. It is a symbol of completeness and perfection. God created the world in seven days, there are seven days in a week, and the Holy Sabbath is on the seventh day. Jesus said you should forgive someone "not seven times, but seventy times seven."

Such thoughts left me floating in space and time until quite a different thought jolted me—*Had the group left for Burgos without me?* Immediately a reversal of the images took place.

As I look back on this experience, I believe that if my imagination had been manifesting seven blazing crosses, they would have disappeared at this thought. But they didn't. They retreated just as they'd appeared . . . seven . . . five . . . three . . . one . . . none, at the same rate with a brief pause in between. It was a perfect orchestration, like a beautiful sunset—or a newborn baby. God had to have been involved. And I knew now, with certainty, that I would soon be a grandfather.

Chapter 36   Beware of the Dog

I FOUND THE GROUP still in the restaurant, paid my bill, and followed Maggie as she led everyone to the church. There, she talked about the beautiful objects on the upper level and in the Chapel of St. Nicholas, restored in 1477 by Queen Isabella. The descent to the crypt was entirely different from what I'd experienced. There were now people and lights in the tomb. Mike and I stood in the background and kept silent. We had both somehow missed the red button at the bottom of the staircase, with the words "*Empujar*" and "Push." Since that button to turn on the lights was so prominent now, it seemed we'd been blinded in our separate descents.

* * *

Arriving in Burgos late that afternoon, we visited the French Gothic Cathedral, a UNESCO World Heritage Site, with its twin, two-hundred-seventy-foot Germanic towers pointing to Heaven. The church houses the remains of El Cid, that famous Castilian knight and warlord of medieval Spain. Although it was one of the most impressive cathedrals I've ever visited, my emotions lagged behind me at the tomb of San Juan de Ortega.

It took us two days to cycle across the windy Meseta, Spain's massive high central plateau, a somewhat barren stretch with a few scattered trees, fields of shimmering wheat, and flocks of sheep that sometimes blocked the road.

Steep, ominous mountains lay to the west one morning as we prepared to mount our bikes. At our first stop to refill our water bottles, Maggie instructed us to find a stone comparable to the magnitude of our sins and put it wherever it would fit—on our bike, pocket, or backpack, depending on its size. Ignoring the solemnity of the moment, I chose a small pebble and placed it in the rear pocket of my cycling jersey.

As we strained to reach the highest elevation, Maggie placed herself strategically with the van at the roadside, her curly blonde hair a tempting lure as she chanted, "Water? Cookies? Bananas? A ride?" When we ignored her offers, she smiled and shouted, "Up ahead is the monument where you'll shed your boulders!"

We soon reached the five-thousand-foot Pass of Foncebadon. The *Cruz de Fierro*, or Iron Cross, sits on a tall pole atop a twenty-five-foot pile of various-sized stones. It's the highest point on the Camino. Several in our group removed a sizable rock from their saddlebag or backpack, scurried up the rockpile, proudly placed it at the foot of the pole, then posed for a photo. Sheepishly, I dropped my pebble at the bottom of the mound, letting it slip through my fingers unnoticed. Having not been to Confession in over forty years, the proper gesture would have required a boulder much larger than I could carry. It made me realize, once again, how undeserving I was of the vision of the crosses I'd seen at the tomb of Juan de Ortega.

With the steep descent to Ponferrada, a city dating to the Roman occupation, we encountered a major change in scenery. We were now on the west side of the Camino's tallest mountains, cycling by fields where cows roamed in green pastures separated by ancient stone walls. This was Galicia, a large province in Northwest Spain with Celtic roots, a distinctive culture, and a language of its own. After reaching the town of Villafranca del Bierzo, again, we began to climb.

The road to O Cebreiro, the highest summit on the Camino after the Cruz de Fierro, followed—a steep climb, eleven miles long, with an average grade of six percent. Many in our group gave in to Maggie's offer and happily opted for the van, but I'd vowed to complete the entire Camino. I'd made my promise to God, and I wasn't about to renege, although it was the most challenging stretch I'd ever climbed. Ashamed of the pebble I'd dropped, I pressed on, fighting off the ever-present leg cramps. Maggie had told us that our reward would be a quaint medieval village with an even quainter legend. And she was right.

I felt exhilarated reaching O Cebreiro. Then, thoroughly alive to our adventure, my achievement, and the crisp and clear air, I went to join the others, who'd arrived earlier in the van. I found them enjoying *Pulpo a la Gallega*, a Galician delicacy of succulent octopus and potatoes in a spicy sauce.

A faint odor of smoke arose from outdoor firepits mixed with the smell of manure from the fields below. Bagpipes sounded in the distance as I relaxed on an ancient stone wall overlooking the landscape, wondering what other wonders remained for our trip. I'd already experienced a miracle and had felt the presence of God, and for that, I was grateful.

We soon checked into our hotel, a rustic lodging set in a former town hall and jail. After a warm shower and short rest, Mike, Carlos, Curt, and I sat at an outdoor table at the hotel's restaurant for a dinner of *Caldo Gallego*—a potato-cabbage-and-bean soup—along with a large plate of octopus and two bottles of hearty Galician red wine. Retrieving his video camera, Carlos asked for my impression of this tiny village.

"We're in O Cebreiro," I said, "at an inn near a little Catholic Church—the oldest on the Camino—where one of the greatest miracles on the Camino took place. It happened in the late 13th century during a severe winter storm. The priest would only say Mass if someone showed up since he didn't believe in the real presence of Christ in the Eucharist. A lone pilgrim came from a village below, and during that Mass, when the priest consecrated the host, there was an actual transformation of the bread and wine into human flesh and blood. The chalice, plate, flesh, and blood are displayed here in the church. I look forward to seeing them and learning more about this miracle."

Until this trip, I'd never believed in what Catholics call "transubstantiation," the conversion of the Eucharist into the body and blood of Christ. But my experience in the tomb of San Juan de Ortega changed me forever. If God could manifest flaming crosses from molecules of nitrogen, oxygen, water, and the CO_2 in the air we breathe, He could place the body of Jesus into the bread, and His blood into the wine of Holy Communion—even though we can't see it.

Faith is a gift. Sometimes it's hard-earned, and sometimes we fall into it, but if we have it, we must treasure, protect, and work to maintain it —if not increase it—for having it once is no guarantee we'll take it to the grave. Which is when it counts.

* * *

The next day's ride was mostly downhill. Rain was predicted, so I pulled my slick yellow rain pants and waterproof jacket from my duffle bag before turning in. It rained hard during the night, and by morning the roads, lined with ancient stone walls, were slick and treacherous. Given the rolling hills, occasional fog, mist, and emerald-green grass, we could have been in Ireland or Scotland. Many Galicians, descended from ancient people, still believed in witches, an uncomfortable thought in such conditions.

We soon left the main road for a timeworn hard-packed dirt path through medieval hamlets of scant stone houses. Wooden rakes and scythes lay about the yards. Random churches dotted the way, where itinerant priests periodically came to say Mass, baptize, and bury the locals. We pedaled slowly, avoiding rocks, ruts, and puddles. Since the day was quite warm, I removed my waterproof jacket but retained my slick yellow rain pants to defend against splashing mud. The path, but six-feet wide, was bordered by crude stone walls. Rounding one corner, I heard a distinctive mooing. Ahead, leading eight oxen, was an elderly man in a torn blue sweater and short-brimmed gray cap, his blue jeans bunched above mud-caked shoes. He used a long pole to keep his balance and prod his animals.

The brown oxen were massive, with long, curved, menacing horns. When they turned sideways, their noses butted one wall, and their long tails brushed the other. To avoid them, I abandoned my bike and hopped the wall to my right, landing feet first in the soft grass of the adjacent field. Mike and Curt followed, leaving their bikes at the mercy of the oxen. Carlos jumped over the opposite wall and, taking his video camera from his backpack, began recording:

I am in my bright red cycling jersey and slick yellow rain pants, a sharp contrast to the emerald grass, black-and-gray buildings, and rock walls. Nearby, Mike is in his black mountain bike shorts and long-sleeved white jersey, blending nicely with the colors around him. About eight yards away, a black and brown German Shepherd lifts his head toward us, turns away, then looks back—directly at *me*. Standing, he shakes off some loose grass and starts forward, faster and faster. Then, a few feet away, he stops, lowers his snout, sniffs my right leg up and down, moves behind me, and raises his hind leg.

Observing the scene through his camera, Carlos exclaimed, "He's peeing on your pants!" I could feel the warmth in my shoe. Then this Galician German Shepherd, having relieved itself, trotted back to recline in his spot by the wall.

"He thought you were a fire hydrant!" Mike said, slapping his hands on his thighs and leaning forward with his hands on his knees. His belly laugh was unrestrained.

"Well, there wasn't much there," I lied. It was a feeble attempt to diminish my embarrassment, my only defense against a humiliation that ranked right up there with the Hopalong Cassidy incident of my childhood. After all my successes in life, why couldn't I conquer the sin of pride, the love of one's own excellence? According to C.S. Lewis, it's the worst of the Seven Deadly Sins. But I hadn't even made a dent. Our talents are gifts from God, and He should get the credit. So I shouldn't be concerned. But that evening, the same sin reared its ugly head again. Carlos had brought his laptop to dinner at the hotel's restaurant, and after dessert, with everyone standing

behind him, he played our encounter with the oxen and the dog. Guffaws
followed with shouts of "Let's see it again!"

I left for my room without saying a word.

* * *

Two days later, on the morning of our last day—Sunday, June 10, 2001—we
reached the foot of the Monte do Gozo, or Hill of Joy, which has a vertical height of two hundred thirty feet. Knowing it was the last hill before
a three-mile descent into Santiago de Compostela, Carlos and I raced the
final thirty yards to the crest. And once again, reaching the summit first, I
raised a fist as "King of the Hill."

"King of the Hill" is one of the many games cyclists play on various
hills along the Camino. But this hill has more significance because of the
euphoria of seeing—for the first time—the three towers of the Cathedral
of Santiago de Compostela above the sprawling city, home to the bones
of the famous saint, after five hundred miles of scenic but often grueling
landscapes.

We pedaled directly into the Plaza del Obradoiro, a massive cobble-
stone space in front of the cathedral's Baroque façade and gigantic twin towers, and stopped for a group photo. In accordance with an ancient ritual, we
then went to the *Oficina de Acogida al Peregrino*—the pilgrims' reception
office—to present our Pilgrim Passport, the *"credencial,"* and receive our
pilgrim's certificate of completion, the *"Compostela."*

Returning to the Plaza, we ascended the two-story, seventeenth-century, Obradoiro staircase to pass through the *Portico de la Gloria*, an elaborate
entry crafted in the late 12th century by the sculptor Master Mateo. Then,
one by one, we paused to place our hands into the smooth grooves of the
center column that holds the carved figure of Saint James, depressions created by millions of pilgrims over hundreds of years.

It was standing-room-only at the Pilgrims' Mass at the Cathedral. I
found a spot on the floor, near the front of the church, with a column to
support my back, that would give me a perfect view of the famous incense
burner—the "Botafumeiro" or "smoke-belcher." About five feet tall, it
weighs one hundred eighty pounds when filled with charcoal, and swings
more than sixty feet high, in a two-hundred-thirteen-foot arc, above the
pilgrims in both transepts of the church.

A nun with a soprano voice began singing in a language I didn't understand, but her love of God was palpable in each word. Moreover, her voice
was amplified, easily heard above the pipes of the massive organ, which

dates to 1700, in a cathedral, the construction of which began in 1075. *Such history and wonderment*, I thought.

To begin the Mass, eight priests, in white vestments trimmed in red, processed with two altar boys along the central nave toward an altar decked with lilies. The Catholic Mass is a ritual presentation of the suffering, death, and resurrection of Jesus, and so participation in it becomes a profound expression of unity between Jesus Christ, God the Father, the Holy Spirit, and the believers in the pews themselves. Many in the congregation did not know this but appreciated the tradition, pageantry, music, and history.

Lectors presented the first and second scriptural readings from the Old and New Testament, and then a priest read the Gospel from the Book of Mark, all in Spanish. Margaret, knowing this would be a special Mass for us, as well as the date we would arrive in Santiago de Compostela, had copied pages for me from her June 2001 *Magnificat* prayer booklet, which contained the readings for that day so that I could follow in English. The final sentence in the Gospel reading was Jesus saying, "For whoever does the will of my Father in heaven is my brother, and sister, and mother." At which my thought was, *Surely, I fall short!* But I was comforted by the thought that, as the priest read from the Gospel of Mark, I was hearing the same words that Margaret would listen to at All Hallows Church in La Jolla just hours later.

Many Protestants believe that Catholics don't read the Bible. It is, I realized, one of the many misunderstandings between Catholicism and the other Christian religions. But as Mark Jorgensen had told me, if you attend daily Mass—as Dad's friend Andy Brose had done for the rest of his life after his miraculous healing from severe asthma—you will hear most of the New Testament and much of the Old Testament read in church every three years before the cycle begins anew.

After the priests distributed Holy Communion, three men in red robes climbed the steps before the altar to grab the enormous incense burner that descended from above on a thick rope. The elaborate pulley system high above dates to the 14th century. The famous silver Botafumeiro, shaped like a large Roman vase, stopped several feet from the floor.

A priest joined the group, lit the charcoal, blessed the incense burner, then backed away, and the source of the burner's nickname soon became evident. As five additional red-robed men pulled on a large ring at the rope's end, a gray cloud of smoke burst forth. As the men pulled down on the ring again and again, the Botafumeiro began to swing from one transept to the other, high above the heads of the astonished pilgrims. It swung for several minutes as the nun with the soprano voice sang, and the massive organ played, filling the thousand-year-old church with smoke, incense, and sacred music. That spectacle alone was worth flying six thousand miles and cycling five hundred miles to participate as a true pilgrim, which I now was, as my *Compostela* attested.

A day later, on our flight to San Diego, as I looked down at the Atlantic Ocean through scattered clouds, the blue water evoked in me a sense of calm and stability. To many Bible scholars, the color blue represents Heaven. What could be more appropriate?

Less than a year earlier, I had returned home from Brazil immersed in the Seven Deadly Sins, projecting my anger toward Margaret for opposing my trip to Rio de Janeiro. That adventure allowed me to tell my friends about the *fio dentals* strolling Copacabana Beach. But I'd omitted to tell them that my gluttony—excessive food and alcohol—had caused the deep sleep that resulted in my missing the commotion of guests escaping a fire in my cheap hotel, putting me in danger of death from smoke inhalation as I descended its spindly wooden staircase in the dark.

But I was married to a woman devoted to God and His teachings, and who honored the vows made on our wedding day. And when the short, portly, perspiring priest—late for the first race at Aqueduct—asked if she would have me for better or worse, she had answered in the affirmative. And she meant it. So when I had returned from Rio de Janeiro, the iciness we had experienced the first two nights melted on the third— the result of Margaret's forgiveness and warmth. Under the covers, she'd placed her hand over mine and squeezed, and I reciprocated.

This time it was much different. I was returning with an amazing faith-filled story and couldn't wait to share my good news with her.

Ten months later, I received grace in its fullest Christian sense. As with Queen Isabella, whose son Juan had been born ten months after her pilgrimage to the tomb of San Juan de Ortega, ten months after I saw the seven flaming crosses, Thomas Blake Sottosanti, a healthy 11-pound baby, was born to Martha and Mark, and I was now a granddad. Just as with my Dad, before encountering the number 653, Mark doubted the power of prayer and its relationship to this beautiful baby boy he'd help create.

But if we're counting miracles here, consider this: Mike Daniels did wonderfully well on our trip, riding in the van only once when Maggie chased us down. Not only was there no sign of his lymphoma at his next exam after our return, but there has never been a recurrence, and he has now been cancer-free for twenty years. For those first three years, however, fearful that his lymphoma would materialize again, he was tested every six months. But in 2004, when his cancer had not returned, and in appreciation for his healing at Lourdes and on the Camino, he decided to become a Deacon in the Catholic Church. He studied for three years, was ordained in 2007, and Margaret and I attended his first Mass, received Communion

from him, and heard his first homily. As a Deacon, he can baptize and perform marriage, funeral, and burial services.

At the end of 2021, Mike said that the Camino de Santiago had saved
his life, and he has Carlos, Curt, and me to thank for it. But in the grand
scheme of things, I realize we had nothing to do with it.

As Mike liked to say, "Remember, John: *Dog*, spelled backward, is *God*."

Chapter 37   Darkening Outlook

ON A TYPICAL WORKDAY, I would descend the staircase of our two-story townhome at 6:30, eat breakfast while reading the *San Diego Union-Tribune*, kiss Margaret, and leave for the office in time for my first patient at 7:30. For some reason, however, on the morning of September 11, 2001, I was ten minutes early, so I sat down in the family room and turned on the television, only to find black smoke filling the screen—billowing against a perfect blue sky. A building was on fire. As the camera moved laterally, a second burning building came into view, its gaping holes emitting black and white smoke that dwarfed that of the Botafumeiro in Spain. The reporter spoke rapidly. Terrorists . . . Twin Towers . . . north . . . south . . . two planes . . . loss of life . . .

I was instantly reminded of the PSA crash site when I'd flown over the North Park area of San Diego in 1978, peering down at the smoke streaming from hotspots below, after body parts of passengers and crew had been taken to the morgue. But what I was witnessing now made me even sicker.

The digital video recorder showed 6:58. A witness was telling a reporter about an attack on the Pentagon, but the screen remained on the burning buildings of the World Trade Center. Suddenly the black smoke spewing from the South Tower's top floors expanded laterally and descended rapidly. The upper half of the building had lost its structural integrity. Fragments of steel, glass, plaster, carpets, desks, and people were plummeting through the black smoke. I'd never seen such horror on television. Margaret joined me, watching in silence.

Then the reporter interrupted the man speaking about the Pentagon. "The World Trade Center is literally starting to crumble." It was 6:59, time to leave for work, and as I walked out the door, I heard a voice saying, "It is falling apart as we watch these pictures live."

As I entered the back door of my office, a voice was blaring from all of our internal speakers. The staff had turned on the radio. "You can see the top portion of the front tower is beginning to collapse . . . good Lord . . . you can see the building falling to the ground in a pile of rubble and a tower of smoke and debris." It was 7:29 in San Diego, but 10:29 in New York City, when the first plane struck. These offices would have been filled with thousands of people going about their daily business.

At my desk, as I tried to process the horror, I reflected on what people will do in most situations to stay alive. In New York that morning, human beings were desperately leaping from windows to escape the unbearable heat, smoke, and flames. I thought of the no-less-desperate patients with terminal cancer who were paying thousands and thousands of dollars for drugs to sustain them for but a year or two, with or without the help of insurance. *Why?* I wondered. Is life a race to be numbered in years, even if it's a life of poor quality? Death can come at any moment to each of us, and eventually will, yet we do little to prepare for it. Why do so many of us live as if we're immortal, without planning for what follows? What if Christ really does pronounce a final judgment to determine our eternal destiny, as the New Testament teaches?

With these thoughts, I realized I hadn't been to Confession since high school. But how could I possibly remember my sins for that many years? The big ones—the mortal ones, which could send me to Hell—were easy. I certainly had accumulated my share of the "Seven Deadlies." But confessing sins of any magnitude to the pastor of one's local church is difficult and embarrassing. Even if I chose to kneel behind a screen to hide my face, my voice would be recognizable to the priest who sees me every Sunday morning when I stop after Mass to chat about his sermon.

Then the perfect solution occurred to me. In early December, I would be in Chicago for a CEOC meeting of the American Academy of Periodontology. So I could go to Confession at the nearby Holy Name Cathedral, the seat of the Archdiocese of Chicago, where there are so many priests coming and going that I'd never see the same one twice—a cowardly plan, to be sure.

I learned that confessions at the Cathedral were heard from 4:00 to 5:15, ending just before the Saturday evening Vigil Mass. As the newly-elected Chair of the CEOC, I could ensure the Saturday afternoon meeting finished on time. And so, my next time in Chicago, on late Saturday afternoon, I was off to confession, entering Holy Name Cathedral—a grandiose Gothic-revival edifice of beige stone bricks, built in 1875— through a massive bronze door, beneath a stained glass rose window and a single bell tower capped by a spire more than two hundred feet high.

Descending a staircase to a long basement hallway, I made my way to a series of small rooms. I chose the shortest line of the five in the hall, silently rehearsing what I would say, although the years of abstinence from Confession had seriously challenged my recall.

The room was small. A large wooden screen held an opaque window within its frame, a well-padded kneeler below it. But off to the left was a chair, an obvious invitation to the brave souls willing to confess face-to-face. *I'll never see this man again,* I thought. *Why not go for it?* So, I bypassed the kneeler and sat down next to him.

The kind-faced, young priest was dressed in black except for his white collar. "Good afternoon," he smiled, looking into my eyes. "Welcome. I'm Father Bob. Please begin."

"Bless me, Father, for I have sinned," I said, remembering the ritual. "It has been forty years since my last Confession, and these are my sins."

"What was that?" the priest said.

"Forty-one, to be exact."

"Well, just tell me your serious sins and a few venial ones."

Once I began, I gained confidence as I listed the transgressions specified earlier in this narrative. The priest appeared interested and compassionate, and I felt better immediately—a feeling difficult to describe. No longer was I concealing something, carrying the weight of my sins. As Maggie had pointed out at the Cruz de Fiero in Spain, the worst sins are symbolically heavy. I'd just lightened my load by turning them over to God, knowing He would forgive me.

The priest then asked why I'd committed such sins, and I confessed that I was helpless not to. "What is your worst sin at this time in your life?" he asked. I responded, "Pride, I think. Because I love it when I'm praised, receive an award, buy a new car, or beat everyone to the top of a hill on my bike."

"Pride is difficult," Father Bob said. "A brain chemical, dopamine, is released when we are prideful, producing a sense of pleasure that creates an addictive 'high' in much the way drugs do. But there's not enough time to discuss this today. So for your penance, say five Our Fathers and five Hail Marys. Do you have rosary beads?" I nodded, and he continued, "Well, also say the entire Joyful Mysteries today. The Church is pleased you have returned."

Sitting in a pew, absolved of my sins, as I prayed the five Our Fathers and five Hail Marys, I experienced an overwhelming sense of forgiveness, peace, and love for God The Father, His Son, and the Holy Spirit. With my eyes closed, I pictured *The Return of the Prodigal Son.* I planned to say the Joyful Mysteries at bedtime, ensuring a restful sleep.

The Cursillo experience had begun the conversion of my heart and soul, and the miracles of the Camino de Santiago catapulted my faith to a new level. I desired to share the gifts that God had given me with those in need. Mike Daniels had recently introduced me to thirty-five-year-old David Rivera—a young Notre Dame School of Law graduate. Wanting to help at-risk children living in the poverty-stricken and crime-ridden inner city, he initiated the tuition-free Nativity Prep Academy in impoverished Logan Heights. Margaret and I agreed we would sponsor a minority student for each year of their education at the school, which emphasized not only reading, writing, and math, but also faith, character development, and elevated self-esteem.

My increased spiritual faith had resulted in better control over much of my behavior—except, as I'd just confessed to Father Bob, for the sin of pride. While my other deadly sins had decreased, my pride had increased. The very nature of pride is insidious, but I was powerless to see it, despite the warning of C.S. Lewis in *Mere Christianity*: "Pride is a spiritual cancer; it eats up the very possibility of love, or contentment, or even common sense."

Since cutting back on my surgical practice, I'd discovered my athletic abilities—something that had been absent my entire life. I took pride in my cycling prowess. Climbing steep hills had revealed my strength and balance to be superior to most people my age, and I reveled in the discovery. Returning from Spain, Mike, Carlos, and I had purchased super-light titanium road bikes with one-inch-wide tires. We signed up with the Leukemia and Lymphoma Society's "Team in Training" program to raise money to fight blood cancers. We'd sent sponsorship letters to friends, family, and even some patients. The Society provided cycling coaches and planned weekly rides to train us for a century ride—a hundred miles or more in a single day—and we contributed the donations we'd received. Training had begun in August, and in November, we completed the "El Tour de Tucson," a hundred-mile ride over flat terrain, except for two 1000-foot climbs.

Cycling soon became an addiction, and I was helpless to stop it because of the highs I experienced relishing my accomplishments. In 2002, I completed "The Triple Bypass," a one-day ride in Colorado—the one-hundred-ten-mile distance from Evergreen to Vail—over three mountain passes, all above eleven thousand feet, including the twelve thousand-foot Loveland Pass. A year later, I finished all five passes of the "Death Ride" in the High Sierra range of Northern California, perhaps the most challenging one-day ride in the U.S., similar to the most demanding mountain stage of the Tour de France. The event sells out each year, and only half of the three thousand riders go the hundred-twenty-nine-mile distance, mastering the total elevation gain of sixteen thousand feet. I repeated the effort the following year and shaved an hour from my time. I was sixty-two then, twenty years older than the average rider in the event. And was I proud of it.

While still celebrating my recent achievement in the "Death Ride," I'd picked up the July issue of the *International Journal of Oral and Maxillofacial Implants*, which contained a paper by Doctors Gregory Vance and Henry Greenwell from the University of Louisville School of Dentistry. They'd done a study comparing my bone regeneration technique with one of the most popular techniques used by oral surgeons worldwide to fill extraction sockets with new bone before placing a dental implant. At four months, the results were analyzed, and the calcium sulfate-containing grafts had 61 percent vital bone, while the alternative technique had only 26 percent. My technique provided a much better environment for dental implants.

Once again, my pride was bursting. The finding of that study should have been revolutionary, but it wasn't. A few days later, Brian Kane called to say that Lifecore Biomedical was selling their Oral Restorative Division to Keystone Dental, including a line of dental implants and my calcium sulfate products. Lifecore wanted to concentrate on its global leadership in manufacturing sodium hyaluronate, a medication for skin ulcers, burn wounds, osteoarthritis, and eye issues. Keystone mainly wanted Lifecore's lucrative dental implant business.

And so, within months of the sale, my royalties, a significant portion of my income, stopped arriving, and my phone calls to Keystone Dental were not returned. I figured my calcium sulfate products would compete against pre-existing Keystone bone regeneration products, which were three to four times more expensive. Rather than deal with that issue, however, especially if my products were better, I believed Keystone had simply decided to discontinue the calcium sulfate line. Reports from friends informed me that the Keystone salesforce reps were telling surgeons that calcium sulfate was "old school" and that their newer products were much better. Once calcium sulfate advertisements and promotions stopped, my invitations to lecture at major meetings began to diminish—another blow to my ego and income.

During my search for academic truth during the twenty-seven years I'd chaired the Annual USC Periodontal Symposium, I'd believed that the truth would prevail, although it might take time. Now I accepted as truth the fact that money could purchase a false truth. Since only a few years were left on my patents to protect a company's interest, I didn't attempt to find a new manufacturer.

Instead, I stayed busy as the 2005 President of the California Society of Periodontists and, with my election to the AAP's Board of Trustees a year later, I would make four or more trips to Chicago and the Ritz-Carlton each of the next six years, with—ironically—more opportunities for going to Confession.

Although proud of my accomplishments and pleased I was donating time to good causes, I felt the financial pressure of a reduced work schedule, the loss of Lifecore's royalties, and diminished speaking honoraria. As the Bible says in the Book of Proverbs, "Pride goes before destruction and a haughty spirit before a fall." Tell me about it!

* * *

Throughout these years, my dislike of seeing medical doctors persisted, whether related to my bad experience at Bridgeport Hospital at age seven or my preference to be the one wearing the white coat. Or maybe it was due to the annual physical being a subtle reminder of an unpleasant aspect of the human condition—the fact of mortality.

For me, seeing a physician was the supreme example of yielding control. I desired permanent invulnerability, to never suffer physical pain, enter a hospital, or have a breathing tube inserted into my trachea, as I had seen done to Dad. Any medical appointment triggered in me heightened anxiety, elevating my blood pressure the moment I approached a doctor's door.

Late in 2005, when my annual lab results indicated that my PSA (prostate-specific antigen) level—at 3.75—was slightly high, I ignored my internist's recommendation to return for a retest in six months. Instead, I began a Mediterranean diet and bicycled additional miles to reduce stress.

More than a year later, however, after finding a new doctor, I was told that my PSA reading was now 4.9 and that I should see a urologist. I was given two names, a gesture that was counterintuitive to my prideful professional self. I would have preferred this doctor say, "The name I'm giving you is the best in the area. I trust this person to do what's best for you."

Leaving the paper with those two names on my desk for months, I did internet research, convincing myself that my problem was *benign prostatic hyperplasia*, a common enlargement that annually afflicts more than two million men in the United States. Moreover, BPH was known to raise PSA levels harmlessly. I also believed that the pounding of my bicycle seat during the seven thousand miles I rode each year was also a factor.

Trading my Mediterranean diet for a vegan diet, except for an occasional seafood meal, I added over-the-counter beta-sitosterol, saw palmetto, and pygeum—a herbal extract taken from the bark of the African cherry tree. Though trained in scientific medicine, I was in total denial about my condition, convinced I could beat my prostate problem independently.

One would think that after my vision in the tomb of San Juan de Ortega, I would have added prayer to my arsenal of prostate-shrinking,

PSA-reducing drugs. But who considers prayer when in denial? My spiritual experience had affected me in other positive ways. For example, I drank much less alcohol, ate more moderately, had a healthier diet, and no longer missed my Mercedes-Benz S-Class. Instead, I felt comfortable driving my Ford SUV—albeit a large one, an Expedition with leather seats, a twelve-speaker Bang and Olufsen sound system, power-folding running boards, and the most powerful engine I could order—with eight cylinders and three hundred horsepower. As I've said, pride is my worst sin.

An elevated PSA aside, I lectured to any group that would invite me, and I occasionally spoke at a prestigious national meeting. In September of 2007, for example, I spoke to more than five hundred general dentists and hygienists at the Annual Session of the American Dental Association in San Francisco; and in October, along with Dr. Maurizio Tonetti, one of Europe's most celebrated periodontists, I planned, chaired, and moderated a session with several thousand periodontists in attendance in Washington, D.C., at the Annual Meeting of the American Academy of Periodontology. As with my upgraded SUV, such exalted positions stoked my ego.

Knowing I wanted a physician I could trust, a friend suggested the Private Internal Medicine Center at the highly-respected Scripps Clinic in La Jolla. I would receive more personalized care and longer appointments in this practice for an additional fee.

"Well, John," Dr. Jonathan Ward began on my first visit to him in January of 2008, "your last PSA, over a year ago, was 4.9, and now it's 6.7. So we're going to have to investigate this further. You're going to have to see a specialist now."

Disappointment overwhelmed me. From my research, I knew the typical approach was to see a local urologist, who'd most likely do a biopsy. Dr. Ward said that a number of his patients had taken that approach, and if cancer was detected, the urologist soon performed surgery to remove the prostate. In some cases, the side effects of surgery had been severe; in others, the cancer returned in a short time because the surgeon had been unable to get all of it once it had escaped the gland. Dr. Ward explained he would use a different approach and recommended I see Dr. Richard Lam at Prostate Oncology Specialists, in the Marina Del Rey area of Los Angeles. He'd had excellent feedback from patients who'd seen him.

In early February, Dr. Lam examined my prostate, using a color Doppler ultrasound unit, while I watched on the monitor. I saw many gradations of gray, with splotches of bright red and gold scattered through-out—interesting, except that this bit of abstract art was my own prostate, not a Jackson Pollock masterpiece.

Dr. Lam explained that the red areas signified hypervascularity and extra blood flow, indicating localized areas of either prostatitis or cancer. There was that word—cancer—the word I feared and despised. "I recommend you see Dr. Duke Bahn in Ventura," Dr. Lam said. "He's very experienced in targeted biopsies."

My PSA that day was 8.0. If I did have prostate cancer, it was growing fast, and if it meant driving four hours to consult the best physician, I was suddenly all for it.

On April 8th, I drove two hundred miles to Ventura. Dr. Bahn, an obvious expert in his field, was very professional. He used a unique guidance technique that allowed him to take only seven core samples from my prostate, whereas most urologists took a dozen or more, creating a greater risk of infection. As I left, Dr. Bahn said, "You seem worried. But, remember, it may just be prostatitis."

I repeated those words on the drive home to San Diego.

A week later—April 15, 2008—I was at the office when Dr. Bahn called. He got right to the point. "Your biopsy report came back, and you do have prostate cancer."

I remained silent as he continued, though it was difficult to concentrate on his exact words—*aggressive, it had escaped the prostate.* I'd become numb, devoid of emotion, filled with fear and anxiety, the opposite of what I'd felt in the tomb of San Juan de Ortega. My life had changed in an instant. I was no longer the person I was before hearing this news. I was a cancer patient, first and foremost, and a periodontist, second.

Like most people in such situations, my initial question was: *Why me?* Then I considered my own case. *Was it the cycling and the pounding of the seat against my prostate? Will I die from this?*

I felt guilty for my denial and failure to take action. When this guilt subsided, an all-encompassing sense of helplessness replaced it. I wished my faith had been sufficiently strong to turn this problem over to God, but it wasn't. The belief that my intellect could solve all problems had been tested and failed.

Fortunately, when the call came on that fateful Tuesday, I was between patients, with only two more examinations to perform, before returning home to tell Margaret the bad news. As always, I knew she'd be supportive, but I could sense myself withdrawing deep within. No matter how hard I tried, I couldn't keep thoughts of surgery, radiation, chemotherapy, sickness, and death at bay. I felt intense fear and wanted to cry, but I somehow managed to repress it. I was unable to express to Margaret what I was experiencing. For someone with such an enormous ego, I became incapacitated.

Unable to sleep, I called my partner, Dr. John Lofthus. "I just received a serious diagnosis of prostate cancer," I told him. "I don't think I can see patients tomorrow. As soon as she arrives, would you have Sarah call my patients and cancel them? I'm not sure how many days off I'll need."

As always, John was gracious, telling me to do as I thought best.

The idea of cancer darkened my mind, and I felt empty, confused, and despondent. Although I wanted to project positivity and confidence, I became quiet, introspective, and sullen. My anxiety increased, and my appetite decreased. What bothered me most was that my cancer had escaped the prostate capsule, leaving me to picture malignant cells coursing through my bloodstream, invading lymph nodes, and entering my bones. Ironically, bone tissue had brought me wealth and fame, and now my own bones could be under assault. And I was powerless to stop it.

A few days later, I had a CT scan—with a contrasting dye—of my abdomen and pelvis. A bone scan followed, for which a radioactive liquid was injected, to look for metastases away from the prostate. Neither test was difficult except for having to lie perfectly still for extended periods.

Both tests—a major relief—were negative.

Nonetheless, I couldn't stop worrying. Prostate cancer is the second leading cause of cancer deaths in American men, right behind lung cancer. My research taught me more than I cared to know about urinary incontinence, chronic diarrhea, erectile dysfunction, and bladder problems. I wanted to live but feared the side effects of treatment.

I scheduled two visits at a prestigious San Diego cancer center during the third week in April. One was with a surgeon who did minimally-invasive laparoscopic and robotic surgery touted as "nerve-sparing," though I knew there were no such guarantees. I will call this surgeon "Dr. X." The other appointment was with a radiation oncologist I'll call "Dr. Y."

"You look worried," Dr. X said, "but I want you to know I can take care of this."

"I'm not only worried about survival," I said. "It's the side effects that bother me."

"With the technique I use, the risk is minimal."

As a surgeon, I knew Dr. X was downplaying the risks. When I'd read my biopsy report, I saw that cancer was found in the adjacent neurovascular bundle.

Two such bundles surround the prostate. I wondered how this surgeon could remove the prostate and get all of the cancer without removing the affected bundle as well. The very thought made me cringe.

"Don't worry," Dr. X said. "You'll be just fine."

The next day, when the medical assistant led me down the long hall-way to see Dr. Y, I realized it was the same hallway where Dr. X had his office. She stopped four doors short. "Well," Dr. Y began, "I see you were in yesterday, and Dr. X recommended surgical removal of your prostate. I can't argue with that, but I can offer an alternative."

I decided to take a more assertive role. "Dr. Y," I interjected. "Look at item four in the pathology report from Bostwick Labs. It says adenocarci-noma is present in the left superior neurovascular bundle. The perineural invasion, found in the prostate itself, supports this finding."

"Let me take another look," Dr. Y said. Returning to my chart, he flipped through its pages, then said, "Who did your biopsy?"

"Dr. Duke Bahn in Ventura."

"He's an amazing guy," Dr. Y said, "the best in the country, the only one I know who can take a transrectal biopsy of a prostate neurovascular bun-dle. Which changes everything, John. You shouldn't have a prostatectomy. It won't get all the cancer, and you'll have side effects from the surgery, and then, when the cancer returns, my radiation to get the rest will add to them."

Dr. Y was compassionate and, like Wally Grossman at Nellis Air Force Base years ago, believed in telling the truth at all costs. The long drive to Ventura had been worth it.

Chapter 38   Spreading the Light

I RETURNED HOME WITHOUT scheduling any further appointments. I'd sent away for a book that hadn't arrived yet, *You Can Beat Prostate Cancer and You Don't Need Surgery to Do It,* by Robert J. Marckini, a prostate cancer survivor who'd had successful proton radiation treatment at the Loma Linda University Medical Center—where I had taught periodontal residents 35-years earlier. I finished the book the day it was delivered.

Meanwhile, Dr. Lam started me on androgen deprivation therapy, known as "ADT." Most prostate cancers thrive and spread with the help of testosterone, but ADT blocks it. He explained that this would temporarily cause the cancer to retreat while I figured out what treatment to pursue. The cancer cells would stop spreading—for a while, at least—as ADT kept them from my lymph nodes.

Now, just as at the University of Pennsylvania, when I felt I'd lost the ability to study after receiving an ill-timed "Dear John" letter before finals and again after my son Mark had called about a possible future without grandchildren, I turned to God, my last source of help only when I realized I was incapable of solving the problem. Since my diagnosis of aggressive prostate cancer, I'd been attending daily Mass at Mary Star of the Sea Church, a white Spanish Mission-style church on Girard Avenue in the center of La Jolla's business district. Though built in 1937, it had retained the architectural style of an original mission, with white stucco, a three-story bell tower, and a chapel with the Eucharist displayed for worship, which in Catholic circles is known as Eucharistic Adoration. Was I hoping for another miracle in such a quaint setting?

At the end of April, at the peak of my anxiety, I received a call from Claudia Bailey, my former dental hygienist. Besides her role in dentistry, she was also a spiritual-but-not-religious Reiki therapist who used the Japanese-developed technique for stress reduction, relaxation, and healing. She'd grown up in Hawaii, the daughter of a lapsed German-Irish Catholic mother, and as a little girl, remembered her mom making anti-Catholic statements. Having a Japanese father might explain her interest in Reiki since *rei* means *the spirit* or *the divine*, and *ki* is *vital energy*. Claudia, whom I'd only seen briefly over recent years, now worked for a La Jolla general dentist, Dr. Ellen Miyashiro. I was surprised when she called the office and asked to speak to me.

"Hello, Dr. Sottosanti," she began. "Long time no see. Dr. Miyashiro said she got a letter from you and that you've taken a sabbatical because of prostate cancer."

"Yes," I said. "That's correct." I'd sent a letter to all my referring dentists, as well as my patients. Emotionally, I was not ready to treat patients. Margaret and I relied on our savings until I knew the treatment outcome.

"I want to let you know that I've become a Catholic. I go to Mass every day."

I couldn't believe it. "How'd that happen?"

"Although my father had died many years ago, I had always been worried about his soul, and I dreamt of him one night. When I woke, I smelled roses—so unusual as there were no flowers or potpourri in my home— and a brilliant light was at the foot of my bed. I sat straight up, and in that light was a beautiful, smiling young woman who looked at me without saying a word. She was dressed in blue and white." Claudia's voice became animated. "I didn't know who she was, but while she was there, I was transfixed. Later, realizing it was the Virgin Mary, I decided to become a Catholic. I did, and I've been going to daily Mass ever since and praying before the Eucharist most days. This morning, I prayed for you and received a message from Jesus. You must go with me to Our Lady of the Rosary Church in Old Town next Monday for the evening Rosary, Mass, and devotions to Saint Padre Pio.

I'd heard about Padre Pio of Pietrelcina, a small town in southern Italy. Born in 1887, he died in 1968. Many believed he'd been blessed with an array of spiritual gifts—the stigmata (the wounds of Christ on the hands, feet, and side), bilocation (the ability to be in two places at once), and the power to heal, prophesize, and read hearts. Reports abounded from Italian citizens that, when they made a dishonest confession, Padro Pio reprimanded them and told them exactly what they'd done. Most days, his reputation had drawn hundreds of the faithful to his confessional.

The following Monday, encouraged by this unexpected reunion with Claudia, I went with her to Our Lady of the Rosary. The church was packed and warm, but the faithful's devotion to Padre Pio was palpable. Afterward, I purchased *Padre Pio's Words of Hope*, edited by Eileen Dunn Bertanzetti, and began to read from it for daily consolation. The book contains one hundred fifty of his meditations, one per page. The one I turned to most, simply titled "Anxiety," says: "Do not anticipate the problems of this life with apprehension, but, rather, with a perfect hope that God, to whom you belong, will free you from them accordingly." A short prayer by Bertanzetti followed. "Dear Lord, forgive me for worrying. Lord, I place my trust in You."

One evening I'd just placed this book down when Margaret entered the room. I'd suddenly experienced a revelation—with clarity and certainty—and wanted to tell her about it.

"How are you feeling?" she asked.

"I need to go to Lourdes," I said. My relationship with Margaret had grown closer since my return from bicycling the Camino de Santiago, as she witnessed and welcomed the changes in my behavior. However, I had been remaining quiet about my cancer's negative impact on my emotions. "Will you come with me? I want to leave in two or three weeks."

"I don't know, sweetie. I've got so many things scheduled. Why do you want to go?"

"I'm confused about my cancer and how to treat it. So many physical and emotional healings have occurred at Lourdes. They get six million visitors a year. There must be something to it. The water the Jorgensens gave us helped Mom when she was dying. Remember?"

"How could I forget? Of course, I'll go."

Two weeks later, on May 22, Margaret and I flew to Toulouse in southwest France, took a two-hour train ride to the small town of Lourdes, and checked into the Grand Hotel de la Grotte. After a short nap, we walked down Rue de la Grotte, past the Lourdes Tourist Office, and found two magnificent basilicas, one atop the other. From a distance, the dual structure looks like the Sleeping Beauty Castle at Disneyland, with its tall middle tower pointing high into the sky over multiple lower spires. The resemblance to Disneyland was so striking that, ever since, I've considered Lourdes a wonderment for spiritual adults.

The Lower Church, the Rosary Basilica, has a semicircular, white marble façade depicting Mary, with the Infant Jesus, handing the Rosary to St. Dominic. Dominic introduced the Rosary in 1208 after experiencing a vision of the Blessed Mother. On both sides of the entrance, a long, curved, stone staircase leads to the Upper Church, the Basilica of the Immaculate Conception, an elaborate Gothic structure consecrated in 1876. This basilica sits on a massive rock above the grotto of Massabielle, where Bernadette Soubirous experienced eighteen apparitions of the Virgin Mary in 1858. Mary had asked Bernadette for a chapel to be built at the site. Little did she know what would be built there. *On second thought, I believe she knew.*

Seven years earlier, before driving up the mountain to Roncesvalles to begin our Camino pilgrimage, Mike Daniels had gone to the baths at Lourdes to pray for the healing of his non-Hodgkin's lymphoma. I could recall his vivid description of the spirituality of the site, especially when bathing in the waters at the grotto. Now *I* was the one with cancer, and I was drawn to the same place.

On the way to the baths, Margaret and I walked down a path with the River Gave to our right and the grotto to our left. A life-sized statue of the Virgin Mary, all white except for a blue sash and a golden rose on each foot, stood in a niche in the rock where Bernadette had seen her apparition. Wheelchairs were aligned before it, their occupants saying the Rosary. Just below was a six-tiered circle of blazing candles, larger at the bottom than the top, resembling a tall, fiery wedding cake.

Adjacent to that were two large caves. According to our guidebook, during the ninth apparition, Mary had instructed Bernadette to dig with her hands in the dirt of the larger of the two—a scene witnessed by an estimated four hundred people. In so doing, she exposed a hidden spring, flowing since then at a rate of seventeen thousand to seventy-two thousand liters daily. In the mid-twentieth century, the water was diverted in two directions. One feeds twenty small fountains, from which pilgrims can draw water to drink, wash, or take with them in bottles; the other leads to sixteen baths built in 1955, eight for men and eight for women. Hundreds of people immerse themselves in these waters daily.

The scene was mesmerizing, but after a few minutes, we moved on. I was anxious to find the men's baths. Leaving Margaret to read on a bench by the river, I followed a large sign— *PISCINES - Hommes*—and was the last one allowed in. A chain is placed across the entrance at 11 a.m., and only those already in the waiting area can continue to the baths. This allows the volunteers to have a lunch break.

Seated at the end of the rear bench, I slid forward eight spots every ten minutes until I moved into the next row. People on my left spoke French, and I heard German up ahead, but the seats to my right were empty. I felt lonely until an elderly priest sat down. I supposed he'd been admitted late because he was a clergyman. Smiling broadly, he addressed me in a delightful Irish brogue. "I'm Father Sean McCartney. What's your name, and where ya from?"

I returned his smile. "I'm John Sottosanti, from California. San Diego area."

"Your first time to the baths, now?"

"Yes, it is."

"Ya here for medical reasons or just makin' a pilgrimage?"

"I've got advanced prostate cancer. It has me worried."

"Well then, John, why don't ya join us tonight? I'm with the Northern Ireland Cancer Pilgrimage. We're having a healing Mass for cancer patients."

"I'll tell my wife," I said. "How should I let you know?

"No need. Just show up at six across the river at St. Patrick's Chapel."

Since I was engaged in conversation, the time passed quickly, and soon it was my turn for the baths. I was anxious about the procedure, but Father Sean said I'd be treated with efficiency, respect, and dignity. One of the volunteers led me into a corridor, pointed to a wide shower curtain, and told me to enter and disrobe to my shorts.

Five minutes later, a similar curtain on the far side of the small room parted, and two volunteers, speaking English with European accents, told me to enter. This next room, with an eight-by-three-foot stone bath set into the floor, allowed for a volunteer on either side. The walls were made of stone blocks quarried nearby. The far wall held a small white statue of Our Lady of Lourdes. Wrapping me in a blue bathing sheet, the two men asked me to drop my shorts and hang them on a wall hook, and I was directed to stand in the cold knee-deep water, make the Sign of the Cross, and say a silent prayer for my intentions, which I did.

Please, God, I prayed. *Heal me of this aggressive prostate cancer.*

The men guided me further into the water and pulled me backward, each taking an arm, briefly submerging my head and shoulders. A volunteer directed me to say another prayer, followed by the Sign of the Cross. Finished, he took my towel, and I grabbed my shorts and retreated to the dressing area. As I did so, I remembered being told by a friend that I'd not need a towel after emerging from the frigid waters. He was right. I recall only a light dampness to my skin as I dressed. But the real surprise was the healing of my heart and spirit—for at that moment, I felt nothing but calm, peace, and love. The experience filled my heart with happiness, wiping away the grief and anxiety related to my cancer diagnosis.

I'd been told that the experience of Lourdes is not for everyone, but it is life-changing for those with faith, belief, and hope. Without these, the water is ineffective. In the words of St. Thomas Aquinas, "To one who has faith, no explanation is necessary. To one without faith, no explanation is possible." Which is certainly the case at Lourdes.

That evening Margaret and I attended the healing Mass. After communion, Father Sean invited all those who were ill to come forward for the sacrament of The Anointing of the Sick. When it was my turn, he recited, "Through this holy anointing, may the Lord in His love and mercy help you with the grace of the Holy Spirit. May the Lord, who frees you from sin, save you and raise you up." He then blessed my forehead and palms, making the

Sign of the Cross on each. For the anointing, he dipped his thumb in Holy Oil—olive oil, blessed by the local bishop.

Later, Margaret and I watched the Marian Torchlight Procession—the most popular event at Lourdes. Introduced in 1863, it takes place every evening from April through October. Thousands begin lining up across the river just before dusk, each holding a lit candle protected from the breeze by a paper sleeve, on which the words of the Marian devotional songs are printed in multiple languages. Once the crowd began walking toward the basilicas, as a guide told us, they would recite the Rosary and then sing the hymns. We were encouraged to climb the steps to the plaza above the Rosary Basilica for a better view. With my arms on the stone railing, I took photos every ten minutes, making a record of the crowd gathering below.

It was breathtaking. Beyond the expansive square was an illuminated, twenty-foot statue of Our Lady of Lourdes—all in white, with her blue sash and golden rose on each foot. She stood in the middle of a wide circle of blooming white roses. Farther beyond, two parallel roads stretched for more than three hundred yards. These were separated by an esplanade of bright green grass and serpentine flowerbeds of red roses. Farther still, high above the valley floor, sat the Castle of Lourdes—the *Château Fort de Lourdes*—on a rocky promontory. Built by the Romans at the strategic entry point of seven valleys, it had been besieged by Charlemagne, then served as a fort and prison. Now it was a museum dedicated to the art, history, and traditions of the Pyrenees.

As the sun fell lower, I breathed the fresh air of the foothills of the Pyrenees. The nearest held the brightest green oaks and beech trees I'd ever seen. As the light grew dimmer, the blue sky, with horizontal wispy clouds, turned illuminated pink, a stark contrast to the shadowy landscape in the hills beneath. At ground level, a parade approached from a distance, a river of dancing lights moving toward the square below us. Marian hymns, sung in many languages by pilgrims from all over the world, rose to our ears.

Hundreds of wheelchairs led the procession, their occupants and caregivers holding candles and singing the words on their globe-like song sheets. As the throng followed behind, the singing intensified, and Margaret and I joined in:

> Immaculate Mary, thy praises we sing;
>
> Who reignest in splendor with Jesus our King.
>
> Ave, ave, ave, Maria! Ave, ave, Maria!

Four men at the very front of the procession carried a five-foot statue of Our Lady of Lourdes, like the one at the grotto. Borne along at shoulder height on an illuminated, covered platform, the Virgin Mary had fresh flowers at her feet and a golden crown on her head.

Then the wheelchairs entered the plaza, lining up in rows at the foot of the Basilica's seven steps. The statue of Mary was now centered on the broad top step, beside a large wooden cross, just short of the arched entrance to the Rosary Basilica. The clergy gathers here to conduct the crowd in singing and to bless the crowd at the end of the evening. By my estimate, there were five hundred wheelchairs in front and eight or nine thousand people behind them. In the dark of the night, we beheld a spectacle of wavering lights—a glorious display of faith in Christ as the light of the world.

I'd arrived at Lourdes thinking that my personal cross—a significant cancer diagnosis—was a heavy one, but when I saw the hundreds of bed-ridden patients, flat on their backs, some on oxygen, pushed around the Sanctuary by volunteer caregivers, my anxiety diminished. Fr. Sean had explained that Jesus helped to heal the sick. He wanted us to do the same and even see Him in them. He quoted Jesus from the Book of Matthew: "As you did it to one of the least of these my brethren, you did it to me." Lourdes was filled with the sickest of the sick. It was a shrine to Mary, but Jesus was present, and it was He who did the healing.

As I looked from our perch, finished with my photography, I took Margaret's hand.

Volunteers throughout the sanctuary were attending to every need of the *malades*. There was no glory or reward for these volunteers—at least not on this earth. This thought brought to mind Viktor Frankl's book, *Man's Search for Meaning*, from which several phrases had stuck with me: "Love is the highest goal to which man can aspire." And, "Even a man who has nothing left in this world still may know bliss, if only for a moment, in the contemplation of the beloved." Such is *agape*—a sacrificial love expecting nothing in return.

* * *

Back in San Diego, I returned to my office, working one day each week, and my staff noticed a significant transformation in me. I was no longer the depressed person they'd seen a few weeks before—self-pitying, mired in thoughts of cancer, suffering, and death, and unable to work with my patients.

Julie Lefever, a devout Catholic who'd been my surgical assistant for many years, asked to see my photos of Lourdes. And so, on a Monday in early June, following our lunch with other staff members around our large conference table, we excused ourselves and headed to the vacant office of our part-time bookkeeper, where I set up my laptop.

In an excited voice, I told Julie about the baths at Lourdes, then showed the pictures of the procession with the wheelchairs assembling. While I hummed along with a few lines of "Immaculate Mary," I realized someone was standing behind us. It was Debra Jo Johnson, our dental hygienist. I'd met "Debbie" twenty-five years earlier when she was married to my partner, Dr. Bruce Johnson. She and Bruce had joined Margaret and me at Jampolsky's Center for Attitudinal Healing at a time when I was unaware of their marital problems. After their divorce, Bruce and I ended our partnership —an unrelated move—and Debbie came to work for me in La Jolla.

She stood behind us now, watching silently, and when I closed my laptop, she left just as quietly. She was an exceptional person—intelligent, compassionate, scientific—a skilled clinician as well. Our relationship had always been professional, and we admired each other's dedication. Debbie had been teaching part-time in a dental hygiene program at Southwestern College in San Diego and several times had invited me to lecture. She'd married Bruce in the Lutheran church, but we had never discussed religion in all the years I knew them.

Five minutes before seeing my first patient, Debbie entered my office and stood at my desk. "Whatever you have, John, I want it. How do I get it?"

I smiled broadly. "It's complicated," I said. "Let's do lunch. How about Friday?" And so, that coming Friday, we met at Jose's Courtroom on Prospect Street—a family-friendly, ocean-view restaurant known for excellent guacamole, enchiladas, and fish tacos. When I arrived, Debbie was seated at a table with her back to the water. I'd brought a yellow legal pad on which I'd scribbled notes. We stuck to small talk until we finished eating, then got serious.

"I stayed up late thinking about what to say," I began. Then I paused, unsure how she'd respond to what came next. "There are many reasons why I think you should become a Catholic. I have sixteen, in fact, written on this pad."

"Tell me."

"First of all, it's the original Christian church, founded by Christ. He gave its leadership to Saint Peter, and there's been continuity ever since. Of course, not all the Popes have been good people. They're just human, like the rest of us, and some were obvious sinners. But the Church is bigger than just one person. It has a two-thousand-year history and thousands of saints. There are two billion Christians in the world, in many denominations, and Roman Catholics make up 60 percent of them."

"I've heard negative things," Debbie said. "Don't Catholics worship Mary?"

"That's a common misconception. While on the cross, Christ said to the Apostle John, 'Behold your mother.' At that moment in time, John represented all Christians. And so, Mary is our mother as well. We respect her but don't worship her. I have a framed photo of my own mother, set in a place of honor, that I see when I enter the house. I have so much love and respect for her, and even though she's passed on, what she taught me helps keep me in line. Mary leads us to Christ, the truth and the light. When Catholics say the Rosary, we relive many of the events in the life of Jesus: his birth, proclamation of the Word of God, agony in Gethsemane, scourging, crucifixion, death, resurrection, and ascension into Heaven."

Debbie looked at me intently. She had such a keen mind and an intellectual curiosity. "What about all the rules and regulations? Doesn't the Church just make people feel guilty? Why can't we pray to God without rules?"

"Jesus had many rules for getting to Heaven. It would be easy to ignore the ones we don't like, just to have our own way. The Magisterium of the Catholic Church is its teaching authority. It consists of the Pope, in communion with the worldwide bishops, and is informed by Sacred Scripture and Apostolic Tradition—what the early Church believed in the years after the death of Christ. Many Protestants think that Scripture is the sole authority, but the Catholic Church, at the Council of Rome in 382, compiled the first Bible by deciding which Scriptures were inspired by the Holy Spirit. Previously, Sacred Tradition determined Christian practices."

Next, I explained the seven sacraments—Baptism, Holy Communion, Confession, Confirmation, Marriage, Anointing of the Sick, and Holy Orders—the backbone of the Church.

"Anointing of the Sick was a beautiful experience for my mother and for me as well at Lourdes. When everything's going well, Debbie, we forget about God, and religion just isn't important. But when we have serious problems, we turn to God for help. Further, we want the solemn events in our life—baptism, marriage, and even our funeral— to be in conjunction with a Catholic Mass because it adds reverence, permanence, and sacredness to the occasion."

Then I told her about the Saints and how comforting it was to know we can ask them for help.

"How does that work? Why not go straight to Jesus?"

I explained that the saints in Heaven intercede on our behalf, offering their own prayers. "Don't Protestants say to their sick friends, 'I'll pray for you?' That's intercession. Why not ask the saints, who have an elevated status?"

Next, I related my experience at the tomb of San Juan de Ortega. My grandson Tommy was now six, and he had two sisters. I beamed with pride and love as I spoke because I felt the Holy Spirit had been involved. I so loved those kids.

Debbie kept on. "Why is it a sin to miss Mass on Sunday?"

"Well, one of the Ten Commandments, given by God to the Israelites, states: 'Remember to keep holy the Sabbath Day.' How do we worship and show love for God without attending Mass? We need to express our love with others who also believe. The concept of community is crucial to the Church. Saint Paul called it the Body of Christ. Jesus is its head, and we are its members. Add the faithful in Heaven and, historically, we're the Communion of Saints."

The Roman Catholic Church, I explained, is the largest non-government provider of healthcare services in the world, with sixteen thousand clinics, fifteen thousand homes for the elderly, and five thousand hospitals, most of them in developing countries. The belief that Christ asked his Church to heal the sick drives this effort.

We'd been talking for at least an hour, and I hadn't yet addressed my notes on the shrines and miracles at Fatima in Portugal or Our Lady of Guadalupe in Mexico City. They'd have to wait for another day. As would my excitement about the Shroud of Turin. For now, I simply said. "Any questions?"

Debbie furrowed her brow. "How do you explain the sexual abuse crisis?"

"I've given that much thought because the Church is such a significant organization for good throughout the world. It promotes good behavior. In many ways, it's in opposition to the liberal agendas of the media and entertainment industry. According to the press, no institution has a worse record of sexual abuse than the Catholic Church. But that's not true."

"Yet it's a problem."

"Yes, but there are two issues. One is the percentage of abusers, compared to other groups, like school teachers and Boy Scout leaders. The other is the bishops' cover-up." I didn't want Debbie to think I was treating the subject lightly because I'd researched it thoroughly and believed I could explain it.

"Most victims of sexual abuse have been post-pubescent males—not young children—as the media insinuates. And much of this involved touching over a victim's clothing."

I related what had happened to me as a fourteen-year-old at the Rudy Molinaro Accordion School in Bridgeport—the time that Gary Vinci, a boy my own age, attempted to molest me in just that way, before I thwarted him.

"Depending upon which survey you look at," I continued, "the priests involved range from two to five percent, which is not that unusual compared to other groups with the same problem. Today, there are more than four hundred thousand Catholic priests worldwide. Do the math. It's easy to print names in the newspaper. Some surveys include cases going back to the 1960s, and many thousands of new priests have been ordained since then. No other organization in the world keeps records like the Catholic Church. Is there a national organization of school teachers that will give you the names and number of its abusers? No. That's true for the other groups as well."

Debbie persisted. "You mentioned the bishops and the cover-ups."

My Nellis Air Force Base Dental Clinic experience had prepared me for this question. "Many large organizations, especially those the public hold in high esteem, become self-protective to conceal their foibles. They take the attitude that the perpetrator has worked hard for the organization, perhaps made a mistake, but can be rehabilitated. I saw that in the Air Force. A Lieutenant Colonel, our Dental Clinic Commander, abused patients—not sexually, but by ordering teeth to be extracted needlessly, so his clinic numbers would look good. He hoped to be promoted to full Colonel, which had eluded him several times. Many of these patients, known in the profession as 'dental cripples,' cannot tolerate plastic dentures in place of their own teeth. But when we exposed our commander, the higher-ups transferred him to another base and later promoted him. It's wrong, as the Air Force and the Church should know."

I felt I'd covered the critical issues. The right to life, the importance of an intact family, the benefits of Eucharistic Adoration, etc., could wait for another day. It was time to address the reason I'd had lunch with Debbie that day. So, I asked her directly, "Would you be interested in becoming a Catholic?"

Debbie's face softened, and she broke into a smile. "I have no idea how."

"That's easy. There's a wonderful Catholic Church in Pacific Beach—Saint Brigid Parish—near your home. The Deacon, Mike Daniels, is a good friend of mine. We cycled the Camino de Santiago together. We'll enroll you in the RCIA program—Rite of Christian Initiation of Adults. I'll be your sponsor, and by next Easter, you can be a Catholic."

* * *

I did become Debbie's sponsor. She attended RCIA weekly, and, in 2009, Margaret and I attended Easter Vigil Mass at Saint Brigid Parish when Debbie was welcomed into the Church. Having studied the Catholic faith, she became proficient and devout, helped with the RCIA program, and read from Scripture during Mass. She was tireless, diligent, and fervent in her endeavor. The sin of sloth, so familiar to me, was simply unknown to her.

Now it was time to deal with my cancer.

After much study, prayer, and consultation, I decided on proton radiation treatment at the Loma Linda University Medical Center. Many people had told me that the treatment offered there was modern, targeted, and compassionate. And because of what I'd experienced at Lourdes and learned since returning home, I knew I wouldn't be facing it alone. I now believed the Father, Son, Holy Spirit, the Blessed Mother, Saint Joseph, and Padre Pio—all to whom I was now eternally devoted—would accompany me on this journey.

And that gave me inner peace.

Made in United States
North Haven, CT
20 June 2024

53863050R00163